INVESTING FROM THE TOP DOWN

INVESTING FROM THE TOP DOWN

A Macro Approach to Capital Markets

ANTHONY CRESCENZI

New York   Chicago   San Francisco   Lisbon   London
Madrid   Mexico City   Milan   New Delhi   San Juan
Seoul   Singapore   Sydney   Toronto

ISBN: 978-0-07-154384-2
MHID: 0-07-154384-8

This publication is designed to provide accurate and authoritative information in regard to the subject matter covered. It is sold with the understanding that the publisher is not engaged in rendering legal, accounting, or other professional service. If legal advice or other expert assistance is required, the services of a competent professional person should be sought.
   —*From a Declaration of Principles Jointly Adopted by a Committee of the American Bar Association and a Committee of Publishers and Associations*

McGraw-Hill books are available at special quantity discounts to use as premiums and sales promotions, or for use in corporate training programs. To contact a representative, please visit the Contact Us pages at www.mhprofessional.com.

This book is printed on acid-free paper.

To Cynthia and our enchanting daughters, Brittany, Victoria, and Isabella, who enrich my life every day and provide me with the greatest possible motivation to work hard, to learn and explore, and to keep challenging myself

To all who, in one way or another, are survivors, and who despite the many obstacles and challenges they face in their daily lives, each day find the inner strength to endure and to excel

To my nurturing parents, Anita and Joseph, who gave me the freedom to think creatively, explore, dream, and have fun—lots of it. To my brother Joseph and my sisters Theresa, Gina, and Nicole, to all of my family and friends, and to the great city of New York

–Anthony Crescenzi

ACKNOWLEDGMENTS

Top-down investing is a by-product of a mindset whereby people take a broad look at the world. Everyone who has this mindset develops it in his or her own way. I would attribute my own development to a number of factors, a few of which many can probably relate to. It starts, of course, with one's parents or guardians, and in my own case my parents helped me immeasurably by giving me free reign to direct my feet and my mind to go in any direction I chose to go. Moreover, my parents planted me and my brother and three sisters into a neighborhood where I was able to have experiences that were a microcosm of the experiences of those found in neighborhoods nationwide, helping to elevate my awareness of the ways in which the masses think, a perspective that is vital to developing views about trends in economies and markets.

The top-down mindset is immensely nurtured when living in countries that encourage free-market capitalism, and no place on earth is better at it than the United States. Capitalist societies such as the United States are most likely to experience change and have transformations that result in changes in the investment landscape, upon which investors feast. I feel fortunate every day to be an American.

Many investors have contributed to the allure of utilizing macro information and secular trends when deciding on investments. An idol of mine in this regard is Bill Gross at Pimco, the manager of the biggest bond fund in the world. He and his colleagues have illustrated the benefits of utilizing a macro approach to the capital markets while also displaying broad knowledge of the products and landscape in which they invest, doing so with great success. George Soros is another great investor I admire who has had smashing success in investing using macro principles.

For the development of my investment approach and in the writing of this book, I would like to acknowledge the work of the researchers at the Federal Reserve, where 200 Ph.D.s produce work available to the general public. The Fed's research can be of great value to anyone who endeavors to know more about the markets, the economy, the Fed, the banking sector, and much more. The Fed's work is easily accessed by subject matter via *Fed in Print*, which can be found on the Internet. Often, the work of the Fed's researchers is showcased in speeches delivered by Federal Reserve officials, and I have benefited greatly from reading these speeches on a regular basis. In particular, the many speeches delivered by former Federal Reserve Chairman Alan Greenspan were immensely beneficial to me in learning more about our capitalist system. Excellent research is also available from the Bank for International Settlements, the International Monetary Fund, the world's central banks, and government agencies.

I would like to thank my employers, Jeffrey Miller and Jeffrey Tabak, for their continued support of my work and for many years having given me the freedom to explore with great liberty the broader capital markets rather than just one area of focus. I thank them also for giving me the opportunity to build the skill set I've needed to build a career on Wall Street and write three books. In the production of this book I would like to thank my colleague Dan Greenhaus, who contributed two chapters in the book and who provides me with research support on a daily basis. Thanks also to my colleagues Pete Boockvar and Charles Campbell for their invaluable insights, to Robert Koggan for so many years of support and guidance, to John Pietanza for elevating the level of my work, to all my coworkers, to Steven Jordan, Nat Lipstadt, and Walter Weil for their wise perspective on markets and the ways of Wall Street.

As for my publisher, McGraw-Hill, I would like to thank Jeanne Glasser for giving me the opportunity to publish and for her guidance as to the direction of the book. Thank you also for your patience! Thanks also to Scott Kurtz and to Laurie Abbate for your support and for motivating me to keep pushing and to do better.

Thanks of course to my three girls, Brittany, Victoria, and Isabella, for giving me the biggest possible motivation of all to do all that I do, and to Cynthia for mothering and nurturing our girls while I worked all these years.

–Anthony Crescenzi

CONTENTS

CHAPTER 1

Top-Down Investing Has Arrived

The world has become more complicated than it used to be, and investing has certainly become more complicated too. Luckily, there has evolved a way to empower investors and make investing simpler, a way of investing that has been around for ages but which only recently has reached critical mass and made it possible for everyone to use. Such is the promise of top-down investing, an investing concept that relies upon indicators which carry implications that are crystal clear and highly dependable thus making it relatively easy to devise investment strategies, especially for those with very little understanding of balance sheets or the world of finance in general. It is an investment approach that also fits perfectly with the evolution of our society, where attention spans for just about everything from television to newspapers and board games have shrunk. It is thematic investing, where an investor buys an idea first and then buys the stocks, bonds, currencies, real estate assets, and other forms of investment that fit with the idea.

Top-down investing is an investment approach that has a multitude of advantages over other styles of investing, including its formidable counterpart, bottom-up investing, which relies mostly upon value investing, an investment approach that begins with scrutiny of the asset being bought. For example, in the case of corporate equities, a bottom-up investor would start with the idea that company XYZ might prosper enough to justify buying shares in the company which appear to hold value relative to the company's prospects. From there, the investor would analyze the company from the "bottom up," looking particularly at the company's balance sheet, its cash flow projections, and so forth, and do so in the context of the share price to decide whether the shares are worth investing in. Yes, this takes a lot of work, and if you do the work, you probably will choose a fairly good number of investments that work. Given the rewards, it seems we should all do the work to ensure that we are making the best possible investment decisions.

The problem with bottom-up investing, however, is that investors don't always have the tools to take on such a task nor do they have the time. How many of us truly know how to pick apart balance sheets? Who really wants to? Who in this day and age really has the time? I say, free yourself from this burden because top-down investing has proven itself to be a terrific way to formulate an investment strategy, and it is a strategy better suited for the twenty-first century than other styles of investing. I make this clear throughout this book.

THE 2007–2008 CREDIT CRISIS, A CASE IN POINT: BOTTOM-UP INVESTING FAILED

Epic were the events of 2007, when in response to the subprime mortgage crisis a full-blown credit crisis developed, requiring extraordinary actions by the Federal Reserve. By August 2007 the crisis was in full bloom, and each day brought its own harrowing episode. Throughout the period there was nary a bottom-up tool to help both in understanding what was happening and how to deal with it, particularly with respect to deciding upon what to do in response to what were very big movements in market prices. Bottom-up value investors were crushed by their approach, which puts valuation ahead of the big picture. Take, for example, the buy recommendations that bottom-up analysts were making on a variety of companies at the heart of the mortgage crisis. In one case, when the credit crisis first swelled in February 2007, one major Wall Street investment firm recommended that investors buy shares in Ambac Financial Group, which were trading at that time at around $90 per share. Through its bottom-up eyes, the firm saw value in Ambac, rating it as "outperform," which is Wall Street jargon for buy. The stock ended 2007 at $25.77 per share and kept falling.

The 2007 credit crisis was a clarion call to embrace top-down investing. When the crisis was in full bloom in August, there

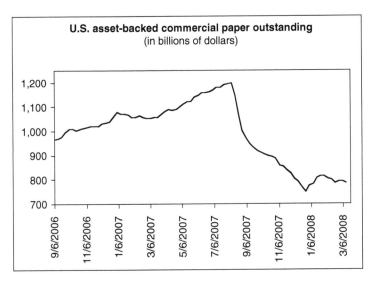

Figure 1.1 The 2007–2008 credit crisis: a top-down clarion call to avoid riskier assets.

Source: Federal Reserve.

emerged a variety of signals about the types of investments to choose and those to avoid. For example, during the crisis it became very difficult for companies to obtain credit, with investors avoiding bonds of almost every variety, including those issued by companies with excellent reputations. Most loathed were issuers with exposure to the mortgage sector, including the commercial paper market where asset-backed securities either having or being perceived as having exposure to the housing sector were avoided like the plague. Figure 1.1 illustrates the abrupt change that occurred in the market for asset-backed commercial paper. As the chart shows, the total amount of asset-backed commercial paper plunged in August 2007, falling 35 percent or about $420 billion over a period of 20 consecutive weeks before stabilizing in early 2008.

Aside from its abruptness, remarkable about the contraction in the commercial paper market was what it said about risk attitudes in general, something that a top-down investor should always be keenly interested in. Here was a segment of a market that had seen only seven defaults since 1970,[1] far less than in other

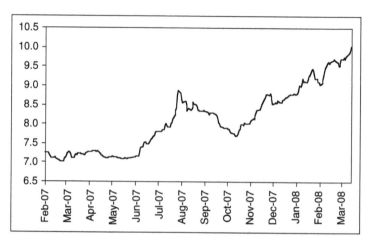

Figure 1.2 KDP High-Yield Index (yield in percentage points).

Note: The KDP High Yield Index is composed of 100 issues making up a broad cross-section of the high-yield market.

Sources: KDP Investment Advisors, Bloomberg.

segments of the fixed-income market, yet investors were fleeing it with reckless abandon. This was a clear top-down signal to scale out of assets that generally underperform when risk aversion increases. One of these was junk bonds, which did very poorly in 2007, particularly beginning in the summer when the credit crisis broadened. Figure 1.2 illustrates this point, showing the increase that occurred in yields on junk bonds during the credit crisis. The junk bond sector was clearly a sector to avoid (given, of course, the fact that bond prices move inversely in relation to bond yields). Bottom-up investors were blindsided during the crisis, lured by the idea that many companies continued to have fairly good cash flow prospects, compelling these investors to buy junk bonds on weakness, a move that would prove a mistake throughout 2007 and early 2008.

The credit crisis also signaled the potential for economic weakness, which manifested itself in a rise in the U.S. unemployment rate, which increased by an amount that since World War II had always been followed by economic recession (see Figure 1.3). For the top-down investor this had a plethora of implications. For

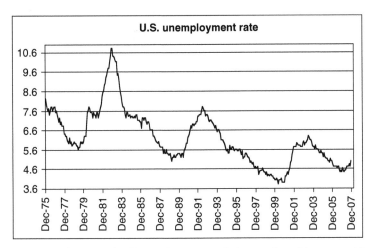

Figure 1.3 Top-down rule: Every increase of six-tenths of 1 percent in the unemployment rate since World War II has led to recession, and the average time between inflections up and recession has been nine months (the most recent inflection up was in March 2007).

Source: U.S. Bureau of Labor Statistics.

example, it was a signal to avoid transportation stocks, which tend to underperform during times of economic weakness and especially during economic downturns, as can be seen in Figure 1.4 on page 6. It was also a signal to buy U.S. Treasuries where, as Figure 1.5 on page 7 shows, yields fell decisively in anticipation of interest-rate cuts from the Federal Reserve, which were expected to be implemented to counter the negative effects of the credit crisis.

There would be many other investment ideas generated by the events of 2007 and 2008, and top-down investors had an edge, not only because top-down investing arms investors with tools that help to indicate what it is that they should be doing next, but also because it is an investment approach that makes investors more prone to look for changes in the big picture that could materially affect the investment landscape, as was the case in 2007. This is one of the reasons why top-down investing is so much better than other investment approaches; it is more dynamic. We talk more about this throughout the book.

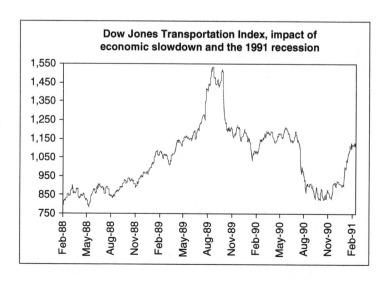

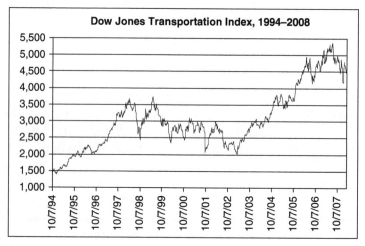

Figure 1.4 In economic downturns, transportation stocks lag.
Source: Bloomberg.

THE GLOBALIZATION OF THE FINANCIAL MARKETS: TOP-DOWN INVESTING IS THE ONLY WAY

Let me get this straight: There are now scores of companies in foreign markets to choose from, abundant challenges presented when analyzing these companies and their markets because of factors

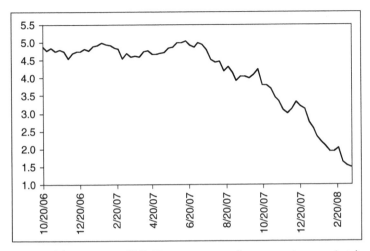

Figure 1.5 Yield on 2-year U.S. Treasury note (in percentage points).
Source: Federal Reserve.

such as language and cultural barriers, as well as questions over how to value securities in foreign markets in light of the fact that what is cheap in one market could be seen as expensive in another. Moreover, there are a swath of asset classes to choose from including commodities and currencies, for example, whose price movements tend to be dictated mostly by macro trends—particularly global ones—and we are supposed to use bottom-up investing as our main approach to constructing a diversified global portfolio? Spare me! In today's integrated markets this looks perilous.

Imagine, for example, a U.S. investor considering buying a stock in Russia. For starters, the investor would, in the absence of research written about the company involved, have to hope that the company distributes or makes available information about itself in English (unless, of course the investor understands Russian). Second, the investor would have to consider investment laws concerning foreign investment in Russia in order to be abreast of the potential impact Russian's laws could have on any investments there. Third, the investor would have to weigh the impact of other laws or decisions that could be rendered at any time by the Russian government with respect to foreign investment, domestic policies, and much more, something that even for insiders is a difficult task. I do not mean to single out Russia; investment returns have been very good there in recent years, and most feel that the prospects for Russia remain good (particularly if the price of oil is high), but what I mean to do is bring to light the idea that every country presents investors with its own set of challenges, whether lingual, cultural, legal, geopolitical, or whatever. In this case the only safe way for investors to get a grip on the big picture is with top-down investing.

THE GOLDEN COMPASSES: KEY INDICATORS

One of the most appealing aspects of top-down investing is the tool-box that this remarkable investing approach arms investors with to enable them to navigate today's complex markets. For decades other investing approaches have for the most part ignored these indicators, which you will find throughout this book and especially in Chapter 14, but doing so in today's global marketplace is igno-rant and does investors a disservice.

In the top-down investor's toolbox is an array of tools, and each and every one of them has a use that when combined makes the job of formulating an investment strategy a snap. I get excited (forgive me, but this stuff is a big part of my life!) when I find a new indicator or when I find a new use for an old one because I know that the indicator will help me to see more clearly the best possible investment alternatives for the situation at hand.

In Chapter 14 of this book we look at 40 of the best top-down indicators, but here are a couple of them now, and a note on how they might be used:

> *Birth statistics:* This is pretty simple. If you knew, for example, how many babies there were in the world, wouldn't you have a pretty good idea about how many diapers would be sold? Or if you knew how many people were going to reach an age where hearing-aid devices normally become necessary, wouldn't you have a good sense as to whether investing in companies that sell such devices might make sense? Sure, it takes a little bit more work to figure out what to do with this kind of information, but it certainly is a great start, which is the whole point of top-down investing—to get you started with a solid investment thesis.

Commercial paper issuance: We saw in 2007 the importance of the commercial paper market to the overall economy, when it began, as I showed earlier, to contract rapidly, unsettling the financial markets and contributing to weakness in the economy. The commercial paper market is a market that for years, virtually unbeknownst to most investors, has correlated strongly with inventory investment, with companies using the issuance of commercial paper to finance short-term transactions, as is required by rules dictated by the Securities and Exchange Commission.[2] What does this mean for investors? When the issuance of commercial paper fluctuates, it casts a compelling signal to the economy, which in turn helps to dictate what types of investments to choose. There are a tremendous number of ideas that result in the different stages of the economic cycle.

YOU'VE SEEN THIS MOVIE BEFORE; YOU WILL SEE IT AGAIN

Those who use technical analysis often use charts to derive a forecast about the future because they generally expect past patterns to repeat. There is a great deal of credence to this, and there are a variety of technical indicators that are true golden compasses, the reasons for which is described in Chapter 12. A few of these indicators are described in Chapter 13 of this book. While I rely upon technical indicators for important signals, particularly on market sentiment, it makes me nervous to put too much weight on them unless they are backed by fundamental factors. For example, unusually high levels of bullish sentiment (a contrary indicator) about a particular commodity carry far more weight when they are coupled with bearish fundamentals such as rising supplies. Still, what I glean from technical analysis as far as it relates to top-down investing is the idea that certain patterns have a strong chance of either repeating themselves or behaving similarly enough to be useful when formulating an investment strategy. With top-down investing, this holds true with the best of the top-down indicators—the golden compasses, each of which has a highly dependable track record of foreshadowing events and aiding the selection of the best performing investments. It is why when a particular indicator behaves a certain way, top-down investors immediately recognize that it is a movie they have seen before. In response, these moviegoers know what to do next. It is one of the more comforting aspects of top-down investing.

BABBLING, BORING BALANCE SHEETS

In a poll of U.S. adults conducted in 2005 by the Associated Press and America Online, by far the subject that respondents said that they hated the most in school was math.[3] This sentiment might be changing if data from the Brown Center on Education Policy are any guide, as it found that math scores for grades 2 and 4 have been increasing steadily since 1990.[4] In fact, according to the National Assessment of Educational Progress (NAEP), which was developed by the U.S. Department of Education to assess what U.S. students know and can do in various subject areas, the increases in math scores seen between 1990 and 2007 indicate that fourth and eighth graders in 2007 knew more than two additional years of mathematics compared to fourth and eighth graders in 1990.[5] Despite these hopeful facts, people just seem to hate math, as the AP and AOL survey and table-talk discussions indicate. This means that there are an awful lot of investors out there who will do whatever it takes to steer clear of math, especially complex math and by all means anything to do with those babbling, boring, balance sheets. There is of course no escaping the use of math when it comes to investing, but most investors can leave the misery of dissecting balance sheets to others if they invest from the top down. We talk more about this in Chapter 9.

YOU CAN DO THE MATH, SO DO IT!

As I said, investors can't escape using math completely; numbers are what make the financial world go around. What astounds me, though, is that people are so loath to do math that they often avoid it almost completely, failing to do the math on big-picture ideas that in concept carry much more weight than the numbers do. The most glaring example I can think of in this regard is the failure by very large numbers of market participants to do the math on the impact that rising energy prices would have on consumer spending and the overall economy when energy prices first began to surge in 2003. It was said about the surge that consumers would buckle, be hamstrung, or otherwise be strained to such an extent that they would almost certainly stop spending on everything else, and the economy would henceforth stop expanding. This idea proved wrong until the end of 2007 when a renewed surge in energy costs combined with the weak housing market, the credit crisis, and other factors produced a sharp slowdown of economic activity. This means that investors who failed to do the math were wrong for about five years. Such was not the case for top-down investors, however, as they had the simple tools needed to avoid this trap, a trap that let top-down traders win investment dollars from the crowd. We talk more about this in Chapter 14.

YOU'RE NOT WARREN BUFFETT—GET OVER IT

Warren Buffett has said that an IQ of no more than 125 is needed to understand and use value investing,[6] the investment approach that involves the selection of stocks in companies trading at levels deemed to be below their intrinsic value, which is determined by comparing a company's share price with its future cash flows. Benjamin Graham, widely considered the founder of the modern concept of value investing thanks to the publication in 1934 of his and David Dodd's groundbreaking classic book *Security Analysis*, depended heavily upon these principles, describing intrinsic value as a company's acquisition or liquidation value, or the collateral value of its assets and cash flow. As Buffett said, applying Graham's principles of value investing requires very little intellectual capacity. Fair enough. The problem, though, is that successful value investing nonetheless requires at least a modicum of intellectual capacity. In other words, while it is probably true that investors need not be rocket scientists in order to have the capacity to apply the principles of value investing, investors nonetheless must have at least some knowledge of it.

Value investing and other investment strategies that depend upon close scrutiny of a company's balance sheet in order to arrive at a yes or no answer on whether to invest have become less viable over the years partly because markets have become more efficient and because of the amount of work now required to conduct a company evaluation that is thorough enough to enable the person doing the analysis to spot opportunities. Graham said as much in 1976 in an interview in the *Financial Analysts Journal,* describing why he was "no longer an advocate of elaborate techniques of security analysis," noting that with so much research being conducted on and off Wall Street that it was unlikely that extensive efforts could generate superior ideas as was the case 40 years earlier when he wrote his book.[7] While today's value investors have found their own ways to overcome this obstacle, this classic investment approach is not for everyone; we are all cut from different cloth. This is one of my main points. You may not now or may not ever possess the knowledge necessary to make you a successful value investor, perhaps either because it is the way you are wired or because you are simply not interested in the rigmarole involved in that style of investing. So you're not Warren Buffett. Don't sweat it; this is the age of top-down investing.

PICK WINNING SECTORS, AND YOU WILL PICK WINNING STOCKS

Studies differ on the amount by which an individual stock's performance can be explained by the performance of other stocks in the sector that it is in, but most agree that it is a large percentage—more than 50 percent. This is intuitive, as it would make sense that companies within an individual sector would be exposed to nearly identical influences, at least as far as the major ones go. For example, home builders are collectively affected by the level of interest rates, credit availability, demographics, housing supply, and so forth. Oil companies are affected by the price of oil. Consumer cyclical companies such as automobile and manufacturers are affected by the ups and downs of the business cycle (more so than other sectors). Exporters are affected by the changes in the value of the dollar. And so forth.

Not convinced yet? Well, consider the financial bubble of the late 1990s and its subsequent bursting in 2000. For a time, owning any stock with a dot-com acronym was like choosing a road to riches. Later, of course, dot-com stocks would plunge, many of them losing all their value. The behavior of dot-com stocks during that period made clear just how important sector performance was to the performance of individual stocks. Many dot-com stocks had little or no real potential to reach profitability (as we eventually learned), yet investors took a leap of faith, betting on the sector, mostly, rather than the individual companies.

In a very different situation that showed why it was better to be a top-down investor than a bottom-up investor, the events of 2007 provide compelling support. Top-down investors watching their golden compasses knew to avoid housing and anything related to housing no matter how cheap companies in the sector might appear because of declines in their stock prices. Top-down investors had a better idea: buy energy stocks. Both of these ideas were guided by macro indicators, as shown in Figures 1.6 and 1.7. In both cases, top-down investors had simple choices about what to do. Investing does not have to be confusing.

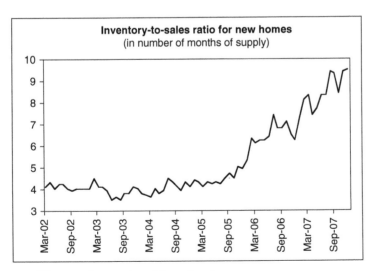

Figure 1.6 The top-down signal to get out.

Source: U.S. Census Bureau.

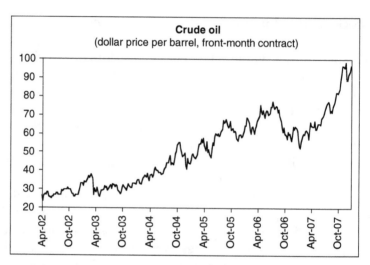

Figure 1.7 The top-down signal to get in.

Sources: New York Mercantile Exchange, Bloomberg.

IT'S THE INFORMATION AGE: TOP-DOWN INVESTORS REJOICE!

When I compare the amount of macro information available to me today compared to the amount available in years past, I want to jump for joy (okay, maybe this stuff gets me a bit too excited, but it truly astounds!). There just is no comparison between today and yesteryear. The reason that I get so excited about this is because as someone who has always approached the markets from the top down, I have always sought as much information as I could find in order to arrive at the best possible conclusion about what might happen next in the economy and the financial markets. This remarkable new era has made available to me information that is rich in both quantity and quality and for which I can find many uses. To me, the fact that the information age has made so much more information available augments my confidence in the ideas I generate.

Today, top-down investors can obtain mountains of information about the economy, the financial markets, specific industries, and specific companies. Information that once was available only through snail mail, telefaxes, or couriers is now just a click away. For example, if I wanted to analyze the supply and demand situation for oil, I could go to a number of Web sites, including the U.S. Department of Energy, the American Petroleum Institute, OPEC, and the International Energy Agency. Each of these Web sites contains data from which a sense of the supply/demand picture can be quickly developed. This can in turn be applied toward investments, not only in the energy sphere but also on the periphery, by selecting or avoiding investments in equities, currencies, and bonds of the largest users of energy, the countries that produce oil. Investment in alternative energy is clearly a macro approach, carrying many advantages over other investing approaches, particularly because it generates a swath of investment ideas around the globe.

Benjamin Graham and his disciples refer to the difference between a company's stock price and its intrinsic value as a *margin of safety*. The idea is that, if their calculations are correct, at a minimum the company's share price will move up toward its intrinsic value, and if the company's intrinsic value increases, its shares will rally even more. It is a sound concept, and it is certainly wise to leave room for error in many walks of life, whether it is running past an oncoming car while crossing the street, making a full stop at a stop sign, or avoiding excessive fats and cholesterol. Taking these actions brings comfort.

These same principles apply to top-down investing where the information age has substantially boosted the degree to which top-down investors can make judgments that result in the best possible investment ideas. The information age brings opportunity, and it brings comfort. There has never been a better time to collect and analyze information, which in the virtual world now sits upon a bountiful table waiting for investors to use it.

MANIAS AND MARKET SENTIMENT ARE A TOP-DOWN AFFAIR

There seems to be no escaping the idea that no matter how sophisticated our society becomes, we still find ourselves getting caught up in the latest craze. It is what led to the dot-com bubble in the late 1990s and the real estate bubble in the latter part of the first decade of the 2000s. I guess we are just human. Apparently no amount of computing power and knowledge seems likely to make us stop.

Since it looks like we will be human for a while longer, we should continue to expect irrational behavior in the financial markets. This means that we must do our best to figure out when it is happening so that we do not get caught up in it and so that we can spot opportunities that result from the irrational behavior of others. The types of analyses required to figure out these sorts of things fall under the top-down umbrella, arming top-down investors with plenty of dependable tools to help in determining whether people are, well, acting human and going to extremes again. Other investment approaches attempt to avoid the sentiment trap by selecting investments that would be protected against most of the vagaries of a market swoon, but they don't do a good job of spotting ways you can profit from or avoid such swoons altogether. We discuss many of the indicators that top-down investors use to assess market sentiment in Chapter 12.

DON'T FIGHT THE FED—OR ANY OTHER CENTRAL BANK

One of my favorite lines uttered so often by those who trade from the bottom up is that they do not care what the Fed is up to because what the Fed does won't affect their investment decisions. Give me a break! There is a wealth of data proving the idea that the Fed's actions have a very large impact on investments. If you don't believe me, then take advice from Federal Reserve chairman Ben Bernanke, who in May 2004, which was about two years before he became Fed chairman, wrote a 56-page research article titled, "What Explains the Stock Market's Reaction to Federal Reserve Policy."[8] Bernanke concluded that, "on average, a hypothetical unanticipated 25-basis-point cut in the federal funds rate target is associated with about a one percent increase in broad stock indexes." It seems to me that any time you can pick up 100 basis points of additional return on your investments, you should try mightily to do so. This is, after all, an environment where finding even a few extra basis points of additional returns have become more difficult to come by, given the increased efficiency of the financial markets. The way that the markets behaved in the aftermath of the actions taken by the Federal Reserve in response to the crisis at Bear Stearns illustrates immensely the importance of the Fed in the investment decision-making process.

There are many ways in which the top-down investor utilizes the actions and the anticipated actions by the Federal Reserve. For starters, as Fed chairman Bernanke found, there is an array of events that typically result from the actions of the Federal Reserve. Aside from added returns to stock market indexes on the whole, individual sectors will tend to perform differently under different monetary policy scenarios. For example, the top-down investor would expect the housing sector and other interest-rate-sensitive sectors to underperform when the Fed is raising interest rates. In addition, in such an environment, the U.S. dollar will tend to appreciate in value.

Central bank watching has now become a global affair, such that investors must now keep tabs on central banks outside the United States, particularly the Bank of England, the European Central Bank, and the Bank of Canada, which during the credit crisis of 2007 cooperated in ways investors only speculated about in the past, for example, by jointly announcing actions to provide short-term liquidity to the global money markets. This increased coordination means that financial assets throughout the globe are subject more than ever before to the very substantial influences of the world's central banks. I am sure we will see more of this in the very near future, including influence by the central banks in emerging economies, particularly in China.

AMERICA'S ATTENTION SPAN FOR INVESTING HAS SHRUNK TOO

There is plenty of evidence to show that Americans have shorter attention spans than they used to, and this has had a profound effect on a variety of entities, including television networks, advertisers, schools, toy companies, food companies, and political campaigns. It seems that keeping peoples' attention has become a chore. Increasingly, people are spreading themselves thinner, spending less and less time on just about everything whether it is watching television, cooking, playing board games, or whatever. The same can be said about investing, with people showing the same proclivity, spending fewer hours polishing up on their investing skills, formulating their investments, and tracking them.

Let's face it, either because you are spreading yourself thinner than before or because you are just not interested in spending more time on your investments, you have got to do all that you can to make sure that the time you do put in on your investments is time well spent.

As with so many other aspects of your life, you need to move quickly and efficiently, and you really can't compromise on this because it is how you want to live your life. You don't want to be bogged down by any one thing because there is too much in this world to enjoy. This is exactly how I feel about things. Like me, you are probably aware of how important it is to make the best possible decisions regarding your investments. It is a major part of your life, yet this feeling of being bogged down can't be escaped. We are quite fortunate, therefore, to have the top-down approach to investing, where the amount of time required to make excellent investment decisions is far less than the time needed with other investment approaches, particularly those that require extensive scrutiny of those boring, babbling balance sheets.

Maybe this seems a bit lazy, but, as I said, this may be how you choose to live your life, and it you might not be lazy at all, just very busy—too busy in light of other priorities you deem higher in importance to find the time to pick apart balance sheets.

The top-down approach is ideally suited for those of you who live your life this way. With just a few big-picture indicators, you can get a grip on your investments and live life the way you choose to. I've given you the concept, which if adopted, will put you well on your way to being a successful top-down investor, and we discuss how to apply these principles throughout this book.

THIS IS THE GOLDEN AGE OF MACROECONOMICS

There is now a wide body of research that refers to the past 25 years as "the great moderation" for the U.S. economy, a name chosen to reflect the decline that has occurred in macroeconomic volatility during the period, specifically with respect to the variability of changes in economic growth and inflation.[9] For example, in one study by Blanchard and Simon, the variability of quarterly output was found to have fallen by half since the mid-1980s, and the variability of quarterly inflation was found to have fallen by two-thirds. Figure 1.8 illustrates the decrease that has occurred in macroeconomic volatility from 1952 to 2002. As the bottom graph in Figure 1.8

shows, the standard deviation of quarterly real gross domestic product (GDP) growth was 4.7 percentage points before 1984, the year often cited as the start of the great moderation, and 2.1 percentage points afterward—a stark change.

Figure 1.8 The great moderation growth in U.S. GDP and consumption in the twentieth century (top chart), and standard deviation of growth and inflation (bottom chart).

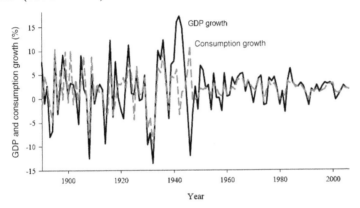

Source: James Nason and Gregor Smith, "Great Moderations and U.S. Interest Rates," Federal Reserve Bank of Atlanta, *Working Paper Series*, January 2008.

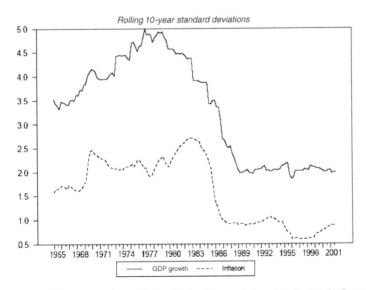

Source: Antonella D'Agostino and Carl Whelan, "Federal Reserve Information During the Great Moderation." *Journal of the European Economics Association*, December 2007.

The decline in economic volatility has many benefits, as the decline should. As Fed chairman Ben Bernanke said in a speech in 2004, the decline in economic volatility leads to "more stable employment and a reduction in the extent of economic uncertainty confronting households and firms." In addition, "lower volatility of inflation improves market functioning, makes economic planning easier, and reduces the resources devoted to hedging inflation risks."[10] These benefits are a major positive to investors who need worry less about the ups and downs in growth and inflation and the effects that these ups and downs will have on financial assets. Today's top-down investors can therefore be more confident than ever about the signals cast by macroeconomic indicators, which tend to result in fairly predictable outcomes.

To further underscore how the macroeconomic landscape has changed in recent years, it is notable that in 2004 the Nobel Prize in economics was given to two researchers who developed a new theory on business cycles and economic policy, placing emphasis away from isolated policy measures toward the institutions of policymaking, which has resulted, for example, in changes in the way that the Federal Reserve is run. In addition, the laureates, according to the Nobel Foundation, "laid the groundwork" for more robust models on the business cycle to include the forward-looking decisions made by households and firms, which these days are sharply influencing the direction of the economy, just as policy decisions by themselves once did. Tellingly, Edward C. Prescott titled his prize lecture, "The Transformation of Macroeconomic Policy and Research," further underscoring these points.[11] What all of this means for investors is that these changes reinforce the idea that top-down investing is an approach that fits with today's more dynamic times, as it is an approach geared toward picking up changes that occur in the big picture that you won't find on company balance sheets.

TOP-DOWN INVESTING WILL LIBERATE YOU

As I have shown, a variety of factors are combining to make the present time a golden period for top-down investing, and applying its principles can be extraordinarily liberating. Who, after all, says that you have to be bound by the exhausting analyses required by other approaches to investing that you either do not understand, do not have the time to understand, or simply choose not to understand? Also, how can we ignore the fact that in today's integrated world a well-diversified portfolio must by definition include investments abroad, which can be selected only by a careful look at the world from the top down? Moreover, we have seen time and time again, via the performance of sectors within the equity market, just how important it is to make stock selections that reflect the outlook for the sectors, which can have substantial influence on the performance of individual stocks. It is also difficult to escape the idea that the information age has made available mountains of useful information to even the simplest folk. The information age is a top-down investor's dream and who doesn't want to live a dream? Investing from the top down is not a cakewalk, of course, and I implore people all the time to "please do the math!" when they are considering the impact of big-picture issues, whether it is the impact of oil on the overall economy or some other factor affecting the markets in ways that may not fit with reality. Luckily, top-down investing equips investors with the numbers they need to "do the math" and arrive at successful investment ideas.

There is a certain calm that comes with investing from the top down that I have tried to portray in this first chapter. I am convinced that top-down investing is the most liberating and effective style of investing available because it not only arms investors with indicators—golden compasses as I sometimes like to call them—whose trends yield unmistakable signals about the best possible investment ideas, but the approach does so without the strains associated with pouring through those boring, babbling balance sheets. It is time you free yourself from the rigmarole of other styles of investing and invest from the top down, where you can do what you do best and think big.

Notes

[1] Crescenzi, Anthony, and Marcia Stigum, "*Stigum's Money Market*," 4th ed. (McGraw-Hill, 2007).

[2] Ibid.

[3] Poll conducted by the Associated Press and America Online, August 2005, http://wid.ap.org/polls/050816school/index.html.

[4] http://www.brookings.edu/~/media/Files/rc/reports/2007/1211_education_loveless/1211_education_loveless.pdf.

[5] http://nces.ed.gov/nationsreportcard/nde/.

[6] Browne, Christopher, *The Little Book of Value Investing* (Wiley, 2007).

[7] Ellis, Charles D., "A Conversation with Benjamin Graham," *Financial Analysts Journal,* 1976.

[8] Bernanke, Ben, and Kenneth Kuttner, "What Explains the Stock Market's Reaction to Federal Reserve Policy?" Federal Reserve Bank of New York Staff Reports, no. 174, October 2003 and March 2004.

[9] Blanchard, Olivier, and John Simon, "The Long and Large Decline in U.S. Output Volatility," *Brookings Papers on Economic Activity,* 1, 2001, pp. 135–164.

[10] Bernanke, Ben, "The Great Moderation." Speech delivered before the Eastern Economic Association, Washington, D.C., February 20, 2004. Available at http://www.federalreserve.gov/boarddocs/speeches/2004/20040220/default.htm#fn1.

[11] Prescott, Edward C., "The Transformation of Macroeconomic Policy and Research." Nobel Prize Lecture, Arizona State University, Tempe, and Federal Reserve Bank of Minneapolis, December 8, 2004.

CHAPTER 2

The 2007 Credit Crisis:
A Case in Point

A true capitalist seeks both shelter and ways to benefit from approaching storms.

During the epic financial events of 2007, an array of indicators forebode the approaching storm, giving top-down investors plenty of opportunity to shield themselves and profit from it. The storm actually began two years earlier when the housing market peaked, when a number of the golden compasses found in Chapter 14 of this book clearly pointed to extraordinarily stretched conditions in the housing market, particularly with respect to home prices. It took time for a host of other indicators to flash danger signs for both the U.S. economy and the financial markets, but the combination of signals stemming from housing and financial indicators gave top-down investors a road map clearer than Google Earth to follow. Pity the bottom-up investors, who by adherence to their notion of value, saw value far earlier than others were ready to believe was there. Top-down investors fared far better.

In 2005, a number of golden compasses signaled danger on the housing front, flashing unmistakable signs of a top in both home sales and home prices. Optimists clung to their views, stating, for example, that there was no precedent for home prices to fall and that shares in home building companies still held "value." One of the indicators flashing warning signs was the National Association of Realtors' housing affordability index, which as its title implies is an index that attempts to measure the degree to which a household earning the median income can afford the purchase of a median-priced home. As Figure 2.1 shows, housing affordability began to plunge in 2005, such that by the middle of 2005 it was at its lowest point since 1991, which was in the throes of the previous housing-market bust in the early 1990s. Boosting the chances of a top was a jump to a record level in the ratio between home prices and incomes.

Top-down investors had additional reasons to believe housing was peaking, not the least of which were the 17 consecutive interest-rate increases implemented by the Federal Reserve over the course of two years beginning in June 2004 and ending in June 2006, and a peak in the Mortgage Bankers Association's weekly mortgage applications index for home purchases, which, as Figure 2.2 shows, peaked in June 2005. By October of 2005 the index dropped below its one-year average, signaling a trend change. In the second half of 2005, the supply of unsold homes also started to trend upward, which according to very basic principles on supply and demand, meant that home prices were likely to fall. The jump in inventories could be seen on several fronts, including inventory-to-sales ratios for new and existing homes, and in Figure 2.3, which shows the amount of existing single-family homes that went unsold.

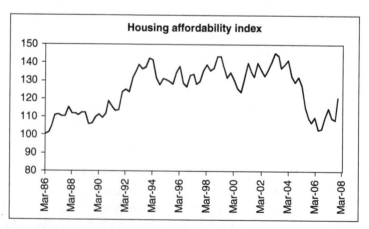

Figure 2.1 Red flag: Housing affordability hit a 14-year low in 2005.
Source: National Association of Realtors.

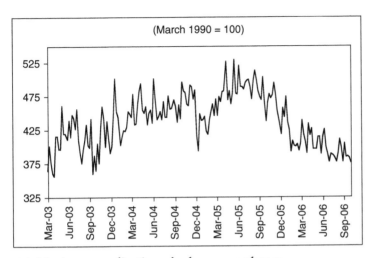

Figure 2.2 Mortgage applications for home purchases.

Source: Mortgage Bankers Association.

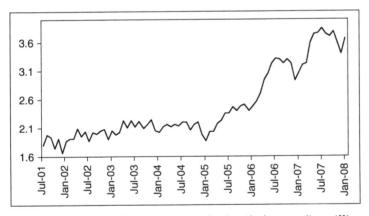

Figure 2.3 Supply of unsold existing single-family homes (in millions of units).

Source: National Association of Realtors.

GLANCE AT A FEW CHARTS; FORMULATE A PLAN IN A SNAP

What is important for readers to pick up from Figures 2.1–2.3 is how quickly a conclusion can be drawn about a particular aspect of the U.S. economy. It literally takes seconds. There's no pouring through reams of data and long-winded analyses, nor is a dissection of company balance sheets required. All that is needed is the right set of indicators and knowledge about what to do when these indicators, particularly those that I am calling "golden compasses," sway one way or another.

As I said, it is fine and dandy to have a reliable set of indicators in hand but to profit from what can be garnered from these indicators requires that investors have a sense for the chain of events that usually follows from trends in the indicators. Gaining this knowledge in no way disrupts a key premise of this book, which is that top-down investing can be applied profitably by all types of investors, including those with either limited knowledge of investing or those who because of lifestyle choices choose not to put their time into learning styles of investing that are deemed more demanding than the top-down approach, particularly those with a heavy emphasis on quantitative analyses—the boring ones especially! What is needed is a simple canvassing of the top indicators—such as those referenced in this book—and how these indicators can be readily tracked. What is needed is convincing evidence on the chain of events that should be expected to follow these indicators. Keep in mind that it is important to blend in trends observed in other indicators, because many indicators work best when combined with others, particularly when a certain thesis is being tested.

FOLLOW THE CHAIN

When signs of a top in the housing market began to mount, top-down investors had an early sense of the very far-reaching effects that the housing sector's decline would eventually bring upon both the financial markets and the economy. This road map would steer top-down investors away from the storm and guide them into more profitable investments. The simplest conclusion was to sell shares in home-building companies, a strategy that would reap massive rewards. And there was plenty of time to implement this strategy, as shown in Figure 2.4.

A major feature of top-down investing is the way in which it leads to multiple trading strategies, often across many asset classes. This results from the way in which top-down investing leads investors to consider the series of events that tend to follow a particular development or a set of facts. These "chain reactions" are

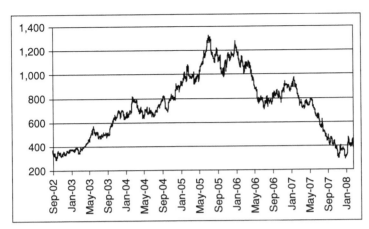

Figure 2.4 S&P Home Builders Index.

Source: Bloomberg.

common in the top-down world, and they are the basis of the investment decisions developed with this approach.

After it became clear that housing would slow down, there was very little inkling that the slowdown would infiltrate the financial sector as deeply as it began to in 2007. There were nonetheless significant amounts of macro information available indicating that the housing sector continued to deteriorate in 2007, chiefly the figures on the amount of unsold homes (see Figure 2.3), which raised the specter of additional price declines, and hence a variety of other scenarios including the potential for knockoff effects on consumers and impact on banks and investors with exposure to mortgage-related securities.

It is important to recognize that bottom-up investors completely missed these facts, which is one of the reasons why many stocks with exposure to housing held up until the summer of 2007 when the credit crisis went into full bloom. For example, shares in government agencies Fannie Mae and Freddie Mac and mortgage insurers such as MBIA Inc. and Ambac, each assigned triple-A credit ratings, held up even longer, not sinking until the final months of 2007. Investors continued to see "value" in these companies because of how the companies were rated and because of perceptions about their balance sheets, considerations heavily relied upon by bottom-up investors. Taking the bottom-up route clearly was the wrong approach, as every top-down indicator pointed to continued deterioration in housing and in the mortgage realm, which kept top-down investors away from the housing-related sectors.

As I said, there emerged a number of indicators that in addition to the dreadful figures on the amount of unsold homes as well as other elements of the supply/demand situation in housing pointed to significant risks for housing and housing-related sectors. The indicators were not housing indicators per se, and they were not indicators that most investors would normally run to when analyzing the housing situation, yet they packed a mighty punch. In particular, there emerged a number of financial indicators suggesting that financial conditions were tightening substantially and would crimp lending in the housing sector. For example, the spread between key money market rates and the federal funds rate widened significantly. Especially troublesome was a jump in commercial paper rates and the London Interbank Offered Rates (LIBOR). The jump in LIBOR is shown in Figure 2.5.

The jump in money market rates was extraordinary, and it was occurring for reasons that gave guidance to investors in terms of how they should weigh the outlook on financial stocks. The root of the problem was the decline in home prices, a macro factor that, as

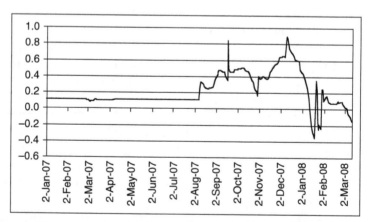

Figure 2.5 Three-month LIBOR minus the target fed funds rate (in percentage points).

Note: The spread moved into negative territory in early 2008 in anticipation of interest rate cuts by the Federal Reserve.

Sources: Federal Reserve, British Bankers Association.

I said before, was clearly signaled by the major housing indicators. Investors were especially troubled over the implications that declining home prices would have on subprime mortgage borrowers, who were also facing sharp increases in their mortgage payments after their so-called teaser rates began expiring. Investors sought answers on three primary fronts:

1. How large was the subprime mortgage market?
2. What amount of subprime mortgage loans might default?
3. Who was left holding the bag with their exposure to subprime mortgage investments?

It was the last question regarding where the losses were that sparked the jump in money market rates, as it resulted in distrust so great that major banks balked at lending to each other. This resulted in virtually unprecedented increases in interbank borrowing rates not only in the United States but abroad, where there were also question marks about who it was that had exposure to the U.S. subprime mortgage market. The dislocation became so great that the European Central Bank (ECB) was forced to inject a record 95 billion euros (131 billion dollars) into its banking system on August 9, 2007, in order to try to stabilize interbank borrowing rates, which had moved significantly above the ECB's target rate, as shown in Figure 2.6. Additional large injections of short-term liquidity continued into the early part

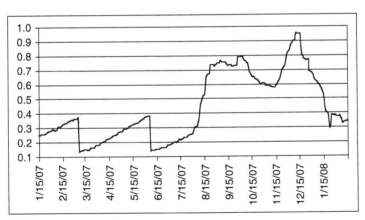

Figure 2.6 Three-month Euribor minus the European Central Bank's benchmark rate (in percentage points).

Sources: European Central Bank, British Bankers Association.

of 2008. On December 18, 2007, the ECB injected nearly $500 billion into the money markets.

For its part, the Federal Reserve was also forced to make mega injections of money into the U.S. banking system, injecting amounts that were at times several times larger than the $9 billion daily average that prevailed in the two years leading up to the crisis. The Fed also devised several strategies to bolster the availability of money for banks in need of cash, including the creation of a term auction facility (TAF), a facility that enables banks to bid for loans from the Fed and which is likely to become a permanent tool for the Fed. By June 2008 the Fed was auctioning $150 billion per month to banks via the TAF. The Fed also created the primary dealer credit facility (PDCF) on March 16, 2008, in order to facilitate J.P. Morgan's purchase of Bear Stearns and provide a backstop to the primary dealer community. In addition to the creation of these facilities and other creative ways in which the Fed sought to provide liquidity and calm the markets, the Fed took potent action by lowering the federal funds rate a full percentage point between September and December 2007, and then by a whopping 125 basis points in January 2008. By April 2008, the Fed had lowered the funds rate a cumulative 325 basis points to 2.0 percent.

None of what has been said here so far relates to bottom-up investing, which was a failed strategy in 2007 and 2008. All of it speaks to top-down investing, where each day brought a new development, and top-down investors were equipped to make the best possible judgments about the actions they should take By "equipped," I am referring to the grasp that top-down investors have of the indicators discussed in this chapter and throughout this book and, importantly, to the general mindset that top-down investors have. For example, top-down investors are always on the lookout for anything that might upset or is altering the landscape, such as the weakening of housing activity beginning in 2005 and the chain of events that followed and resulted in the credit crisis of 2007.

BEYOND THE HOUSING CRISIS, THE FUTURE OF HOUSING FROM THE TOP DOWN

There are a variety of indicators available that investors can utilize to form an outlook on how the housing situation will play itself out and the strategies that best fit the outlook. It is a comforting thought to know that such indicators exist, and this is one of the major allures of top-down investing.

Demographics: A Powerful Tool

In early 2008 pessimism about the outlook for housing and its potential impact on the economy was extraordinarily high, as was evident on a variety of fronts, including the behavior of housing-related stocks, credit default swaps, the performance of financial shares with housing-related exposure, and the general tone of the financial markets, which was extremely anxious. Yet there existed a set of top-down data that pointed to an eventual stabilization in housing and its impact on the economy that in the years following the publication of this book will be almost impossible to ignore. One of the most glaring sets of these data can be gleaned from one of the golden compasses—population and demographic statistics. The premise on this one is simple: if the number of people entering prime home-buying ages increases, then household formation will increase, which in turn should increase the demand for housing. By this same logic, if there are more babies in the world, then the demand for diapers will increase. Demographic data such as these can yield powerful clues about future demand trends on a variety of goods and services, and the conclusions drawn from demographic information are incredibly sound, as they are based on simple facts about human existence and cultural factors, such as the fact that in the present day babies wear diapers.

For housing, the age group that matters most in terms of developing a forecast for housing demand is the group aged 25 to 30. Those are the years, of course, when people start buying homes of their own. Another age group that matters especially now because of the group's growing numbers is the group aged 50, especially those aged 55 and up, chiefly because people aged 55 and up account for substantial amounts of the second-home buying activity in the United States.[1] Figure 2.7 shows by age group the share of households that owns second homes.

Birth statistics from the U.S. National Center for Health Services indicate that the number of people in both of these important age groups will be rising at a pace that will be quite supportive of housing demand in the years following the publication of this

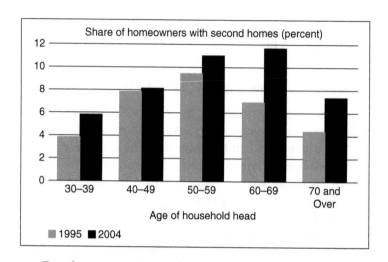

Figure 2.7 People over age 50 are the biggest second-home buyers.

Note: Second homes include fractional ownership in timeshares and vacation properties.

Source: Harvard University, *"The State of the Nation's Housing, 2006,"* Joint Center for Housing Studies of Harvard University.

book. This stands in stark contrast to the demographic influences that followed the last bust in the housing market, which occurred in the early 1990s. Back then the number of people in the age group 25 to 30 fell by about 14 percent owing to influences relating to the end of the baby boom, which occurred between 1946 and 1964. In other words, the number of people born between the years 1965 and 1969 fell by 14 percent compared to the period 1960 to 1964. This meant that the number of people that would turn 25 in 1989 would exceed the number of people turning 25 in 1990. Take it from me. I learned firsthand how powerful this influence would turn out to be. I purchased my first home in 1989—right on target at age 25. There were a lot of people like me—those of us born in 1964, but I had no idea how few of me—those turning age 25—there would be in the several years that followed my home purchase. Had I only known then what I know now! If I did, I would have recognized that the many problems facing the housing market at that time would take a very long time to dissipate, owing partly to unfavorable demographics. I wound up selling my home in 1997 at a loss of more than 30 percent.

The table has turned on demographic influences, and the interest rate picture is also better, owing to entrenched views about favorable inflation trends and greater trust in the Federal Reserve, so there is now a better chance at a recovery in housing despite the many obstacles that exist. These obstacles of course must be weighed, but it is difficult to ignore the basic facts surrounding the need for shelter. With respect to demographics, keep this fact in mind for the next 10 years: the number of people aged 25 to 30 will increase by close to 15 percent through 2015,[2] birth statistics indicate. Moreover, there will also be a sharp increase in the number of people aged 55 and up, owing to the aging of the baby boomers. Therefore, given that in the time ahead there will be more people in the age groups that matter, it stands to reason that there will be plenty of buyers to absorb the excess housing supply that built up after the housing bubble burst in the early 2000s.

A New Indicator: The Subprime Reset Schedule

In addition to favorable demographics, it is predicted that in 2008 and 2009 the housing sector will be set to become less hamstrung by resets on subprime mortgages, which in the early part of 2008 saw rates pushed higher on about $40 billion of subprime mortgages per month. This impaired the ability of many homeowners to pay their bills and consume goods and services. By early 2009 the reset figure moves closer to zero, raising the odds of a bottoming of this very negative influence on both housing and the economy.

It is important to note that the reset figure is a macro figure that surfaced only recently, which highlights the dynamic nature of top-down investing and the need to stay abreast of the issues of the day in order to locate macro indicators that can help you navigate through the new situations that arise. Because of their prominence, figures such as these eventually move into the mainstream for a while before fading again, so they have to be picked up quickly. Often they will appear in news stories, and credible news organizations will often cite where they found the data, which is the best place to go to find out more about them. For the housing sector, Fannie Mae, Freddie Mac, and the Office for Federal Housing and Oversight are usually good places to start, but as I said, many indicators that come into vogue will eventually be found just about everywhere, including in a wide body of research and studies such as those conducted by the Federal Reserve, major colleges, and political think tanks.

No Doubt: Humans Need Shelter

Finally, another factor set to reduce the housing sector's drag on the economy was the level of housing starts, which by early 2008 had fallen close to its lowest point in 50 years of record-keeping, to a pace of 954K in March 2008 before rebounding only slightly in subsequent months. Following top-down logic, it is almost impossible to fathom starts moving much lower in the time ahead given that household formation tends to increase by about 1.2 million per year. Moreover, it is important to keep in mind that housing starts include homes torn down and reconstructed, activity that adds no new net supply to housing. This figure tends to run at around 200,000 units per year, which means that housing starts of about 1 million annually boost the number of homes that can be lived in by only about 800,000, a figure well below household formation. Where pray tell will the other 400,000 households go? Well, into the excess supply of unsold homes that burdened the economy in 2007 and 2008.

Top-down indicators such as these enable investors to stay calmer than other investors and allow them to spot opportunities better. In the case of the recent housing crisis, the data cited here are the type that top-down investors dream about: because the data have sturdy logic and because the conclusions drawn from them conflict with the consensus, they provide the opportunity to enter into good investment ideas. In early 2008, data such as these gave top-down investors a means of removing themselves from the thicket of worrywarts and the basis to consider conditions that could well turn out far different from what just about everyone expected at that time.

MORE LESSONS FROM THE CREDIT AND HOUSING CRISES OF 2007 AND 2008

The seismic events of 2007 spurred sustained tremors throughout the world. The events affected the world economy and its financial markets and had a major impact on the U.S. political landscape, with the U.S. economy becoming the public's top concern as the 2008 election year rolled on. Given the way in which the credit crisis, the housing crisis, and other macro events such as the surge in energy costs affected the world in 2007 and 2008, it is difficult to fathom how some investors can turn their backs on macro events when it comes to their investment decision-making process. Heaven help them.

In this book and in other investment books, nearly all of what is discussed relates to the financial markets and the economy. This is as it should be because the books are geared toward those topics. Not to be lost, however, and never lost in the mind of this still-humble Wall Streeter is that there are people behind every number and that when these numbers move around, lives are affected in one way or another. In 2007 and 2008, the lives of many people were affected in major ways. Families were displaced from their homes amid the massive wave of foreclosures, and others were strained by significant increases in their mortgage payments and the cost of filling up their gas tanks. Rising unemployment broke the hearts of laborers, many of whom had to suffer the pain and worry of how to feed their children and give them a better life. This is not the place to pontificate, but I am giving it all I've got to convince you, the reader, that by grasping the big picture, you will be able to clearly see every little detail that you thought you could only get from the bottom up. The more that you take to looking at the world from the top down, the more that you will see the far-ranging implications of everything that happens in it, right down to the joys and the tears that every event or trend entails.

The View from the Top Down: Three Musts for the Macro Maven

Decide: Is this a macro moment?

1. *When big events occur, seek both protection and profit.* Each situation is different, but there will undoubtedly be big winners and big losers from the fallout of these events as was the case with the credit crisis in 2007.

2. *Glance at a few charts; make a plan in a snap.* As with a map, a collection of a few of the best charts can help steer you into the most profitable investment strategies. Each chart tells a tale, and I am not talking about technical analysis here; I am talking about the deep underlying messages that many charts contain because of their wide-ranging implications.

3. *Follow the chain all the way to the last link.* Envision the series of events that will follow the trends that you observe. Think deeply. Think as many steps down the road as you can and coordinate your conclusions with those of the markets to time your entries and exits to make them the most profitable.

THE GOLDEN COMPASSES:
THE TOP TOP-DOWN INDICATORS

- *Housing affordability index.* We all live on a budget of some sort. If we Americans can afford something, we buy it. If we can't, we don't, except during credit bubbles such as the one that led to the subprime mortgage crisis. The ups and downs in this index therefore will tend to yield indisputable implications for future housing demand.

- *Mortgage applications index.* When an application of any kind is filed, it suggests an attempt to do something, which in the case of mortgage applications means that a prospective home buyer is interested in obtaining a mortgage to purchase a home. These data have proved reliable since the early 1990s in signaling changes in home sale activity, and the data are available weekly, hence providing early clues on important trend changes.

- *Inventory-to-sales ratio for new and existing home sales.* There are no simpler principles in economics than those that surround issues related to changes in supply and demand. When supplies are up, prices fall. When supplies are down, prices rise. Demand up, prices up. Demand down, prices down. Got it? You probably got this one many years ago. For housing, the inventory-to-sales ratio is your guide to a key influence on home prices.

- *Commercial paper.* This is a terrific indicator for a variety of situations. When tracking credit conditions, it is an excellent gauge of the amount of anxiety that exists in the markets because commercial paper is not backed (it is unsecured) by anything. As a money market instrument, commercial paper yields clues about interbank funding conditions, chiefly with respect to LIBOR and federal funds, the two sources of money that keep banks running.

- *LIBOR.* We just mentioned this one, but it is such an important indicator that it is worth mentioning over and over. In 2007, widening yield spreads between LIBOR, which can accurately be called the world's funding rate, and the federal funds rate signaled trouble in the banking system in the United States and abroad that for top-down investors was impossible to miss. LIBOR is almost always close to the federal funds rate, so when it moves higher, it not only signals growing distrust about the health of the financial system (because lenders are showing caution and charging more for loans), but it also flags the potential for problems in the economy, because many debtors have debts tied to LIBOR.

- *Demographics: birth statistics.* There are a plethora of uses for birth statistics. Basically, if you can figure out how many people there are in a particular age group, you can drum up a wide variety of investment ideas. For example, if you knew how many babies were born 22 years ago, you would have a good sense of how many new entrants there would likely be into the labor force. For housing, we showed that the two important age groups are groups 25 to 30, and 55 and up. Birth statistics are incredibly useful because people are prone to do things that are incredibly predictable, like seeking shelter, eating, dressing themselves, and all those obvious sorts of things that have tremendous investment implications.

Notes

[1] Much research exists on this including this study: see http://www.jchs .harvard.edu/publications/markets/son2006/son2006_homeownership_ trends.pdf.

[2] Data from the National Center for Health Statistics: http://www.cdc .gov/nchs/births.htm.

CHAPTER 3

Globalization Makes Top Down a Must

Market capitalism has gone global; the investment implications are enormous and skew toward top-down investing.

We have all heard the line, "The world is getting complicated." In many respects this is certainly true, but the investment world, which in many respects has become far more complicated, is actually getting less complicated in other ways, thanks to top-down investing, which is being underpinned by the information age, the integration of the world economy and its financial markets, and the spread of market capitalism. Gone are the days when the notion of "investing abroad" would send shudders up and down investors' spines. Now investors have to ask "how?" We all know the answer to that; it is almost second nature. Moreover, investing abroad doesn't bring anxiety; it brings calm because when we invest abroad, we feel good that we are diversifying our investments. There is also a feeling of excitement that comes with investing abroad because we feel as though we are participating in the remarkable success stories happening off our shores and quite simply also because we are intrigued about foreign countries. It is why we travel the globe in such large numbers.

GOSUDARSTVENNYI KOMITET PO PLANIROVANIYU, GOOD RIDDANCE!

During the Cold War, Western bloc countries sought to learn as much as they could about their Eastern counterparts, including information about their economies. It was a formidable task given the misinformation that the Eastern bloc dealt out on a regular basis and the inaccuracies contained in the data they produced. The West poured enormous resources into its efforts to learn about the Eastern economies yet there was never much confidence that they were getting it right. If all the efforts of the Western world could not solve the mystery about what was happening in the economies of the Eastern world, then how could ordinary investors figure it out? They couldn't, really. Between the lack of information and the formidable barriers that existed to investing in the East, investors stayed away. Not that there was any reason to invest there, unless you wanted to make a bet on just how far the East would lag the West on big-picture matters such as output per capita, technological advances, productivity, employment, and so forth.

In his recent book, former Federal Reserve chairman Alan Greenspan highlights the difficulties that existed during the Cold War in trying to assess Eastern economies. Greenspan recounts, for example, his stint from 1983 to 1985 on President Reagan's foreign intelligence advisory board (PFIAB) when he was asked to review U.S. assessments of the Soviet Union's ability to handle economically the ramping up of U.S. armament.[1] Reagan's theory, of course, was that the Soviets would fail to keep up and would blunder under the weight of their own failure, forcing them to fall or negotiate with the United States. Either way, the Cold War would end.

Greenspan describes the effort to assess the Soviet Union's economy as "Herculean," saying that, "Once I dug into the project, though, it took me only a week to conclude that it was impossible: there was no way to assess their economy." One of the reasons for this, Greenspan notes, was the Soviet Union's state planning agency, Gosudarstvennyi Komitet po Planirovaniyu, or Gosplan for short. One of Gosplan's roles was to produce economic data, which Greenspan considered "rotten." This was unfortunate, given that Gosplan played a major role in deciding what would be produced and where and at what price at practically every factory in the Soviet Union. Greenspan knew that he could not accurately project whether the U.S. arms buildup would put unbearable pressures on the Soviet economy, but he was confident the data-starved Soviets couldn't either.

Throughout the Cold War, Western countries knew to discount the economic data that were spit out by Eastern bloc countries. Alan

Greenspan had done a bit of discounting of his own as part of his work for the PFIAB, assessing estimates of GDP and productivity in Eastern countries. In a striking example of the poor quality of information that existed before the fall of the Berlin Wall, Greenspan notes that many experts had estimated East Germany's GDP per capita to be roughly 75 to 85 percent of that of West Germany. Greenspan found those estimates difficult to believe, and when more reliable statistics poured in after the Berlin Wall fell, it was felt that productivity in East Germany was only about a third of West Germany's and that as many as 40 percent of East Germany's factories were obsolete.

The Cold War was a dark period in many respects. Two vastly different economic systems vied to be the one on top by the end of the twentieth century, and it was market capitalism that won out over central planning. It was the birth of a new era for investors, and it did not take long for once-in-a-lifetime opportunities to develop.

IT'S A BIGGER WORLD; THINK BIG

The ending of the Cold War created vast markets that did not exist before, bringing with it a large set of investment choices. Investors these days are investing in the stocks, bonds, and currencies of the countries that are benefiting from the rapid growth of free-market capitalism. Quite commonly, investors are also investing in the many commodities that have increased rapidly in price as a result of the global upswing. One of these commodities is of course oil, which reached $100 per barrel in early 2008.

Russia, which is the world's second largest oil exporter and holds the world's largest natural gas reserves, was a major beneficiary of the surge in energy prices, with its economy expanding by more than 7 percent in both 2006 and 2007,[2] the fastest of any of the G8 countries.[3] The boom brought Russia back from the brink after the country had defaulted on roughly $40 billion of its debts in 1998. At that time Russia held just $10 billion of international reserves, but by the beginning of 2008 Russia's reserves had soared to over $475 billion,[4] a mighty cushion against economic risks and a dollop certainly large enough to support solid levels of economic growth for quite some time, particularly given the size of Russia's economy, estimated to have been $1.251 trillion in 2007.[5] Now you know where your money went when you filled up your car at the gas station!

Top-down investors, always mindful of the broad implications of macro developments such as fluctuations in the price of oil, knew to consider investments in countries such as Russia that were accruing enormous benefits from the surge in the price of oil. Investors lucky enough to have bought shares representative of gains posted in Russia's RTS index saw whopping gains of 3,400 percent! Of course, this is an extraordinary example—shares in Saudi Arabia gained 574 percent during the same period, and gains on other types of top-down investing ideas are not likely to be as fruitful. I mean to emphasize the idea that something so simple as extrapolating the likely impact of a run-up in the price of oil can yield excellent investment ideas. In the case of the surge in energy costs, the amount of investment ideas that top-down investors were able to generate extended well beyond the terrific investments that were made in the oil-producing nations. In particular, there were big gains to be had in shares of producers of alternative energy, including solar, for example. For example, shares in First Solar, a designer and manufacturer of solar modules followed closely by investors in solar stocks, saw its shares gain 1,235 percent in the five-year period ended December 31, 2007. Other ideas included the purchase of bonds in the emerging markets as well as their currencies. In both cases, investors saw big gains.

The growth of free-market capitalism and the opportunities generated by it are likely to continue in the years ahead for many reasons, not the least of which is the acceleration in productivity gains worldwide. Productivity gains are at the heart of increases in standards of living, as they are at the root of increases in income gains. It is estimated that global productivity growth nearly doubled in the 10 years ended in 2005, rising to 2.3 percent per year from 1.2 percent in the 1980s,[6] with the gains occurring mostly in emerging markets such as China, India, and Eastern Europe, as shown in Figure 3.1. The prospects of continued increases in global productivity look good for the years ahead. The Federal Reserve Bank of Dallas believes that globalization boosts productivity in 10 ways, as shown in Table 3.1.

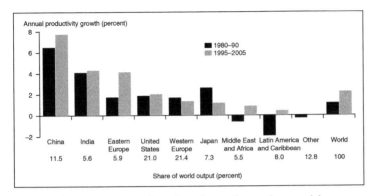

Figure 3.1 Productivity is accelerating throughout the world.

Source: Federal Reserve Bank of Dallas, 2006 annual report, available at http://www.dallasfed.org/ fed/annual/2006/ar06e.pdf.

Countries That Reform Deserve Your Money

In the global march toward market capitalism, countries that continuously move toward a market-based system will be strong candidates for your investment dollars. Efforts to impede the spread of capitalism should be taken as a red flag to avoid such countries. A good guide to the top-down factors to look out for when assessing a country's financial system should include following[7]:

- The degree of respect for property rights.
- The strength of the country's legal system.
- The degree of tolerance for and handling of corruption.
- The quality of financial and economic information.
- The degree of corporate governance.
- The quality of regulatory oversight of the nation's banking system.

Alan Greenspan has frequently identified property rights as one of the most crucial elements needed for the development of an economy, noting that, "It was an unrelentingly embarrassing stain on the Soviet Union's central planning that a very substantial percentage of its crops came from 'privately owned' plots that covered only a fraction of the tilled land."[8] In addition to property rights, Greenspan notes three other important characteristics influencing global growth: (1) the extent of competition domestically,

T A B L E 3.1

Globalization Raises Productivity and Reduces Cost in 10 Ways.

Factor	How It Works
Lower communication and transportation costs	Consumers benefit directly when moving information and goods across international borders becomes cheaper. Communication and transportation drive the other factors in this guide, offering even greater potential for higher productivity and lower costs.
Better production functions	When communication and transportation are cheap and easy, firms have access to productive inputs anytime, anywhere. Firms can develop and manage production functions less constrained by skills, work hours, cost and availability of local labor. They're also less reliant on local resources and capital.
Stronger competition	Increased competition makes it harder for firms to raise prices when costs rise, forcing managers to find better ways to produce. Those who do, survive; those who don't are eliminated. In this way, production is constantly transferred to the most efficient, adaptable and innovative firms.
Greater specialization	People and nations become more efficient when they concentrate on what they do best and meet other needs through trade. Output increases with equal or less labor input—a pure productivity gain. Even better, specialization focuses attention on specific tasks, leading us to think more deeply about how to improve production processes. What stimulates innovation raises productivity growth.
Larger market size	The bigger the market, the greater the potential sales and profits. Market size stimulates innovation and business formation by offering inventors, entrepreneurs and capitalists greater return for their ideas, effort and risk.
Extended economies of scale	Most knowledge-intensive goods are produced under conditions of high fixed and low marginal costs, which create substantial economies of scale. Larger markets expand producers' reach, allowing them to spread the fixed costs over even more customers. The results are lower unit costs of production and lower prices for consumers.
Broader capital markets	Access to global capital enables entrepreneurs to shift productive assets to uses with the highest returns, wherever they may be.
More contestable markets	In a world of isolated nations, a supplier in a small country may have substantial monopoly power. Integrating economies puts producers everywhere in competition, with access to a virtually limitless supply of capital. The threat of new entrants discourages suppliers from charging too much.
Greater knowledge spillovers	The transfer of productive knowledge makes economies more efficient. Knowledge has long moved across borders through trade (embodied knowledge). Now, more of the spillovers are general information and research (disembodied knowledge), creating larger economic ripples.

(*continued*)

T A B L E   3.1
_____

(Continued)

Factor	How It Works
Spread of nonrivalrous consumption	Products are nonrivalrous when one person's consumption doesn't diminish another's. TV, movies and the Internet are examples of nonrivalrous goods that can serve additional customers without significant additional costs, thereby contributing to lower costs as they speed around the globe.

Source: Federal Reserve Bank of Dallas, 2006 annual report, available at http://www .dallasfed.org/fed/annual/2006/ar06e.pdf.

and, especially for developing nations, the extent of a country's openness to trade and its integration with the rest of the world; (2) the quality of a country's institutions that make an economy work; and (3) the success of its policymakers in implementing the measures necessary for macroeconomic stability.

How does a top-down investor assess whether these elements are in place when evaluating the viability of an investment in a particular country? Well, the top-down investor need only scan the news and a read a few stories about the country's corporate sector, specifically looking for a sense of capitalist verve, in addition to stories that discuss the country's economic and monetary policies. Further checking can be done on the Web sites of the various central banks, which will often mention world economies and financial systems in their economic research. Some of the best research and statistics can be found on the Web sites of the Bank for International Settlements, the United Nations, the International Monetary Fund, and, interestingly, the U.S. Central Intelligence Agency (CIA), which maintains a "world factbook" containing mountains of information and data about every country in the world in a very easy-to-grasp format. The behavior of a country's financial markets can also be very telling, of course.

In This Era of Globalization, Bottom-Up Investing Fails

I can't fathom how anyone would want to stay with investment approaches that predate globalization, a truly seminal event that is likely to shape the course of history, economically and politically, throughout the twenty-first century. Bottom-up investing is poorly suited to the current era, as it fails to equip investors with the many tools they need in order to spot opportunities throughout the globe. To be frank, bottom-up investing in this era of globalization is for those who want to think small and prefer to shun the extraordinary investment opportunities created by the spread of market capitalism. Top-down investing is for those desiring to think big, and it is for profit.

OVER THERE? WRONG! WE'RE ALL IN THIS TOGETHER

During the Asian financial crisis in 1998, I would awake each day to financial news on Bloomberg radio, which I had set as my wakeup call on my alarm clock. I set it for a time of the morning when there was likely to be a review of overnight developments and a preview of where U.S. markets were expected to open, which like today can be assessed by a gander at where S&P 500 futures are trading. The Asian financial crisis was a doozy of a crisis, which had its roots in the collapse of the Thai Baht in 1997, when the Thai government allowed its currency to float, sparking a devaluation of the Baht. The contagion quickly spread, and several Asian economies quickly slipped into recession. South Korea, which at that time had the world's eleventh-largest economy, was on the brink, unable to pay its debts. It required a $55 billion support package from the International Monetary Fund, the IMF's largest-ever rescue. Russia, as I mention earlier, eventually defaulted on its debts.

The episode was as epic as the financial world had ever seen, and each morning I was given a new lesson about just how integrated the world's financial system had become. The unsettling unease that I felt and the ping in my chest would stay with me throughout the day, a feeling of anxiety that I vividly remember to this day. Although I still check where S&P futures are in the early morning, I stopped waking up to financial news soon after the Asian financial crisis ended. Now I awake only to music and nature sounds.

Although 1998 was harrowing, it was, as I said earlier, a time when it became clear just how integrated the world's financial system had become. There would be enormous benefits to come from the strides made in globalization, including the gains in global productivity and output. Another benefit that has accrued has been a

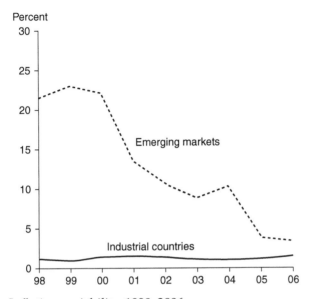

Figure 3.2 Inflation variability, 1998–2006.

Source: International Financial Statistics, IMF. Measurement is in percent, measured as standard deviation. Adapted from a speech by Mark Siegel that appeared in the Federal Reserve Bank of San Francisco's *Economic Letter*, November 23, 2007.

decrease in the variability of inflation, particularly in the emerging markets, as shown in Figure 3.2.

The 1998 Asian financial crisis reflected growing pains that would subside for a while, but like anything it has had its ups and downs. In early 2008 one of the least appealing aspects of the increased interconnectivity that exists among global markets surfaced again, with markets swooning across the globe in one of the worst Januarys on record—and all because a couple of million people did not pay their mortgages on time! It's hard to imagine the U.S. mortgage dilemma affecting the world's 6 billion inhabitants for long, but the impact was stark. (This is the type of mindset that a top-down investor must have, always putting events in perspective; in this unusual case weighing the impact that the fate a couple of million households can have on 6 billion people. Of course, a sense of what others think of each situation is important, and market conditions should always play a major role in any investment decision. But when there is a strong base case for an investment, what others are thinking matters only in terms of the timing of the investment.)

The events of 1998 and then again in 2007 and 2008 clearly illustrate why it is so important to stay focused on global markets, as markets are now intertwined and events abroad can have a major impact on your investments. It would be foolish to turn a blind eye to this reality, and those who have done so have been blindsided as a result. Those not hurt by the effects of these crises missed the opportunities they generated worldwide.

THE GLOBE IS EASIER TO SEE FROM AFAR

From the ground, we can't see the rest of the planet; we can only see it from afar. It is no different when it comes to investing abroad. We can't see the forces shaping movement in the world's financial markets unless we take a broad, macro look at the world. There are a variety of ways in which you can do this, and, as I said earlier, there are a number of institutions that provide large amounts of both data and research that can help you to make more sense of the world.

This leads to an obvious question: What types of data should you look for? The simple answer for a top-down investor is to look for anything of a macro nature that you can get your hands on. Some of the best data are those related to simple supply-and-demand statistics. For example, it is important to always know the amount of supply and demand for petroleum each year and the trends expected in the time ahead. The global supply-and-demand picture for oil is a terrific example of how global factors are shaping major trends that affect not only the financial markets but also the way we live. For oil, this is something that has been obvious since the oil crises of the 1970s. Knowing the simple facts on the supply-and-demand balance for oil can lead to wide-ranging investment ideas. Here is just a small sample of where the investment chain leads:

- Oil producers and gas service companies.
- Alternative energy companies.
- Energy commodities.
- Currencies of oil-producing nations.
- Equities within oil-producing nations.
- Bonds within oil-producing nations.
- Oil and gas service companies within oil-producing nations.
- Inflation-indexed bonds.

- Gold.
- Corn and sugar producers.
- Corn and sugar commodities (because high gasoline prices boost the production of ethanol).
- Meat producers (because corn prices boost feed costs).
- Consumer stocks, particularly discount retailers (because high gasoline prices sap the discretionary incomes of those in the lower-income brackets most of all).
- Chemicals and plastics companies (high energy prices boost the price of making these products, thus hurting companies in these fields).

Sometimes the big-pictures ideas generated by the top-down investment approach arrive from financial indicators. For example, many investment ideas can be developed from the numerous data and analyses available from the Bank for International Settlements (BIS), the international organization that endeavors to foster monetary and financial cooperation and which serves as a bank for central banks. The BIS is the world's oldest international financial institution and, with its main office in Basel, Switzerland, is at the heart of international cooperation on Basel II, the international banking agreement that sets capital standards for banks worldwide.

Among many other things, the BIS keeps tabs on the amount of money that crosses international borders, which is aptly referred to as *cross-border deposits*. These data can be used in a variety of ways, as shown in Chapter 14. One way to use the data is as a gauge of the strength of the global economy and on its ability to withstand stress. For example, data from the BIS show that at the end of the June 2007 cross-border deposits totaled a whopping $30 trillion, an increase of $5 trillion from the previous year.[9] What this means is that $30 trillion was deposited across borders by banks in the host countries included in the BIS survey. An example of a cross-border deposit would be monies from a Middle Eastern bank deposited in a bank in China.

When cross-border deposits increase rapidly in size, it indicates that there is a surfeit of cash being generated worldwide, most likely because of rapid growth in the world economy. To be sure, we can measure the relative strength of the world economy by other means, but what these data tell us that GDP and related data do not is the extent to which economic activity is rising fast enough to boost incomes and profits by an amount large enough to produce a surplus of internally generated funds. In other words, when cross-border deposits rise, it tells us that sufficient capital exists within each of the respective countries on the aggregate and that investors are searching for opportunities abroad. In a case such as this, where cross-border deposits are strong, if domestic economies were to weaken, these deposits could be either withdrawn or new deposits scaled back (more likely) to nurture growth back in the home country. So, when cross-border deposits are large, it means that there is plenty of money out there that could be redeployed if necessary to support global growth.

Another way to use the data is to find out which countries are making the largest number of cross-border deposits and which countries are receiving the largest number. The depositors are apt to be countries experiencing strong growth, usually those with trade surpluses, which in recent times generally means countries in the Middle East. On the receiving end have been emerging economies such as those in Eastern Europe, which in the second quarter of 2007 received about $50 billion in new cross-border deposits, roughly half of all new net deposits into emerging economies. Countries in the Baltic states and southeastern Europe have been the biggest recipients within Europe. Bulgaria and Romania have seen particularly large flows, probably because of their recent ascension into the European Union. For top-down investors these data yield important clues about where it is that they should consider putting their money. Bulgaria and Romania? Who would have thought? Certainly not the bottom-up investor.

The Most Liquid Investment Ever

I love this top-down idea: invest in companies that have strong positions in the water industry, including those that purify, desalinate, and disinfect water as well as those that play a major role in the world's water infrastructure. This is a macro idea with a global imperative that can't lose because of water's essential role in sustaining life. Demands upon the global water supply are far greater than most think, which is what is creating this investment opportunity.

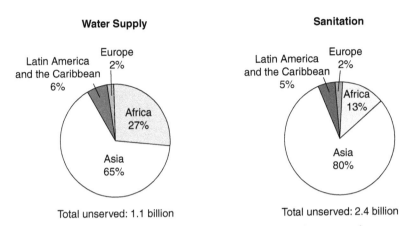

Figure 3.3 Water supply and sanitation, distribution of unserved populations by region.

Source: WHO/UNICEF Joint Monitoring Programme (2002), extracted from WWDR1, "Water for People, Water for Life" (UNESCO-WWAP, 2003). United Nations Educational and Cultural Organization, World Water Assessment Programme: http: available at //www.unesco.org/water/wwap/facts_figures/ basic_needs.shtml.

According to estimates from the United Nations, around 1.2 billion people, about a fifth of the world's population, live in areas where the limits of sustainable water use have already been reached or breached. U.N. Secretary-General Ban Ki-moon, speaking at the World Economic Forum in Davos, Switzerland, in January 2008, emphasized these facts, noting that, "A recent report by International Alert identified 46 countries, home to 2.7 billion people, where climate change and water-related crises create a high risk of violent conflict. A further 56 countries, representing another 1.2 billion people, are at high risk of political instability. That's more than half the world."[10] Ki-moon noted that the conflict in Darfur, while affected by a number of factors, began because of factors related to a drought there. Figure 3.3 illustrates the vast degree to which the world's water needs are unmet.

Further adding to strains on the world's clean water supply is the recent surge in energy costs, which has motivated farmers to produce food used in the production of ethanol and other biofuels. To emphasize the strain posed, Dutch Crown Prince Willem Alexander, who in 2007 headed the U.N. Secretary-General's advisory board on water and sanitation, attending the 2007 World Water

Week conference in Stockholm, told the Associated Press that "The amount of water needed to produce the biofuels for a tank of an SUV equals the amount of water needed to feed one person on grains for a whole year."[11] In light of continued efforts to boost the production of biofuels, this is a strain that is almost certainly being underestimated.

Out of Necessity, the World's Central Banks and Regulators Are Joining Forces

An extraordinarily compelling reason why in the twenty-first century investors must adopt top-down investment principles is the increasing alignment of the world's central banks and bank regulators. The alignment has been decades in the making, but it has become increasingly necessary since the fall of communism and the resulting ascension of market capitalism. Major events such as the 1998 Asian financial crisis and the 2007 credit crisis have created urgency for central bankers and regulators to coordinate their policies. It is no longer safe, for example, for the world's financial system to be kept under the guise of multiple regulatory practices now that the system is so deeply integrated.

Recent events glaringly illustrate this point, particularly with respect to the varying rules that govern the accounting of off-balance-sheet vehicles such as structured investment vehicles, the conduits that in 2007 were wrought with funding problems after it was disclosed that these conduits had exposure to the U.S. subprime mortgage market. Investors were alarmed to discover that major banks such as Citibank had large exposures to structured investment vehicles (SIVs) and that the SIVs were involved in such risky investments, forcing banks to eliminate their SIVs. The credit crisis also illustrated the need for more uniform regulations on the disclosure of basic data on assets deemed risky or difficult to value in the open market. A regulatory response by institutions such as the Bank for International Settlements and the International Monetary Fund should be expected, which means that more of what happens at the world's financial institutions will be coordinated, thereby increasing the need to stay on top of the big picture.

The same can be said about the world's central banks, which through their coordinated actions to provide liquidity to markets that were starving for it in 2007 and early 2008, showed a degree of coordination rarely seen. This was abundantly evident in the announcement on December 12, 2007, by the Federal Reserve of an agreement between the world's major central banks to take actions to add temporary liquidity to the world financial system:

> Today, the Bank of Canada, the Bank of England, the European Central Bank, the Federal Reserve, and the Swiss National Bank are announcing measures designed to address elevated pressures in short-term funding markets. Actions taken by the Federal Reserve include the establishment of a temporary Term Auction Facility (approved by the Board of Governors of the Federal Reserve System) and the establishment of foreign exchange swap lines with the European Central Bank and the Swiss National Bank (approved by the Federal Open Market Committee).

In separate statements, the Bank of Japan and the Swedish Riksbank said that they welcomed the announcement.

Given the increasing degree of coordination among the world's central banks, the adage "Don't fight the Fed" has broadened considerably. It is no longer enough to be a Fed watcher; investors must also keep an eye on the ways in which foreign central banks are coordinating with the Fed. Their collective actions could have deep ramifications for the world economy and your financial investments. We talk more about this in Chapter 6.

There Is So Much More

The discussions earlier in this chapter on oil, cross-border deposits, and water were put there not only to provide a few specific ideas that can be generated by using the top-down approach toward investing, but they were put there mainly to show how a top-down investor looks at the world and the wide variety of ideas that can be generated from a few simple and easy-to-obtain facts. There really is so much more out there. Globalization has literally been going on for thousands of years—the Romans built a vast transportation network of roads, for example—but only recently has it changed the landscape so immensely that investors must forever change their way of investing.

The View from the Top Down: Three Musts for the Macro Maven

Global investing is by definition a top-down affair.

1. *Glasnost is here! Dig in!* The ending of the Cold War has finally made it possible to learn more about what is happening in countries such as those in the Eastern bloc where both opportunities and accurate data used to be scarce. This transformation is in its infant stages. Don't miss this extraordinary opportunity.

2. *Catch up to globalization.* The spread of free-market capitalism and the increased integration of the world's financial system have rendered bottom-up investing a failed strategy for the twenty-first century. Top-down investors must stay mindful of how global influences will shape their investments.

3. *Look at the world from afar.* As I said earlier, you can't see much of the Earth from where you are; you have to look at it from afar in order to see it better. It is the same with investing. The more that you look at if from afar, the more you will see. Supply and demand for commodities, for example, can no longer be analyzed on a domestic level; the global equilibrium level is what is most important in terms of discerning price trends. Utilize global financial indicators such as cross-border deposits to gauge the global economy and hot spots.

THE GOLDEN COMPASSES: THE TOP TOP-DOWN INDICATORS

- *Cross-border deposits.* This is one of the best indicators around, and it is one that only the most astute players on Wall Street use, which makes it even better since we all should endeavor to find indicators that are diamonds in the rough. Simply put, cross-border deposits represent all monies deposited, well, across borders. Countries experiencing an influx of money have money to burn, a sign of good times for that country. The recipients of the money are also a good bet. These days money is flowing from oil producers to emerging markets, Eastern Europe in particular.

- *International reserves.* International reserve tallies often correlate with cross-border deposits but not in every case. Oil producers, for example, have in recent years been flush with cash, which often turns into cross-border deposits. An exceptional case of the lack of correlation between reserves and cross-border deposits is China, which often sees net inflows of money despite the country having massive amounts of international reserves, which totaled nearly $1.5 trillion at the beginning of 2008. The more a country has, the greater the ability the country has to wield power, both economic and political.

- *Energy prices.* This is an obvious one, but the global implications from an investment perspective are widely unappreciated. Top-down investors know to look at the broad swath of investments affected by higher oil prices including alternative energy, foodstuffs, foreign currencies, foreign bonds, emerging markets, and consumer stocks.

- *Water demand.* Some of the best top-down indicators are those that relate to the most basic elements of human life, such as the need for food, water, and shelter. Water is something that most of us in the industrialized world take for granted, but the tide is turning, so to speak, on the situation, with water-related topics set to move increasingly close to the forefront in the time ahead.

To these I would add the Baltic Dry Shipping Index and yield spreads between emerging markets bonds and U.S. Treasuries. Both are discussed in Chapter 3 and Chapter 14.

Notes

[1] Greenspan, Alan, *The Age of Turbulence*, New York: The Penguin Press, 2007.

[2] Energy Information Agency, Department of Energy Web site, http://www.eia.doe.gov/emeu/cabs/Russia/pdf.

[3] The G8 is jargon for the "Group of 8" countries, which consists of the United States, the United Kingdom, France, Germany, Italy, Canada, Japan, and Russia.

[4] The Central Bank of Russia Web site; http://www.cbr.ru/eng/.

[5] U.S. Central Intelligence Agency Web site; www.cia.gov.

[6] Federal Reserve Bank of Dallas, "Globalizing the Knowledge Economy, 2006 annual report, 2007.

[7] Mishkin, Frederic, "Globalization and Financial Development," from a speech he delivered on April 26, 2007.

[8] Greenspan, Alan, *The Age of Turbulence*.

[9] Bank for International Settlements, *Quarterly Banking Report*, December 2007.

[10] Remarks delivered at the World Economic Forum in Davos, Switzerland, January 24, 2008.

[11] *Boston Globe*, August 15, 2007. "Dutch Prince Favors Food over Biofuels." By Karl Ritter, Associated Press.

CHAPTER 4

Thematic Trading
and Investing

Hey, Joe! You know those trends you've been noticing? Buy 'em!

If there is one thing that the average Joe can notice it is a major trend. Why? Because we average Joes *are* the trend; we make them. They are certainly not made by the Harvards; there just aren't enough of them. But there are plenty of us. As the proprietors of trends, we therefore have no excuse for missing them and the investment opportunities that go with them. Of course, I am talking mostly about trends that affect domestic markets, but we mighty folk are also at the root of trends happening throughout the world. In cases where our collective might is not as influential as it might otherwise be, as investors we have to do a bit more work in order to understand the powerful trends that are changing the landscape enough for us to take notice and then decide where to put our money. Still, there are an enormous number of opportunities available to us if we catch onto the right themes. Fellow Joes (and Josettes), as everyday men and women it is time you took advantage of your ability to understand the world as only you can and adopt a key principle of top-down trading: thematic trading and investing.

WHAT IS THEMATIC INVESTING?

Thematic investing is a form of top-down investing that develops investment ideas based on major trends, changes in government regulatory and tax laws, and global influences on economies and

markets that are powerful enough to override numerous other factors as considerations in the investment decision-making process.
With thematic investing, you embrace ideas first and then invest in
the specific investments the ideas lead to.

Thematic investing has at its roots themes that are very macro
by nature but that also can be spotted on a micro level. In addition,
a major characteristic of thematic investing is that it is a form of
investing that can be influenced by a wide variety of factors, including trends in consumer spending, social issues such as "go green"
initiatives, economic trends as diverse as surges in mortgage refi-
nancings, the corporate restructuring imperative that began in the
early 1990s, or global factors such as China's ascension and globalization. There are a wide variety of themes to latch onto. The key is
to catch them early and to avoid the largest pitfall of thematic
investing: investing with an overly exuberant herd.

There has never been a better time to adopt the principles
of thematic investing. Not only has it become easier to spot the
themes that move markets, but it has become easier to invest in
these themes without having to gamble on specific companies,
which, when it comes to emerging themes, often have a tendency to
fall by the wayside and get shaken out. Today, you can make investments that reflect the many themes that are fundamentally altering
the landscape for economies and the industries within them.
Finally, thanks to a plethora of exchange-traded funds (ETFs) and
mutual funds, and reduced barriers to investing abroad and in
financial instruments previously accessible only to professionals,
thematic investing has come into its own.

WHY THEMATIC INVESTING HAS BECOME A MUST

Let me ask you this: do you value your time? Of course you do! So
does everybody else. One aspect of thematic investing is that it can
help save some of your precious time. This is not the main reason
that you should adopt the principles of thematic investing, but it is
an appealing one. The reason that thematic investing is a time-
saver is because it is a strategy designed to bring to light powerful
investment opportunities by unearthing broad-stroked ideas that
can be quickly understood and analyzed. This is certainly an

appealing idea in a day and age when people are feeling stressed more by problems related to their personal time than their financial situation.

Thematic investing often crosses into familiar territory, into ideas that people can personally relate to, which can save them time. These might include the things that people are buying or the social issues of the day, such as the recent wave of interest in "go green" initiatives. Moreover, the themes themselves are often quite personal, because they can relate to one's retirement planning, saving for college, and saving for a home, among many other themes that often dictate an investor's investment strategy.

Major Themes Are More Likely to Develop and Be Stronger in Today's Integrated World

In Chapter 3 we discuss why globalization has made top-down a must in today's increasingly integrated world. The idea that investments are influenced increasingly by global forces is compelling, and it is making other investment approaches look increasingly obsolete. This has become particularly clear since the early 1990s, which, when it comes to historical timelines, was basically just yesterday.

Since the early 1990s, the world has seen remarkable change, with vast numbers of societies embracing the principles of market capitalism. Changes have also been substantial in industrialized nations, as evidenced most prominently by Europe's shift to a single currency in January 1999. The European Union has broken down numerous walls, creating competitive pressures and putting companies on a more equal plane, making it more likely that trends occurring in a single country or industry might spread elsewhere, which of course increases the allure of thematic investing.

The lowering of trade barriers throughout the globe has also increased the likelihood that major themes will cross borders and industries. Trade barriers have been moving inexorably lower for years, and the trend has accelerated, in part because of efforts by the World Trade Organization, which has for years worked at liberalizing world trade. The WTO's efforts began with the General Agreement on Tariffs and Trade (GATT), which had its roots in 1948, and then the so-called Uruguay round from 1986 to1994 (and subsequent negotiations of that round), and the current effort, the

Doha Development Agenda, which was launched in 2001.[1] Although the WTO was not established until January 1, 1995, its original trading system, GATT, was its original framework. Particularly important in recent years was China's ascension into the WTO, which, after 15 years of negotiations, took place on December 11, 2001. Now that China is required to adhere to rules governing inclusion in the WTO, economies and markets will become even more integrated, which will further pressure nations and private industry to adopt strategies that collectively are likely to have enormous impact.

The 2007–2008 credit crisis promises more uniform and hence far-reaching cooperation on both monetary policy and bank regulation, adding another crucial element to thematic investing. The world's financial regulators and central banks are now likely to more closely coordinate their policies, either directly or indirectly in response to events they see as having global repercussions. This means that the collective actions of the world's central banks and influential regulatory and financial institutions, such as the Bank for International Settlements, the World Bank, and the International Monetary Fund, will be stronger than ever.

Capital Is Crossing Borders More Than Ever, Boosting the Size of the Crowd

The ease with which capital can be transferred across borders represents another compelling reason to embrace thematic investing, as the number of capitalists seeking the best possible investments is larger than ever, making it likely that when strong themes emerge, there will be a tidal wave of support for those themes. I emphasize again the need to be careful about latching onto trends that are sated with speculative investors. There are many ways to spot when speculative fervor gets too hot, chiefly through market sentiment, as we discuss in greater depth in Chapter 12.

Financial Innovation Has Tilted Toward Thematic Investing

As we show in Chapter 5, a revolution has taken place in the financial markets in recent years, with investors increasingly embracing top-down principles of buying ideas rather than buying specific companies. Investors everywhere are expressing their sentiments about major themes by buying exchange-traded funds (ETFs) and mutual funds, financial products where the investment possibilities grow by the day. For example, using ETFs, investors can place bets on themes as wide-ranging as those that relate to gold, timber, grains, livestock, orthopedic repair, clean energy, the so-called BRIC nations (Brazil, Russia, India, and China), cardiology, ophthalmology, biotechnology, U.S. Treasuries, and so on. There almost literally is an ETF or a mutual fund for just about every sort of investment, including many investments that are outside of the traditional realm of stocks and bonds. These days money is flowing freely into commodities, real estate, foreign stocks and bonds, and other types of investments previously accessible only to market professionals. This means that theme-based investments are likely to be major drivers of the performance of more narrow investments such as specific stocks. ETFs themselves are influencing market prices when they are established, as has been the case with ETFs for commodities, which results in large purchases of commodities by the sponsors of the ETFs, thus influencing the prices of these commodities. The surge in energy prices that took place in 2008, particularly in the spring, is a case in point. Lacking attractive alternatives, investors flocked to commodity ETFs.

The Information Age Will Synthesize Trends

It is human nature for people to look at what others are doing when they are considering how they should themselves behave. In fact, this is a major feature of theories of consumption patterns in the United States presented by famed economists such as John Maynard Keynes[2] and Milton Friedman,[3] and J. S. Duesenberry.[4] Here is the consumption theory put forward by Keynes, which is often seen as the root of the so-called *permanent income hypothesis*:

> The fundamental psychological law, upon which we are entitled to depend with great confidence both *a priori* and from our knowledge of human nature and from the detailed facts of experience, is that men are disposed, as a rule and on the average, to increase their consumption, as their income increases, but not by as much as the increase in their income (*The General Theory of Employment, Interest and Money*, 1936, p. 96).

Duesenberry theorized something a bit different, arguing that individual consumption patterns were influenced by the consumption patterns of other people. This theory relates to a principle we can all relate to, which is the desire to "keep up with the Joneses." Anyone recently compelled to buy an iPod, an iPhone, a flat-screen television, or a digital camera can relate to this theory (as can the wave of people who for some reason were compelled to buy Crocs!) Duesenberry's theory is more formally known as the *relative theory of consumption*:

> The strength of any individual's desire to increase his consumption expenditure is a function of the ratio of his expenditure to some weighted average of the expenditures of others with whom he comes into contact (Duesenberry).

The fact that people are more aware than ever of what their neighbors are up to should sharpen the tendency for trends to permeate quickly and pervasively. This goes for consumable goods and services as well as for endeavors related to social, ethical, and political considerations. All this means that thematic investing is apt to have greater underpinnings in the information age. This is an area where the average Joes will have very significant insights, as they will be at the frontline of these themes.

TYPES OF THEMES

There are more viable themes than there is room in this book to list, many of which relate to the many ETFs I mention earlier, but Table 4.1 on page 63 shows a collection of themes, some of which come and go.

Past Themes That Worked

Following is a chronological collection of themes that worked, many of which were obvious from the get-go:

1940–1952: Government spending on World War II and postwar reconstruction will pull the U.S. economy out of the depressed economic years of the 1930s. It did.

Early 1970s: The baby boom that began in 1946 will lead to sharply increased levels of household formation in the early 1970s and spur an unprecedented housing boom. This is

TABLE 4.1

A Sample of Different Types of Themes

Theme	Implications
People are concerned about their lack of personal time and want to find ways to manage their time better and get help.	Personal service providers and producers of automated services will be winners. Sellers of devices that improve a person's efficiency will win.
The U.S. population is aging.	Very broad. The U.S. health-care system will see strong growth. Retirement planners will be in demand. Vacation homes will sell faster. Much more!
People have become enamored of flat-screen televisions.	An obvious one. Producers of flat-screen televisions and their components will prosper, as will some television sellers.
Gasoline prices are fluctuating.	Very broad. Car buyers will shift from large cars to small cars and vice versa depending on the price of gas. Discount retailers and other consumer companies will be affected.
In a more competitive global environment, companies will need to create more brand recognition.	Advertising firms will prosper. Media companies that receive advertising revenue will benefit.
Productivity is rising at a fast pace.	Inflation will be low, corporate profits will be high, and personal income growth will be strong. The economy will prosper.
There is a supply-and-demand imbalance for oil.	Oil producers and oil-producing nations will prosper. Consumers will be losers. Alternative-energy companies will thrive.

precisely what happened when those born in 1946 and the several years after that grew up and moved into homes of their own. Housing starts went from 1.085 million in January 1970 (when those born in 1946 had turned 24) to a whopping pace of 1.494 million in January 1972, a record that stands to this day despite the fact that the overall U.S. population has grown by about 100 million people since then.[5] This shows the power of demographics.

Early 1990s: The ending of the baby boom years in 1964 (my year!) will lead to sharply decreased levels of household formation in the early 1990s and spur weakness in housing activity. As the last of the baby boomers, poor me was the last

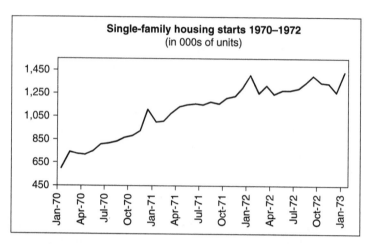

Figure 4.1 Baby boomers start buying in 1970.
Source: U.S. Department of Commerce.

one in on that cycle, buying a home in 1989 right on schedule at age 25 only to see my home's market value plummet. A lesson learned for sure. Figures 4.1 and 4.2 show the housing cycle of the early 1970s and 1990s.

1995–?: The technology shock will boost nonfarm business productivity in the United States and lead to a period of fast

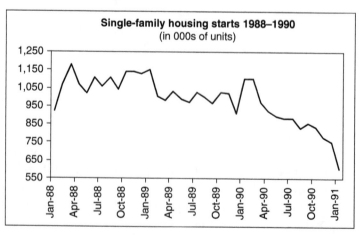

Figure 4.2 As boomers passed their prime home-buying years, the buying spree ended.
Source: U.S. Department of Commerce.

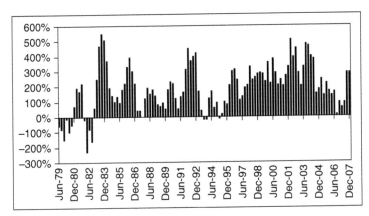

Figure 4.3 Nonfarm productivity (annualized gains on quarterly basis).
Source: U.S. Bureau of Labor Statistics.

gains in corporate profits, personal incomes, and GDP. This is precisely what happened minus the two interruptions related to the financial bubble of the late 1990s and the housing bubble of the early 2000s. Figure 4.3 shows the rapid productivity growth since 1995, and Figure 4.4 shows the rapid growth in corporate profits that the productivity gains contributed to.

2001: China's inclusion in the World Trade Organization in December 2001 will lead to more rapid growth in China. Does anyone doubt this one? Forget the charts.

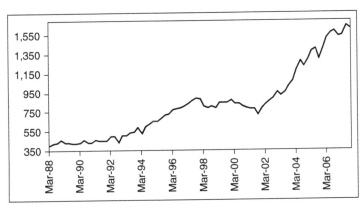

Figure 4.4 U.S. Corporate Profits (in billions of dollars).
Source: U.S. Bureau of Labor Statistics.

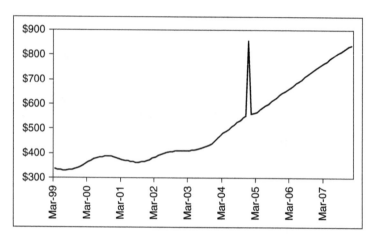

Figure 4.5 Household dividend income (in billions of dollars).

Note: The spike on the chart occurred in the fourth quarter of 2004.
It relates to a special dividend paid by the Microsoft Corporation.

Source: U.S. Department of Commerce.

2003: Dividend tax cuts in 2003 will spur more rapid growth
in dividend payments. This is precisely what happened, as
Figure 4.5 shows.

2008–2009: The U.S. economy and its financial system will be
spared a deep recession by big Fed rate cuts, fiscal stimulus,
continued productivity growth, lean business inventories,
strong global growth, and massive injections of money from
sovereign wealth funds. The jury is still out!

THEMES FOR TODAY

As I said before, at any point there is a wide variety of themes
strong enough to change the landscape and cut across industries
and countries. Many types of investment strategies can be developed from these themes, whether in company stocks, bonds, foreign currencies, commodities, foreign stocks and bonds, and so on.
Here are a few examples of themes likely to have staying power in
the years ahead:

- The aging of the U.S. population and lifestyle choices will
  boost demand for so-called lifestyle drugs. These include
  drugs for depression (Zoloft and Prozac), smoking

(Zyban), weight loss (Alli), hair loss (Rogaine), cholesterol (Lipitor), and erectile dysfunction (Viagra).

- The aging of the U.S. population will increase the amount of migration of people to states with relatively warmer temperatures (Figure 4.6).
- Vast pools of international reserves will support a secular upswing in global economic activity, particularly in emerging industries and markets.
- Strong growth in the global economy and the spread of free-market capitalism will continue to forge upward mobility in emerging markets and support a secular upswing in commodity prices.
- High energy prices will continue the worldwide push for alternative energies, transforming the issue of global warming from a scientific issue to an economic one.
- Surging demand for clean water will boost economic and political pressures worldwide to invest in water infrastructure.

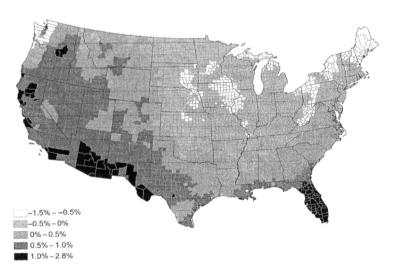

Figure 4.6 Expected population growth from weather (1970–2000) (Fitted annual population growth rate, controlling for coast, topography, initial density, concentric population, and industry).

Source: Jordan, Rappaport. "Moving to Nice Weather," Federal Reserve Bank of Kansas City, Research Working Paper, January 2006.

THE FOUR-STEP PROCESS IN THEMATIC INVESTING

As you have seen, adopting the principles of thematic investing is relatively simple. Sometimes the best themes are right in front of you. This could be because you are personally playing a role in shaping the theme, whether it is because of the things you are buying, the social issues you interested in, the way you are choosing to spend your time, or the things that you do because of the age group you are in. (I don't mean to say that you are necessarily following the crowd—to each his own—but you certainly have insight into what people your age are doing.) Other sorts of themes can be found with even a light familiarity with domestic and global affairs. In cases where the themes aren't so obvious, you have to stop and think a bit deeper and check the indicators, especially the golden compasses shown throughout this book and listed in Chapter 14.

There are four main steps needed to successfully adopt the top-down principle of thematic investing:

1. *Identify the theme.* Seek out themes by identifying those products, concepts, and social issues that are strong enough to affect industries and economies domestically and/or internationally.

2. *Follow the chain of events the theme creates.* As we discuss in Chapter 2, a key principle of top-down investing is the idea that macro events spark a series of events with numerous investment implications. With thematic investing, you must envision the series of events that will follow the trends that you observe. Think deep.

3. *Identify the optimal investments within the chain.* You must weigh which of the investment possibilities will be the most profitable while also finding the right ones for your financial situation.

4. *Carefully build the position.* Begin to build your position, taking into consideration how the investments appear to be valued. (Is there excessive bullish or bearish sentiment built into the price? Is its P/E high or low? How's the dividend? How does the yield spread on its bonds look? If a physical asset, has its price been ramped up recently, or has it been sullied by deep pessimism?) Continually assess

whether the theme is holding up and build your position with an eye on exiting when the theme seems to be weakening or when there is excessive appreciation of the idea and prices have ramped up.

The View from the Top Down: Three Musts for the Macro Maven

Keep it simple. Most trends are obvious—invest in them.

1. *Embrace thematic investing.* History has shown that many of the most obvious and simple-to-understand themes were a terrific basis for profitable investments. Seize upon these opportunities.
2. *Use your power; you* are *the trend.* You are on the front line of many major trends that influence the financial markets. Recognize that you and others like you are what is behind these powerful trends and seize on their investment themes.
3. *Cheer the growth of themed financial instruments.* This is a golden age for thematic investing thanks to ETFs and other new products that allow you to invest easily in stock sectors, stock indexes, bonds, foreign currencies, commodities, real estate, and many other investments previously difficult to access. Macro investors should use these incredibly liberating tools.

THE GOLDEN COMPASSES: THE TOP TOP-DOWN INDICATORS

- *Demographics, the migration south.* Figure 4.6 illustrates quite clearly the penchant for people to move to relatively warmer climates. It is important to have a sense for the growth rates of the age groups that tend to be inclined to migrate southward, chiefly retirees.
- *The Joneses.* Duesenberry theorized that the inclination of people to spend is affected by the spending patterns of other consumers that individuals come into contact with. This means that spending patterns are likely to be affected

by trends that catch on. Thematic investing gears investors to spot these trends.

- *The World Trade Organization (WTO).* Changes in international trade laws have for many years had a profound impact on the international economy, producing clear winners and losers. In addition, inclusion in the WTO has the potential to elevate a nation's economic status, as was made abundantly clear after China was made a member in December 2001.

Notes

[1] World Trade Organization Web site: http://www.wto.org/english/thewto_e/whatis_e/tif_e/fact1_e.htm.

[2] Keynes, John M., *The General Theory of Employment, Interest and Money* (London: Macmillan, 1936).

[3] Friedman, Milton, *A Theory of the Consumption Function* (Princeton, NJ: Princeton University Press, 1956).

[4] Duesenberry, J. S., "Income—Consumption Relations and Their Implications," in Lloyd Metzler, et al., Income, Employment, and Public Policy (New York: W. W. Norton, 1948).

[5] U.S. Census Bureau statistics.

CHAPTER 5

Thematic Investing Using ETFs*

Seek out ETFs that enable forays into asset classes, economies, and themes previously shut to investors.

As we discuss in Chapter 4, there has never been a better time than the present to adopt the principles of thematic investing, particularly because it has not only become easier to spot the themes that move markets, but it has also become easier to invest in these themes by using products such as exchange-traded funds (ETFs). Today, investors of all sizes are able to embrace top-down principles of buying ideas rather than specific companies, bonds, commodities, currencies, and much more. These days money is flowing freely into commodities, real estate, foreign stocks and bonds, and other types of investments previously accessible only to market professionals.

Ever since State Street Bank & Trust originated the Standard & Poor's depositary receipts (SPDR) S&P 500 index in 1993, the popularity of ETFs has increased rapidly, particularly over the past few years. Data from State Street indicate that in 2007, ETFs held $608 billion in assets, a 45 percent increase compared to a year earlier.[1] In addition, the number of ETFs outstanding increased by 270 to 629,

---

*This chapter was contributed by Dan Greenhaus, an analyst and trader in the Equity Strategy Group at Miller Tabak + Co. Dan previously worked for Credit Suisse First Boston in its high-yield research department. Mr. Greenhaus obtained his MBA from Baruch College in 2006 and is currently a Chartered Financial Analyst (CFA) candidate.

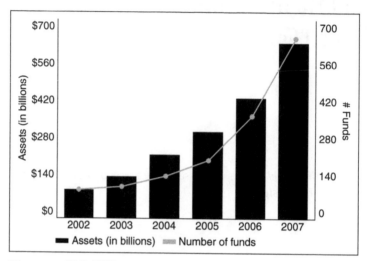

Figure 5.1 U.S. ETF asset growth.

Sources: Anderson, Tom, "US– Listed ETF Industry Review and 2008 Outlook," State Street Global Advisors, January 2008, and Bloomberg. Data through December 2007.

and trading volume increased by 14 percent to a daily average of $58 billion. Despite this rapid growth, which is illustrated in Figure 5.1, many individual investors still don't understand ETFs and their potential benefits, particularly in terms of how ETFs can provide both capital gains opportunities and diversification benefits.

ETFs IN A NUTSHELL

By their technical definition, ETFs are investment companies legally classified as open-end management investment companies or unit investment trusts. ETFs do not sell individual shares directly to the public and issue their shares only in large blocks known as *creation units*. Institutions generally purchase the creation units with a basket of securities that mirrors the ETF's portfolio and then split the creation unit and sell the individual shares on the secondary market.[2]

In plain English, ETFs are index funds that track a basket of stocks which provide an investor with exposure to a particular area of the market while reducing the potential risks of investing in a single company. They provide an investor with an efficient, low-cost approach to asset allocation, while achieving a level of portfolio diversification that would otherwise be far more difficult to obtain. ETFs are similar to open-end mutual funds in that regard; however, they often provide similar exposure at lower costs. Moreover, unlike mutual funds, which are priced at the end of each trading day, ETFs trade in the open market throughout each trading day and, because of factors related to supply-and-demand fundamentals, often deviate to some degree from their net asset value.

ETFs also provide a number of other benefits to investors, such as potential tax advantages when compared to standard mutual funds, although this can vary from one investor to the next. For example, with actively managed mutual funds, the sale of securities within the fund sometimes triggers capital gains distributions to shareholders, an event with tax consequences. Such a distribution does not exist with most ETFs, and the only capital gains tax considerations that exist occur with the sale of the ETF, an occurrence at the discretion of investors rather than the mutual fund portfolio managers. Although ETFs generally do not distribute capital gains, roughly 18 percent of all ETFs tracked by Morningstar Inc. in 2007 distributed some amount of capital gains to investors. That represents an increase compared to 2006, when only 6 percent of ETFs distributed capital gains. Only 3 percent of ETFs did so in 2005.[3] To be sure, the capital gains that ETFs distribute do not tend to be large, but they are distributions nonetheless. Morningstar Inc. notes that 49 percent of the funds that made any distribution at all made distributions equal to 1 percent of assets, or more.

A Few Perceived Disadvantages to ETFs

As with other investment vehicles, there are disadvantages to ETFs that investors must consider. For one, while some ETFs, such as the aforementioned Standard & Poor's depository receipts, trade tens of millions of shares per day, others trade far more infrequently. Increasingly, this is occurring because of the rapid introduction of ETFs we cite earlier. Investors are having difficulty keeping up with the almost daily introductions, keeping awareness low for some ETFs. In other cases, ETFs are being introduced in areas where investor interest is likely to be very narrow, thus limiting trading volume. Low trading volumes tend to be associated with wider bid/ask spreads than is the case with more liquid stocks, thus eroding the amount of profit that can be realized on an ETF investment.

A negative cited by some observers that is not easily backed up is the idea that ETFs lack diversification benefits. This narrow view rests on the notion that some of the more narrowly focused ETFs invest too heavily in a small group of companies with as few as five or ten companies making up the bulk of the investment. Despite this contention, this is a feature that actually makes such ETFs attractive because they provide investors with exposure to specific sectors, some of which are risky, doing so without investors having to commit capital to single companies, which could be a riskier strategy than owning the seemingly narrowly diversified ETF. An example would be the Deutsche Bank AG Climate Change Fund, which pledges to invest "at least 80% of net assets in companies engaged in activities related to climate change."[4] The climate change fund focuses on small and medium-sized companies in emerging areas that are often deemed risky. What is attractive here is the ability to invest in a basket of relatively risky companies rather than one relatively risky company. This provides investors with protection against potential failures within the group, which often occur in emerging industries. In situations such as this, it is much safer to buy into the theme, as expressed by investment in the group, than to gamble on which of the companies within the group will survive both the extreme competitive pressures that are found in emerging industries and a future shakeout of the industry. Ultimately, any singular investment, whether it is in shares of an individual company or in an ETF, by definition lacks diversification. It is within the context of a well-diversified portfolio that ETFs can be utilized by investors without the fear of being exposed to a potentially risky investment when that investment is held in isolation.

ETFs ARE IDEAL FOR TOP-DOWN INVESTORS

By allowing investors to diversify their risks, ETFs are ideal instruments for investors seeking a top-down approach to investing. As we've said before, at its core, with top-down investing you invest in a theme or an idea rather than investing in a specific company, a commodity, a currency, a bond, or the like. Top-down investors invest in very wide variety of ideas ranging from those that relate to demographics, the influence of commodities prices on sovereign wealth funds, new advances in biotechnology, or perhaps economic activity in Eastern Europe or Asia.

The ability to invest in diverse themes and also obtain diversification benefits are two of the biggest allures of ETFs. Many investors are attracted to ETFs also because they simply don't have the time to commit to other investing approaches. These investors would rather invest in the market as a whole rather than getting wrapped up in the ongoing analyses necessary to maintain portfolios developed from the bottom up, for example.

Investing in the market as a whole has proven to be a good strategy for many investors. For starters, numerous studies have pointed out that individuals, including mutual fund managers, do not outperform the broader market over extended periods of time. To highlight this, Morningstar's Web site outlines 18 different strategies for domestic stock funds from simple long-short to technology-specific funds. In the five years ending December 2007, the best-performing fund classification was natural resources which was up over by 30 percent, and the second best was communications, which was up by almost 25 percent.[5] Conversely, the S&P 500 increased by about 70 percent over the same five-year period. An investor looking for exposure to the S&P 500 could simply purchase the ETF for the S&P 500, SPDR, achieving a return almost identical to the market as a whole, with none of the company-specific risk associated with individual names. Perhaps you would like to track only the S&P 100, the Russell 2000, the Wilshire 5000, or some other index. Whatever index you wish to track, ETFs allow you to do so.

As we've noted, reducing company-specific risk is an important feature of ETFs and a crucial part of portfolio diversification. Investors who utilize ETFs give themselves an added layer of diversification. For example, with respect to health-care stocks, which are typically viewed as defensive stocks, not only can investors add this relatively safe sector to their holdings, but by using ETFs, investors can also neutralize an individual stock's performance on the return of their portfolios.

One such example would be the impact that both the Iraq war and rising oil prices have had on investors' awareness of "green" companies. Increasingly, investors have put their money in companies that either produce or use renewable energy. Powershares, an asset management firm headquartered in Wheaton, Illinois, offers investors the ability to gain exposure to renewable energy through its ETF called the Wilderhill clean-energy portfolio, trading under the ticker PBW. According to Powershares, the Wilderhill clean-energy portfolio is designed to "deliver capital appreciation through the selection of companies that focus on greener and generally renewable sources of energy and technologies that facilitate cleaner energy."[6] Its two largest holdings are Emcore Corp and American Superconductor Corp., two stocks that feature a high beta, which is a measure of the variability of a stock in relation to a benchmark (S&P 500), to a level that is north of 2.0. Stocks with a beta of 2.0 are twice as volatile as the stocks in the S&P 500. In fact, the top five holdings in this particular ETF all have betas above 1.75, which obviously means that each individual name would be considered "risky" in its own right, should you choose to invest in one of them individually. By investing in the ETF instead, the investor reduces the individual stock variability and instead focuses only on the beta of the ETF as a whole.

REACH BEYOND FAMILIAR TERRITORY WITH ETFs

New ETFs are being launched almost every day of late, and they exist for virtually vast numbers of trading strategies. A new concept, for example, is the idea of "life cycle" ETFs, which are geared toward investors planning for retirement. This is just one of many new concepts that reaches beyond equities and gives investors the opportunity to gain exposure outside traditional asset classes. Even in familiar asset classes such as municipal bonds, there are new ideas. For example, a recent launch of an ETF for municipal bonds gives investors an alternative to municipal mutual funds while charging a smaller fee, sometimes as little as .20 to .28 percent, which is well below the average for all mutual funds, which is around 1 percent of the funds managed.[7]

In an increasingly intertwined global economy, achieving a level of international diversification in one's portfolio is no longer an option; it's a necessity. Even a few years ago, achieving this level of diversification would prove both problematic and costly. But the advent of ETFs has reduced the cost substantially and with far less work required of investors.

Those who subscribe to certain portfolio theories have for years touted the benefits of portfolio diversification as a means of reducing a portfolio's overall beta and improving its risk/return profile. In the past, diversification may have meant holding energy stocks as well as retail stocks, or holding both consumer discretionary and health-care stocks. Today's integrated world and the burgeoning opportunities that have developed from the spread of market capitalism force investors to think beyond these traditional means of diversification. This means, for example, that investors need to look beyond their shores to gain exposure to foreign economies and their stocks, their bonds, their currencies, and the commodities they produce. While such diversification may be easy for the institutional investor, individual investors may find it more difficult and more expensive, and it is in these circumstances in which ETFs really provide enormous benefit.

One final example of the allure of ETFs is the experience that ETF investors have had with China, which of course has emerged as an economic powerhouse on the global stage. You are all familiar with headlines about China's double-digit economic growth rate. A top-down investor can easily gain exposure to the Chinese stock market by utilizing ETFs. One such ETF is the iShares Trust FTSE/Xinhua China 25 fund, or the FXI. The ETF is designed to mimic the performance of some of the largest companies in the Chinese market. It is difficult to imagine making the foray into individual stocks themselves in a land notorious for its inaccessibility to investors outside the country.

Amidst all their benefits, if nothing else ETFs have emerged as a liberating investing tool. Not surprisingly, investors are increasingly taking advantage of the vast array of ETFs now available, seeking capital gains, diversification benefits, and a means of investing in themes and entering markets that seemed out of reach even just a few years ago.

The View from the Top Down: Three Musts for the Macro Maven

ETFs fit perfectly with top-down investing and vice versa. It has never been easier to both broaden the asset classes you can invest in and diversify within these asset classes.

1. *Keep up with the newest ETFs.* A new ETF was issued on average every business day in 2007 across all asset classes and across the globe. It pays to keep up with the newest products and look for products that enable investments in areas where the barrier of entry was previously very high.

2. *Be leery of some narrowly based ETFs.* The rapid growth in the number of ETFs is occurring in part because of enthusiasm toward the product, which raises the risk that some ETFs will be issued that eventually either fall out of favor or carry excessive liquidity risks. Investors need be on the lookout for these.

3. *Span the world for ETFs.* Investors can easily gain exposure to foreign markets using ETFs. Investors should have on their watch list ETFs for countries where EFTs do not exist or exist with limited exposures, and ETFs for countries whose prospects might change quickly as a result of important events such as the signing of free-trade agreements (see Chapter 8), entry into the World Trade Organization, commodity price trends, geopolitical developments, and so forth.

THE GOLDEN COMPASSES: THE TOP TOP-DOWN INDICATORS

- *Cross-border deposits and impact of commodities prices.* To pick the best ETFs, investors should invest in countries that stand to benefit not only from increases in commodity prices but from cross-border flows that work their way into other countries. For example, there are a number of countries in the former Eastern Bloc that are benefiting from cash flowing in from the Middle East, which obviously has been benefiting from the surging price of oil.

Notes

[1] State Street Global Advisers, "U.S.-Listed ETF Industry Review and 2008 Outlook," January 2008. State Street report, available at http:// www.ssga-funds.com/library/mkcm/Outlook_2008_01.15.2008REVCCRI1200502543 .pdf.

[2] Adapted from the Securities and Exchange Commission's Web site; http://www.sec.gov/answers/etf.htm.

[3] Ian Salisbury, "ETFs Harbor a Little Surprise," *Wall Street Journal*, January 16, 2008.

[4] See https://www.dws-scudder.com/usmfWeb/dyn/fundShell/index.jsp? coreFundkey=4528&fundCat=4.

[5] See http://news.morningstar.com/fundReturns/CategoryReturns.html.

[6] See http://www.invescopowershares.com/products/overview.aspx?ticker =PBW.

[7] Shefali Anand, "Municipal Bonds Are Awkward Fit in ETF World," *Wall Street Journal*, October 20, 2007.

CHAPTER 6

Central Banking Is
a Top-Down Affair

The more fully the public understands what the function of the Federal Reserve System is, and on what grounds its policies and actions are based, the simpler and easier will be the problems of credit administration in the U.S.

—Federal Reserve Board annual report, 1923, p. 95

Whoever controls the volume of money in any country is absolute master of all industry and commerce.

—James A. Garfield, 20th President of the United States

Ever since President Woodrow Wilson signed the Federal Reserve Act of 1913 at 6:02 p.m. on December 23 of that year, the Federal Reserve has been evolving into one of the most powerful institutions in the United States and the world, for that matter. The act established the Fed with the goal of providing stability to the U.S. financial system, which at that time had no official backstop in the event of financial crises. The act stated that the Fed would "provide for the establishment of Federal reserve banks, to furnish an elastic currency, to afford means of rediscounting commercial paper, to establish a more effective supervision of banking in the United States, and for other purposes." Other purposes, indeed. Ever since that important day in our nation's financial history, the Fed's role has expanded greatly to the point that its influence now stretches across the globe.

For investors, whose money now spans the globe, the idea that the Fed's influence has broadened worldwide must be taken into account when investing domestically and abroad. In addition, it is imperative for investors to recognize that investments across all asset classes are being influenced by unprecedented degrees of coordination among the world's central banks. Some investors will say that none of this matters to them, that they don't pay attention to all the gibberish and drama that surrounds the Fed. To each his own, I suppose, but history has shown that investors, mindful of the adage "Don't fight the Fed," have been able to put together dependable investment strategies to both protect themselves and profit from the Fed's policy cycles. As we discuss later, there are new variables in the equation, chiefly the integration of the world financial system, the Fed's growing toolbox, more forceful strategizing by the Fed, and increased transparency at the Fed. But at the end of the day we are still facing a Fed with the power to move markets. The same can be said of central banks abroad, where their influence has grown mightily in places we would not have expected even ten years ago, including Moscow, Brazil, the Middle East, and Asia, particularly China. Central bank watching has always been a top-down affair. The integration of the world financial system has made it even more so and it is why it is imperative to gain an understanding about how these powerful institutions work, how they are operating in this new era, and how they move markets.

THE FED'S *RAISON D'ÊTRE*

Over time, new legislation has molded the Fed's role into the institution we know today. There were two particular additional acts of Congress that refined and supplemented the objectives of the Fed, as originally stated in the Federal Reserve Act of 1913. The acts were: the Employment Act of 1946 and the Full Employment and Balanced Growth Act of 1978 (sometimes referred to the Humphrey-Hawkins Act after its original sponsors). These two acts restated the Fed's objectives to include economic growth in line with the economy's growth potential; a high level of employment; stable prices (in terms of the purchasing power of the dollar); and moderate long-term interest rates.

From the Fed's vantage point, its duties fall into four general areas:

1. Conducting the nation's monetary policies by influencing the money and credit conditions in the economy in the pursuit of full employment and stable prices.

2. Supervising and regulating banking institutions to ensure the safety and soundness of the nation's banking and financial systems and to protect the credit rights of consumers.
3. Maintaining the stability of the financial system and containing systemic risk that may arise in financial markets.
4. Providing certain financial services to the U.S. government, to the public, to financial institutions, and to foreign official institutions including playing a major role in operating the nation's payment systems.

Of the four, the first is the most prominent and is the one that gets the most attention in the financial markets by far. The main tools available to the Fed for implementing policy are open market operations, reserve requirements, and the discount rate. More recently, the Federal Reserve began auctioning loans via a term auction facility (TAF), a strategy the Fed adopted in December 2007 and expanded in 2008. In March 2008 the Fed added to its toolbox, establishing a Primary Dealer Credit Facility, which provides credit to investment banks in exchange for securities. The facility was established to help finance the rescue of Bear Stearns. On paper, authority for policy-making at the Fed is widely diffused throughout the system. In practice, however, this authority has gradually been centered in the Federal Open Market Committee (FOMC), which was established to oversee the Fed's open market operations. Members of the FOMC include all seven governors of the system, the president of the New York Fed, and the presidents of four of the other eleven district banks; the last of which serve on a rotating basis. Every member of the FOMC has one vote, but it has become tradition that the chairman of the board of governors plays a decisive role in formulating policy and acts as chief spokesperson for the system, which is why this position is viewed as one of high power and importance.

THE FED DOES NOT CHANGE INTEREST RATES BY FIAT

The primary policy tool available to the Fed is its so-called open market operations, the ability to create bank reserves in any desired quantity by monetizing some portion of the national debt. The Fed could in theory monetize anything—scrap metal to soybeans—but it has stuck largely to Treasury IOUs because there has never been any shortage of them; also, they are highly liquid, so the Fed can sell them with as much ease as it buys them. In formulating policy, the first question the Fed faces is what macroeconomic *targets* to pursue. There are various possibilities: full employment, price stability, or a "correct" exchange value for the dollar. The achievement of *all* of these targets is desirable. However, since the Fed has only *one* powerful string to its bow—the ability to control bank reserves and thereby money creation by the private banking system—and given that the fact that the Fed now targets interest rates rather than reserve levels, the Fed must conduct its open market operations in a way that strikes the right balance first and foremost via the appropriate target rate, the federal funds rate, which is the rate that banks charge each other for loans and the rate to which many other interest rates are tied.

Once the Fed has chosen its policy targets, it faces a second difficult question: What policies should it use to achieve these targets? For example, if it wants to pursue a tight money policy to curb inflation, does that mean it should force up interest rates, or what?

Not surprisingly, the Fed's answers to the questions of what targets it should pursue and of how it should do so change considerably over time. One reason is that external conditions—the structure of financial markets and the state of the domestic and world economies—are in constant flux. A second reason is that central banking is an art form that's not fully understood, and the Fed's behavior at any time is therefore partly a function of how far it has progressed along its learning curve.

Whatever its ultimate macroeconomic goals may be, the Fed currently states its immediate policy objectives in the policy statements that follow its policy meetings. It does so primarily by indicating a target level for the federal funds rate. As I said in the section heading, the Fed does not change interest rates by fiat. The Fed does not just announce a change in interest rates and then it happens. In order for the Fed to adjust the level of the federal funds rate, it must do something more than just talk. In particular, in order to adjust the level of the funds rate, the Fed must alter the level of bank reserves in the banking system. It is simple economics 101: in order to change the price of anything, some change in the equilibrium between supply and demand must occur. It is the same with federal funds. In order to change its price, the Fed must adjust its supply. This means that if the Fed desires to lower the fed funds rate, the Fed must inject reserves into the banking system (which become available for lending in the federal funds market) such that the supply of federal funds increases and the price (the rate) is lowered. Conversely, in order to raise interest rates, the Fed must reduce the supply of reserves by draining money from the banking system to decrease its availability and raise its cost.

The process I have just described is very important for top-down investors to grasp. Investors do not always see it in the way described here. They think that a rate announcement is just a rate announcement. They don't see that it is much more than that. Each and every time the Fed announces that it has decided upon a change in interest rates, it must do something to make it happen, namely either add money to make the funds rate fall or drain money to make the funds rate rise. When the Fed takes these actions, a whirlwind of chain reactions takes place, affecting the economy and the financial markets. As I will show, there is no denying this impact and the advantage that top-down investors have when it comes to the Fed's rate cycles.

IMPACT FROM THE TOP DOWN: THE TRANSMISSION EFFECTS OF MONETARY POLICY

Monetary policy tends to work with an uncanny degree of simultaneity that any top-down investor can take advantage of. Of course, no two financial episodes are exactly alike, especially with respect to the magnitude of reactions to changes in Fed policy, but the direction of the reactions that tend to follow changes in Fed policy is more predictable than many realize. For example, when the Federal Reserve lowers interest rates, both nominal and real interest rates (nominal rates minus inflation) tend to fall, the yield curve tends to steepen, and spread products (corporate bonds, agency securities, mortgage-backed securities, and the like) tend to outperform Treasuries. In addition, equity prices tend to rise. All these responses help the Fed to achieve its desired goals on growth and inflation and are a part of a number *transmission effects* that ripple through the financial system first and then through the economy.

There are five main ways in which the Fed's interest-rate changes work their way into the economy:

1. Stock prices.
2. Credit spreads.
3. The value of the dollar.
4. Lending standards.
5. Capital formation.

These transmission effects can significantly affect the extent to which the Fed is successful in achieving a desired outcome. For example, if the transmission effects are strong—in other words if the impact on the transmission channels shown above is significant—the more effective the Fed's rate actions will be and the less the Fed will need to do. Basically, the markets will have done the heavy lifting in such a situation. On the other hand, if the transmission effects are weak, then the Fed will have to do more. What is most relevant for the top-down investor to remember in this regard is to be sure to monitor the extent to which the transmission effects are working or not working. Once you have done that, you can place bets on how the flow of economic data will affect the financial markets.

For example, consider a situation where the Fed has lowered interest rates yet stock prices have fallen, the dollar has rallied, credit spreads have widened, and lending standards have tightened. In a situation like this, it is likely that the Fed will have difficulty reviving economic growth and will pursue more interest-rate cuts. This is an ideal situation to buy short-term Treasury securities, which tend to perform when the Fed is lowering interest rates. In addition to this, betting against cyclical shares such as technology shares, retail, and financial stocks in favor of defense stocks such as utilities and drug stocks would make sense.

If it seems far-fetched for this type of situation to arise, it's not. It happened in 2001 amid the bursting of the financial bubble and then again in late 2007 and early 2008 despite virtually unprecedented interest-rate cuts by the Federal Reserve. In 2001, Fed chairman Alan Greenspan, having learned from his experience from the 1990–1991 recession as well as from the Bank of Japan's failure to move quickly to reverse its prolonged economic downturn of the 1990s, began cutting interest rates aggressively starting on January

3, 2001, following an emergency convening of the Federal Open Market Committee (FOMC) via conference call, announcing a 50-basis–point cut in the federal funds rate. Greenspan's Fed would cut the funds rate 11 times that year by 475 basis points to 1.75 percent and eventually bring the funds rate down to 1 percent in June 2003, its lowest level since 1958! Alan Greenspan felt that interest rates had to be cut more aggressively than usual, telling the FOMC in its January 3 conference call that, "The same technology that was boosting productivity growth might also be speeding up the process of cyclical adjustment."[1] Greenspan argued that a just-in-time economy, the phrase used to describe the way in which companies these days produce goods in response to demand rather than in anticipation of demand, demanded just-in-time monetary policy.

Wealth Effects

Despite Greenspan's aggressive moves, atypical reactions were occurring in the financial markets after rate cuts began in 2001. Equity prices fell, credit spreads widened (credit spreads represent the yield difference between Treasuries and other fixed-income securities such as corporate bonds and mortgage-backed securities), and the dollar rallied, as shown in Figure 6.1. Each of these reactions tightened financial conditions, which is to say that financial market conditions were having a negative influence on the economy. For example, the decline in stock prices was diminishing household wealth which resulted in negative *wealth effects*. This means that consumer spending was being negatively affected by the stock market's decline. In fact, many studies indicate that for each dollar decline in household wealth resulting from a decline in stock prices, consumers cut their spending by about 3–5 cents over time.[2] With the value of equities held by households having fallen by about $2 trillion in 2001,[3] the decline in stock prices threatened to cut consumer spending by about $80 billion, an amount roughly equal to a full percentage point of GDP. The wealth effect is a concept that is important for top-down investors to always be mindful of. When a top-down investor sees a swoon in stock prices, one of his or her first thoughts should be on the impact that the movement could have on consumer spending. From there, a wide variety of other thoughts should come to mind that lead to numerous investment ideas.

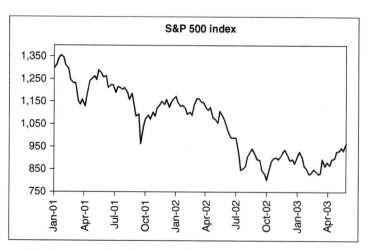

Figure 6.1 Fed rate cuts in 2001–2003 failed to rally equities.
Source: Bloomberg.

Impact of a Weaker Dollar on the U.S. Economy

Also imparting a negative influence on the economy in 2001 was a rally in the U.S. dollar. The Federal Reserve's trade-weighted dollar index increased by about 7 percent in 2001, which meant that the prices of goods sold to the United States from abroad became more affordable to U.S. consumers. When this happens, U.S. consumers tend to buy relatively more foreign-made products, thereby weakening economic activity at home. The strengthening of the dollar in 2001 was unusual, as central bank rate cuts tend to result in a weaker domestic currency mainly because low interest rates spur investors to eschew currencies in countries where interest rates are falling in favor of currencies in countries where interest rates are higher. In addition, rate cuts usually signal weak domestic growth, reducing the allure of investing in countries that lower their interest rates. The rally in the dollar was yet another headwind for the Fed to fight, making it necessary to cut interest rates to unusually low levels. As a general rule, keep in mind that for each 5 percent change in the value of the dollar the impact will be roughly the equivalent of a 50-basis–point cut in the federal funds rate. That is enough to affect GDP by roughly a half percentage point over two years.[4] In 2007 and 2008, weakness in the U.S. dollar helped offset many of the headwinds faced by the U.S. economy by adding almost a percentage point to GDP.

Impact of Credit Spreads

To add to the headwinds from other segments of the financial markets that were occurring in 2001, credit spreads widened dramatically, making it more costly for companies to raise money for expansion. This, too, was unusual, as Fed rate cuts tend to make people more optimistic about the outlook for corporate revenue growth, alleviating the primary concern that investors have when they buy corporate bonds, namely future cash flows. All a bond investor ever worries about is getting his or her money back. The primary factor causing this unusual movement in 2001 was the bursting of the financial bubble as well as the risk that it and the economic recession might spark deflation in the prices of goods and services. If it did, company revenues might decline, making it difficult for companies to repay their debts. Investors hence steered clear of corporate bonds and bought Treasuries instead, pushing up the cost of capital and forcing many companies to either cut back on their expansion plans or scrap them completely. Some companies simply failed to launch.

Top-down investors need to be mindful of the impact that credit spreads can have on the economy and on the signal sent by the markets regarding risk taking. When credit spreads widen, it unequivocally indicates that companies will be paying more to carry their debt as long as the widening exceeds any decline that might be occurring in Treasury yields. Top-down investors must then consider whether there are any offsets to the economic drag that the wider credit spreads are creating (such as Fed rate cuts and fiscal stimulus). If there are none, then it can be quickly assumed that the economy will be worse off. Of course, if credit spreads tighten, then this means that the cost of capital has fallen, which should lend support to economic activity, as was the case in the years following the 2001 recession.

Keep in mind that, when credit spreads widen, it is important to determine whether the widening is because of a liquidity shock, as was the case in 1998 and 2007–2008 when investors expressed concerns about the U.S. and global financial systems and the availability of money, or because of a credit-quality shock, as was the case in 2001. The distinction is important because it has been found that liquidity shocks tend to cause a bigger decrease in corporate bond issuance than do credit-quality shocks, even though credit spreads will tend to widen more when concerns over credit quality are foremost. Top-down investors must therefore make this distinction in order to decide upon what kind of impact that shock will have on the economy. This is not difficult, as the news surrounding these events will make it obvious, as was the case in 2007 and 2008 when the difficulties that financial entities were having in obtaining liquidity were all over the news.

I have one last point regarding the distinctions between liquidity shocks and credit-quality shocks: regardless of whether bond issuance falls because of a liquidity or credit-quality shock, in both cases the impact of a decline in corporate bond issuance needn't have substantial impact on the economy unless the decline in issuance is prolonged, say beyond three months. This is because most firms do not tap the bond market for money all that often. For instance, Harrison found that only between 5 and 10 percent of low-grade issuing firms issue bonds in any given quarter and that only around 10 percent issue bonds over a 12-month horizon.[5] One implication of this is that the impact on liquidity from shocks may be more troublesome for investors and trading activity than the impact that a decrease in bond issuance would be for the economy. Central bankers and top-down investors can nonetheless track credit spreads and bond issuance as a gauge of the secondary market and the many signals it casts with respect to concerns over liquidity, credit, and the economy.

Impact of Globalization on the Transmission Effects of Monetary Policy

Fed policy does not work in a vacuum. Globalization has added significant challenges to the formulation of monetary policy. Frederic Mishkin, a member of the Federal Reserve's board of governors and the Federal Open Market Committee and a respected academic, analyzed the impact of globalization on the transmission of monetary policy in a speech he delivered in September 2007.[6] Mishkin notes four key questions surrounding the impact of globalization on the monetary transmission mechanism:

1. Has globalization led to a decline in the sensitivity of inflation to domestic output gaps (the difference between actual and potential output) and thus to domestic

monetary policy? In other words, has globalization made the Phillips curve flatter? (The Phillips curve gauges the correlation between unemployment and inflation.)

2. Are foreign output gaps playing a more prominent role in the domestic inflation process so that domestic monetary policy has more difficulty stabilizing inflation?

3. Can domestic monetary policy still control domestic interest rates and thereby stabilize both inflation and output?

4. Are there other ways, besides possible influences on inflation and interest rates, in which globalization has affected the transmission mechanism of monetary policy?

With respect to the first question, which basically asks whether globalization has reduced inflation pressures at home resulting from gaps between the output of goods and services and the economy's ability to produce goods and services—the output gap, it certainly seems possible since consumers can buy goods and services from abroad more than ever these days, thus reducing domestic price pressures. Mishkin argues, however, that the main factor reducing these price pressures has been better monetary policy and the improved inflation expectations that it has engendered. This makes sense since we have indeed witnessed a more stable mindset on inflation, the result of many years of successful Fed policy, particularly during the tenure of Alan Greenspan, who helped break the back of inflation expectations.

On the second question, Mishkin points to evidence suggesting that extra slack in countries abroad "has superseded domestic slack as a key determinant of domestic inflation." This means that if countries abroad have lots of spare capacity, it will help alleviate capacity constraints at home, thus curtailing price pressures. We have seen this in recent years in the outsourcing of production abroad.

The third question is one that has been posed increasingly in the early 2000s. It deals with the idea that globalization has rendered Fed policy impotent. Many note, for example, that in 2004 the Federal Reserve's efforts to boost long-term interest rates to slow the economy failed because foreign investors were investing their large pool of savings into U.S. Treasuries, thus pushing long-term rates lower. Alan Greenspan referred to this as a "conundrum," which he made the subject of an entire chapter in his recent book, *The Age of Turbulence*. There is little doubt that foreign investors, who hold about half of all Treasuries outstanding, played a major role in keeping long-term interest rates down. It can nonetheless be argued, as Mishkin does, that central banks such as the Federal Reserve are still in control of short-term interest rates, which means that the Fed can still affect the cost of money and that the Fed is still quite relevant.

The fourth question is an interesting one that top-down investors will have to be particularly watchful for, especially since it is apt to be unpredictable. The basic premise with this one deals with the value of the dollar, with the theory being that Fed rate cuts will weaken the dollar and Fed rate hikes will strengthen the dollar. As I showed earlier, this was hardly the case in 2001, underscoring the idea that it is a linkage that may not always work. In 2007 and 2008 it was a much different story, with the dollar weakening sharply in response to signs of weakening U.S. economic growth and Fed rate cuts.

The dollar's sharp decline highlights one of two main ways in which influences related to the increased role of globalization are affecting the transmission of monetary policy through foreign exchange rates. In particular, it is possible that the increased flow of capital across borders is resulting in more rapid adjustments in foreign exchange rates to rate changes implemented by the Fed and the world's central banks. Adding to this effect is the decline that has taken place worldwide in the so-called "home bias," which is the preference that investors tend to express for keeping money in their own backyard, namely their home country. A second way in which globalization is affecting the transmission of monetary policy is by intensifying the impact of changes in exchange rates that occur as a result of changes in monetary policy. This intensification is occurring because of the expanded level of global trade. In other words, because international trade represents a larger share of global economic activity than ever before, when foreign exchange rates move up and down in response to changes in monetary policy (or for any other reason for that matter), the impact on economic activity is apt to be greater.

THE IMPORTANCE OF TRACKING TRANSMISSION EFFECTS

To sum up, top-down investors should always be mindful of the transmission effects of monetary policy, keeping an eye to determining the likelihood that the Federal Reserve will be successful in achieving its goals on growth and inflation. In cases where the transmission effects look small, expect more aggressive Fed rate actions and for a slow response in the economy and on sectors within the equity market. For example, if as in 2001 it appears that the transmission effects are reducing the effectiveness of Fed rate cuts, expect deeper rate cuts. Under this scenario, Treasuries will rally, and the yield curve will steepen. In addition, the outlook on corporate profits will be weaker than otherwise, hurting so-called high-beta stocks (stocks whose movement tends to exceed that of the overall market in both directions), and shares of companies in cyclical industries. Defensive shares will outperform most other sectors, particularly cyclical stocks. In cases where the transmission effects are strong, expect the Fed's goals to be reached faster so there will be a quick end to Fed actions. Probably in all cases it makes sense to believe that at the end of the day the Fed will eventually reach its goals. It is the timing and magnitude that are open to question.

THE FED'S IMPACT ON THE STOCK MARKET

As I said, it is important for top-down investors to gauge the transmission effects of the monetary policy to develop a clearer picture of where the economy is headed and to determine just how much more work the Fed may have to do. Implicit in all of this is the idea that there is a timing element that will be important to get a handle on in order to time your investments well. In this section we focus a bit more on the impact that the Fed's rate actions tend to have on equities beyond what I have already indicated.

Bernanke's Take

Everyone's got an opinion on whether or not the Fed has any impact on equities prices, including Fed chairman Ben Bernanke. He has studied the issue and has concluded that there is indeed an impact. Suffice it to say that when Bernanke either boosts or lowers interest rates, he expects that the equity market will respond, particularly to surprise rate changes.

In a 56-page study published in 2004, Bernanke found that, on average, a hypothetical unanticipated 25-basis-point cut in the federal funds rate target is associated with about a 1 percent increase in broad stock indexes.[7] This finding helps to explain the surprises Bernanke sprung upon the markets in the 2007–2008 rate cut cycle, in particular the extraordinarily large 75-basis-point intermeeting rate cut the Fed announced on January 22, 2008, and the additional 50 basis points of cuts just two weeks later. The January 22 cut was 25 basis points more than the market expected, as was the Fed's September 18, 2007 cut of 50 basis points. The Fed also announced a number of creative approaches to providing liquidity to the financial markets, in particular major lending facilities designed to supply collateralized loans to banks and investment banks. In light of these surprises and Bernanke's 2004 study, a little knowledge about a Fed chairman's past works can go a long way!

Support for Bernanke's findings can be found in many studies. Rigobon and Sack, for example, found that a 25-basis-point *increase* in the federal funds rate results in a 1.9 percent decline in the S&P 500 index and that it has an even larger impact on the Nasdaq—2.5 percent.[8]

The Fed's Impact on Stock Sectors

Another conclusion drawn in Ben Bernanke's 2004 study on the impact of Fed policy on stock prices was that the reaction to surprise rate changes differed across stock sectors, which was consistent with widely accepted notions. Bernanke found that high-tech and telecommunications sectors reacted most to surprise changes in monetary policy, while the energy and utility sectors did not appear to be significantly affected. Figure 6.2 illustrates Bernanke's findings. Although the illustration is a bit technical, pay attention to the scale of impact that the chart suggests.

As I mentioned, Bernanke's findings fit with widely accepted notions. Navarro, illustrated these beliefs in the chart shown in Figure 6.3.[9] Keep in mind that while the chart does not directly

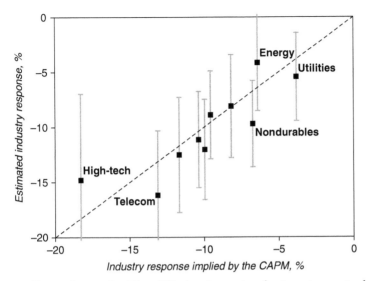

Figure 6.2 Bernanke study: The differing impacts of rate cuts on stock sectors. The figure depicts the one-month responses of the Fama-French industry portfolios to a one percentage point federal funds rate surprise. The values on the horizontal axis are the industry stock return responses implied by the capital asset pricing model (CAPM). The vertical axis values are estimated industry return responses. The vertical gray lines represent the 80 percent confidence intervals associated with the estimated industry responses.

Source: Bernanke, Ben, and Kenneth Kuttner. "What Explains the Stock Market's Reaction to Federal Reserve Policy?" Federal Reserve Board of Governors, *Finance and Economic Discussion Series*, March 2004.

relate to the Federal Reserve, there is the widely held presumption that the Federal Reserve's monetary policy cycles play a major role in the ups and downs of the business cycle.

Top-down investors mindful of the impact that the Fed's policy cycles have on the business cycle will be successful in formulating investment strategies that are both timely and that have lasting impact on their portfolios. For example, an investor, after having assessed whether the Fed's rate changes are transmitting in the ways we discussed earlier, would then decide upon sectors to both overweight and underweight riding these positions into the next stage of the cycle. In cases where the Fed is lowering interest rates,

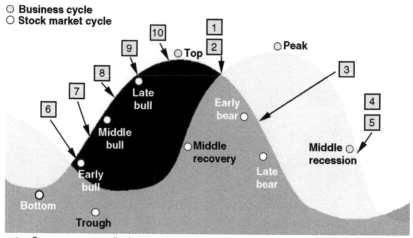

1. Consumer noncyclicals (e.g., food, drugs, cosmetics)
2. Health care
3. Utilities
4. Consumer cyclicals (e.g., autos, housing)
5. Financials
6. Transportation
7. Technology
8. Capital goods
9. Basic Industry (e.g., aluminum, chemicals, paper, steel)
10. Energy

Figure 6.3 The business cycle and the stock market cycle.

Source: Peter Navarro, *If It's Raining in Brazil, This Must Be Starbucks*, McGraw-Hill, 2002.

this means that investors would, as Bernanke's research indicates, buy technology stocks in anticipation of a rebound in economic activity. The transportation and capital goods industries also tend to perform well early in the cycle. In contrast, defense industries tend to underperform, particularly shares in consumer noncyclicals and health-care industries.

It is important to keep in mind why it is that equity prices respond to the Fed's rate changes. I bring this up because most investors sometimes only consider the impact that interest rates have on the economy, which is perfectly okay, but it is also important to think about the impact that rate changes have on risk attitudes. In particular, investors must consider the risk premium that is built into equity prices and how this might change as a result of changes in interest rates. The *equity risk premium* basically measures the amount of return that investors expect to receive over and above the risk-free rate of return, which is typically defined as the yield on three-month Treasury bills. When investors become risk takers, the risk premium rises, with investors paying less for stocks than they otherwise would. If this sounds a bit confusing—the idea that a rising equity risk *premium* results in a lower stock price—it is perhaps more easily understood if you think about what potential buyers are demanding of those who sell them stock. When buyers demand increased compensation for risk, they pay lower prices, basically demanding that sellers compensate them for the increased risk that they see in owning stock. By paying lower prices for stocks, buyers exact a "premium" from the sellers of stock. Conversely, when investors are risk-averse, they demand a smaller amount of compensation for the risks they see. This means that they become willing to pay higher prices, believing that equities carry relatively less risk than before. This happened in 1999 and 2000 when stock prices soared, with investors perceiving very little risk in owning stocks, a belief that was way off the mark.

The equity risk premium will fluctuate for a lot of reasons, and the Federal Reserve is one of them. In his 2004 study, Bernanke cites two ways in which Fed policy affects equities. For starters, changes in monetary policy could affect stocks directly by influencing the interest costs and balance sheets of publicly owned firms. In other cases, monetary policy can affect the willingness of investors to take risks—the equity risk premium. Bernanke notes that by affecting the equity risk premium, the Fed can affect the level of precautionary savings. In other words, when the Fed alters monetary policy, investors could be incited to increase or decrease their savings, hence influencing investment and consumption and the pace of economic activity.

Top-down investors should constantly weigh how the Fed's rate actions will affect risk attitudes, not only toward stocks but toward other asset classes as well. It is an important judgment to make not only as a means of determining the right mix of asset classes, but also to select the right mix of investments within each asset class. For example, Fed rate cuts that boost risk taking would be a reason to not only buy stocks, but to buy stocks deemed risky compared to the overall market, either those with high betas or in a highly cyclical industry that correlates well to the economic cycle.

The Production Cycle, the Fed, and Stock Prices

Equity prices often move higher or lower in response to the Fed's interest-rate changes, doing so in anticipation of a change in the economic climate and the outlook for corporate profits, which is the main driver of stock prices. This anticipatory response works well, most times, as the economy eventually responds to the Fed's interest-rate changes, although just when the economy responds depends on many factors, such as the transmission effects mentioned earlier. Top-down investors can gain an edge on predicting just when the Fed's rate changes will have their intended effect by monitoring the transmission effects of monetary policy and by tracking the production cycle, which is at the root of what sustains economic expansions. In doing so, you can make more timely choices of stock sectors.

The production cycle is an easy top-down process to understand. When you track it regularly, you will rarely miss its signs and its many investment implications. It is a cycle that I have found to be extraordinarily dependable since the early 1990s. Basically, what the production cycle entails is a cycle of increases or decreases in production, income, and spending. When the economy is expanding, a virtuous cycle of self-feeding increases occurs. In downturns, the virtuous cycle becomes vicious until something (the Fed, usually) comes along to break it. The production cycle is self-feeding because increases in production generally require an increased number of workers, which means that when companies decide to raise output (of goods and services), they are likely to either boost the size of their labor force or extend the workweek of their existing workforce. This process boosts income growth, which translates into higher spending, requiring additional increases in production, which spur another cycle of increases in production, income, and spending.

Top-down investors can track this process by comparing spending levels to output. When spending breaks either higher or lower relative to output, output will inevitably follow, mainly because companies do not want to be left in the dust and lose market share to their competitors. Importantly, the financial markets will be ignorant of this process and behave as if they have been hoodwinked by reacting to the economic calendar, which is laden with data that reflect on the production end of the economy. A few samples include the Institute for Supply Management (ISM) index, durable goods orders, factory orders, industrial production, the New York Empire survey, and employment data such as jobless claims and payroll employment; these gauges tend to reflect changes in output. What smart investors should do is think from the top down and expect that changes in spending patterns will ultimately feed through to production into widely followed data. I actually feel glad, most times, that U.S. statisticians have barely tinkered with the economic calendar over the years despite the fact that the U.S. economy has shifted increasingly to a service-oriented economy. As a result, we top-down investors have an edge because most investors will be obsessed with data that are on the so-called back end of the economy, while we will be watching the front end— the spending side—and the factors that will affect spending.

The best numbers to track in this regard are the figures on consumer spending. In particular, weekly data on chain store sales are of immense value. You really can't get closer to consumers than you do by looking at how they spent their money over the previous weekend. These data are released by a few retailers on Monday mornings, but the best data are the statistics released every Tuesday morning by the International Council for Shopping Centers (ICSC), which releases data on the aggregate weekly sales of dozens of the nation's top retailers. Also important to watch is the weekly data on mortgage applications released every Wednesday by the Mortgage Bankers Association. The data yield clues on home buying. A third indicator is automobile sales, which are released at the start of each month by the major automobile manufacturers (paid subscribers to a variety of data providers can get sales statistics more frequently). So there's your list: store sales, car sales, and home sales. You really don't need much more than that to get a bead on the consumer, but take all that you can get.

There is no exact science to making judgments about how spending is faring relative to output. It is more important to get a "sense of the data" especially as they relate to how the data are being perceived in the financial markets. Generally speaking, however, it is not difficult to know when spending and production are diverging or when something is happening on the spending side that could, well, change everything. For example, at the end of 2007, data from the ICSC indicated that same-store chain store sales were increasing at a pace of about 2.5 percent and then in January 2008 at a pace of only 1.5 percent compared to a year earlier, a paltry pace compared to normal rates of closer to 3.5 percent or so. Being below trend, it was difficult to envision how the production end of the economy could show any lasting strength. If it did, then companies would likely get stuck with an unintended buildup of inventories. In cases such as this, top-down investors would expect weakness in the statistics released throughout the factory-laden economic calendar. This is exactly how events played out. As for a turn in conditions, in a case such as this top-down investors should be on the lookout for an uptick in spending. For example, if chain sales were to strengthen back to 3.5 percent, to a top-down investor there would be no getting around the idea that production schedules would eventually ramp up. In turn, so would economic data, which, to investors outside the top-down realm would come as a surprise, resulting in an uptick in stock prices and in cyclical shares in particular.

THE FED HOLDS BIG SWAY IN THE BOND MARKET

Few factors move the bond market more than the Federal Reserve does. The Federal Reserve's ability to alter short-term interest rates and the impact this has on the bond market and the financial markets in general is immense. The Fed's impact on the bond market is particularly visible in the following:

- Nominal interest rates (actual rates).
- Real interest rates (actual rates minus inflation).
- The yield curve.
- Yield spreads between Treasuries and other fixed-income products such as corporate and agency securities.

Nominal Interest Rates

It's pretty easy to understand how the Fed's rate changes affect *nominal interest rates,* which refer to actual levels of interest rates. When the Fed adjusts short-term interest rates, market interest rates

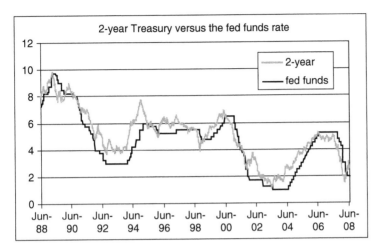

Figure 6.4 Treasury yields are closely correlated with the fed funds rate.
Source: Federal Reserve.

adjust accordingly, particularly for money market instruments. There are several reasons for this. First, yields on short-term maturities are largely determined by the cost of money, which is principally determined by the federal funds rate, the interest rate the Fed controls. Figure 6.4 clearly shows the tight relationship that exists between the federal funds rate and short-term maturities such as the two-year Treasury note. Top-down investors mindful of this relationship should buy short-term maturities when the Fed is cutting interest rates.

A major principle to keep in mind is the fact that yields on Treasury securities rarely fall below the fed funds rate except when the Fed is expected to lower the funds rate. In fact, over the past 18 years, the 10-year Treasury has dipped below the funds rate on only five occasions, each time within six months of an interest-rate cut. The reason for this is that Wall Street finances its vast holdings of fixed-income securities at interest rates that are roughly the same as the fed funds rate. This means that when Treasuries yield less than the funds rate, dealers purchasing Treasuries using borrowed money incur what is known as *negative carry*, which is to say that it costs them money to hold the securities. Traders don't want to see their profit-and-loss statement in the red every day, which is why they avoid buying Treasuries that yield less than the fed funds rate except when they believe that Fed rate cuts will eventually lower their borrowing costs, which will result in *positive carry*.

Real Interest Rates

The Federal Reserve has a great deal of influence on the level of *real interest rates*, which is defined as nominal interest rates minus inflation. Real interest rates tend to rise when the Fed raises interest rates and fall when the Fed lowers interest rates. There are a few reasons for this. First, when the Fed embarks on a course to move interest rates either up or down, bond investors begin to anticipate additional interest-rate adjustments by pushing moving nominal interest rates either up or down more quickly than changes occur in the inflation rate. Second, the Fed endeavors to engineer either low real interest rates when the economy is weak, or high real interest rates when the economy is strong. It does so in an attempt to achieve a certain degree of equilibrium between savings and investment in the economy. A third way in which the Fed affects the level of real interest rates is through its credibility as an inflation fighter. When bond investors have confidence in the Fed, real interest rates tend to be low. This is because investors tend to demand less of an interest-rate premium over and above the inflation rate when they are confident inflation will be kept low. Of course, the opposite holds true when Fed credibility is low.

The Yield Curve

One of the biggest influences on the shape of the yield curve is the Federal Reserve. The Fed affects the yield curve largely through its control of short-term interest rates, as we can see in Figure 6.4. A second way in which the Fed influences the yield curve is by affecting inflation expectations, which have a large bearing on the behavior of long-term interest rates, particularly compared to that of short-term interest rates. If investors are confident the Fed will be able to contain inflation, this will tend to keep inflation expectations low, resulting in low long-term interest rates and a relatively flat yield curve. On the other hand, if the market lacks confidence in the Fed's ability to fight inflation, the yield curve will be steep, reflecting the market's uncertainty about the inflation outlook.

The yield curve is also affected by the bond market's expectations of future Fed policies. In theory, since long-term interest rates are thought to reflect expectations of future short-term interest rates, the yield curve reflects expectations on future Fed rate actions. There's one important point to remember in this regard. The degree to which the market embeds future Fed rate actions into long-term interest rates will depend a great deal upon the degree to which inflation expectations are well anchored. In other words, if inflation expectations are well anchored, then the number of interest-rate adjustments the market will expect will tend to be smaller. If inflation expectations are not well anchored, then any rate changes will have an amplified effect on market interest rates.

The Fed's Impact on So-Called Spread Products

The Federal Reserve can greatly influence the amount of yield spread between Treasuries and other fixed-income securities, including corporate and agency securities. Since these so-called spread products are deemed riskier than Treasuries, their yields tend to fluctuate accordingly as perceptions about the risks of holding these securities change. These perceptions change especially when views about economic growth change. After all, what concerns investors most when they invest in fixed-income securities other than Treasuries is getting their money back. Fed rate cuts tend to cause a narrowing of credit spreads, although as we saw in 2007 and early 2008, over six months of Fed rate cuts failed to stop a sharp widening in credit spreads. The key, then, for top-down investors is to expect a narrowing of credit spreads when the Fed cuts rates, but to expect the narrowing to be delayed until market sentiment toward the economic outlook improves.

THE FED'S IMPACT ON OTHER ASSET CLASSES

We have thus far discussed the Federal Reserve's impact on stocks, bonds, and foreign exchange rates, three of the top transmitters of the Fed's monetary policies. Secondary to the impact on these asset classes is the Fed's impact on other asset classes, including commodities and emerging markets. The Fed's primary influence on these asset classes is tied to the impact of monetary policy on economic activity, which can significantly affect the balance between supply and demand for commodities, thus affecting prices. The problem with this statement, of course, is that in today's integrated world the Federal Reserve's impact on commodities has weakened, although with the United States representing 20 percent of global economic activity, the relationship has not broken down entirely. Moreover, the increased integration of the global economy means that the world's economies are likely to move more synchronously than ever before, which makes it likely that the world's central banks are likely to be more in sync than ever before.

As a result of the increased integration of the global economy and the increased synchronicity of monetary policy that the integration implies, at the very least it could be said that economic activity in the United States and the monetary policies adopted by the Fed are apt to be a microcosm of the situation globally. There is also no escaping the idea that the Fed and the world's central banks have retained their ability to influence market psychology, as there remains an obsession in the financial markets over the outlook for monetary policy in the United States and abroad. Moreover, there continues to be strong evidence of correlation between the value of the U.S. dollar and commodities prices, which have moved accordingly with changes in monetary policy (this was seen with a vengeance in the first half of 2008 when commodity prices surged following the Fed's aggressive rate cuts).

The Impact of Money Growth on Commodities Prices

Guiding a key top-down principle with respect to commodity prices is Milton Friedman's famous dictum, "Inflation is always and everywhere a monetary phenomenon."[10] This theory has credibility when we look at what happened in countries that experienced rapid increases in the money supply and rapid inflation over the past century, including, for example, Germany in the 1930s, and Brazil and Argentina from 1989–1991 and then again in the early 2000s. The theory also seems to make sense because it is difficult to envision how the demand for goods and services can rise without the presence of money. Charts that track year-over-year growth in the money supply versus year-over-year changes in the consumer price index do in fact show strong correlation, as shown in Figure 6.4. The strong correlation means that monetary aggregates such as M1, M2, which are the Federal Reserve's main gauges of the money supply, and the monetary base, remain important indicators despite having been discarded by many observers because of perceptions about their reduced correlation with GDP. This is especially true of the global scene, where the correlation appears to remain strong, as implied by the European Central Bank's continued emphasis on money supply and extreme examples such as Zimbabwe, which in 2008 was in the midst of hyperinflation amid rapid expansion of its money supply growth. Who would have thought?

Of course, when we say that there is correlation between money supply growth and inflation, we are making the assumption that the Fed and the world's central banks influence the growth of the money supply. This is not a difficult theory to substantiate, and there is a great deal of research supporting the idea. The fact is that only banks can expand the money supply, but it is the Fed that has control over the amount of new money that enters the banking system via its open market operations, which means that the Fed effectively controls the growth of the money supply.

The Fed Affects Risk Attitudes, Influencing Many Asset Classes

Earlier in this chapter we discuss the equity risk premium, which has been shown to be a major factor behind stock valuations. A risk premium exists in most other asset classes as well and is a major determinant in their valuations. The Federal Reserve substantially influences risk attitudes both by altering expectations on economic growth and by affecting the decision to either save or invest, which is accomplished by changes to the fed funds rate. For example, when the fed funds rate is abnormally low, as was the case beginning in 2001 through early 2005, investors push further out on the risk spectrum in search of higher yields—a *yield grab*. This means that in the fixed-income market, when the Fed lowers rates, investors will increasingly seek out higher yields in instruments such as emerging markets bonds, junk bonds, and other securities deemed relatively risky. As we mention in the discussion on the equity risk premium, this does not always happen immediately, as we saw in 2001–2002 and 2007–2008, but it does have a strong tendency to happen eventually.

Top-down investors need to respect the idea that while there is a strong correlation between Fed policy and the risk attitudes expressed by financial markets, there is often a delay in the relationship. Investors therefore must time their investments to match turns in the macroeconomic climate, an exercise that is at the heart of much of this book.

MORE TOP-DOWN IDEAS ON THE FED

I've got more to say on the Fed, but frankly there is not enough space in this book to say it. However, I want to get across a number of top-down concepts on the Fed which I believe are very important to remember when you're planning your investment strategies. Some of these ideas have not been tested—they're new, which is one reason why they don't yet deserve a lot of space. Nevertheless, a good top-down investor is always on the lookout for new ideas about how to view the world and apply it to investing. Here goes:

> *B-52 Ben.* This is the name coined by my astute colleague Peter Boockvar, our equity strategist, to describe the aggressive rate cut actions taken by Fed chairman Ben Bernanke in 2007 and 2008. The nickname is a twist on the nickname more commonly used to describe the chairman, Helicopter Ben, a nickname he was given following a speech he delivered in 2002 to describe actions the Fed could take to help an ailing economy. The "helicopter" notion is one actually first described by Milton Friedman. The concept I want to get across in this space is the idea that the Federal Reserve, having gained from its experiences and the experiences of other countries, might now be embarking on a path to adjust interest rates more rapidly in order to align these rates more quickly to levels that past experience would suggest they need to be brought to in order to bring about a particular economic outcome. In other words, gradualism, such as was seen in the early 1990s when the Fed cut the funds rate by just 25 basis points on nearly 20 occasions, is out, except in cases where more careful rate moves are needed to fine-tune the level of economic activity. For the

Treasury market, this means that top-down investors should choose short-term maturities when the Fed looks set to cut rates or when it begins cutting interest rates. For stocks and other asset classes, top-down investors should expect more speedy economic recoveries. This means choosing economically sensitive stocks in consumer cyclical, financial, and technology industries, as well as making bets on corporate bonds and commodities prices.

A more transparent Fed creates volatility. There are a lot of benefits to a more transparent Fed, but there has been a downside: more volatility in financial markets. We investors need not know the Fed's every thought. We do not need to know what it thinks of this and what it thinks of that. If we were privy to the Fed's every thought, we would be whipsawed. So, while I agree with the first old credo shown at the very start of this chapter, for the sake of a more stable investment climate, I hope the credo is combined with a dash of the one below:

Never explain, never excuse.

—An oft-repeated line by Montagu Norman, governor of the Bank of England 1921–1944, who was known for his reclusiveness

The Fed might miss the next bubble. There is a distinct predilection at the Fed to pay too little attention to the inflation that occurs in financial assets compared to that of real assets. This is something we saw during the financial bubble in 2000, for example, and then again a few years later during the go-go years of the credit bubble that burst when the housing market went south. I feel it imperative that central bankers pay more attention to inflation in financial assets and to realize that inflation in financial assets can be just as great a source of instability as inflation in real assets, as these recent episodes have clearly shown. The Fed should reconsider the idea that it can't know a bubble until it is over. Give me a break! What top-down investors should be on the lookout for is inflation in financial assets that is left unattended by the Fed. In other words, there is more than one sort of inflation to worry about, no matter what the Fed says.

The Fed and politics are closely aligned. The conventional wisdom is that the Fed is an independent body, and we have seen since Bill Clinton's administration tremendous respect for this principle. There nonetheless remains a strong connection between Fed policy and politics, although it is an indirect connection. History has shown that the impact of the actions taken by the Federal Reserve has helped shape the political landscape. For example, by delaying an economic recovery, the very slow pace of Fed rate cuts entering the 1990 election may have hurt President Bush's chances for reelection. In the 1990s, President Clinton was strongly helped by an era of low interest rates, which he helped engineer through strong fiscal discipline and encouragement of productivity-enhancing investments. Top-down investors, mindful of who holds power in Washington, should always consider how the Fed's monetary policies might influence the political landscape by way of impact on the economy.

The View from the Top Down: Three Musts for the Macro Maven

Don't fight the Fed!

1. *Always remember that the Fed does not change rates by fiat.*
   When the Fed wants to raise or lower interest rates, it
   does not simply announce the change and it magically
   happens. The only way the Fed can adjust the level of
   interest rates is by either adding or draining money from
   the banking system. Top-down investors should be
   mindful of the fact that the Fed's rate announcements are
   not headlines; something very real happens that
   eventually has substantial impact on the economy and
   the financial markets.

2. *Fit your portfolio to the monetary policy cycle.* There is plenty
   of evidence to suggest that there is a strong linkage
   between financial assets and the Fed's monetary policy
   cycles. For example, short-term Treasury notes are closely
   linked to the level of the fed funds rate, as is the
   performance of stock sectors, corporate bonds, and other
   asset classes. Top-down investors should be aware of how

financial assets tend to perform during the various periods of the monetary policy cycle.

3. *Be watchful of the "transmission effects" of monetary policy.* To gauge the timing of when the Fed's rate changes will achieve their intended effect, always beware of the transmission effects of monetary policy: the impact of rate changes on stocks, credit spreads, and foreign exchange rates in particular. This will help you to assess the need for further rate actions and thus help you to decide what the Fed will do next, which can be applied to a number of different investment strategies.

THE GOLDEN COMPASSES: THE TOP TOP-DOWN INDICATORS

- *Money aggregates.* History has shown that economic growth and inflation are tied to growth in the nation's money supply. Today's investors should expand their money supply toolbox by looking not only at M1, M2, and the monetary base, but by focusing also on bank credit and bond issuance, which will help in determining the net amount of credit formation taking place. Money makes the world go around, as they say.
- *The transmission mechanisms.* We discussed this one a good deal. The bottom line is that it is extremely important to track how changes in Fed policy are affecting the financial markets and what this will mean for the economy and the relative performance of financial assets.
- *Flow of funds report.* Produced by the Fed, this report is loaded with information about financial assets. In this report you can see breakdowns of the holders of specific financial assets as well as what else these entities hold. This helps in determining the impact of changes in the values of financial assets on the holders of these assets. There is also a terrific one-page summary on the assets and liabilities of the household sector.

- *Two-year Treasuries to fed funds.* As we show in Figure 6.4, the correlation between the two-year Treasury note to the federal funds rate is very tight, and Treasuries rarely trade below the fed funds rate except when rate cuts are expected. By following the two-year note, you can get a strong sense of where the markets expect the fed funds rate to go and make strong judgments about whether the entire Treasury yield curve is fairly valued—as the two-year goes, so goes the Treasury market. You can also use the two-year as a basis for judging whether Fed rate expectations are off the mark.

Notes

[1] Greenspan, Alan, *"The Age of Turbulence,"* The Penguin Press, 2007.

[2] For example, Case, Karl, John Quigley, and Robert Shiller, "Comparing Wealth Effects: The Stock Market versus the Housing Market," *Advances in Macroeconomics,*(The Berkeley Electronic Press, 2005); Ludvigson, Sydney, and Charles Steindel, "How Important Is the Stock Market Effect on Consumption?" Federal Reserve Bank of New York, *Economic Policy Review,* July 1999, pp. 29–51.

[3] Data from the Federal Reserve Board of Governors' *Flow of Funds Accounts of the United States,* March 2002; available at http://www.federalreserve.gov/releases/z1/default.htm

[4] Lettau, Martin, Sydney Ludvigson, and Charles Steindel, "Monetary Policy Transmission through the Consumption Wealth Channel." Federal Reserve Bank of New York, *Economic Policy Review,* May 2002.

[5] Harrison, Paul. "The Impact of Market Liquidity in Times of Stress on the Corporate Bond Market: Pricing, Trading, and the Availability of Funds." Paper presented at the Bank for International Settlements' Third Joint Bank Conference on Risk Measurement and Systemic Risk, 2002.

[6] Mishkin, Frederic. "Globalization, Macroeconomic Performance, and Monetary Policy," from a speech delivered at the Domestic Prices in an Integrated World Economy Conference, Washington, D.C., September 27, 2007.

[7] Bernanke, Ben, and Kenneth Kuttner, "What Explains the Stock Market's Reaction to Federal Reserve Policy?" Federal Reserve Board of Governors, *Finance and Economic Discussion Series,* March 2004.

[8] Rigobon, Roberto, and Brian Sack, "The Impact of Monetary Policy on Asset Prices," Federal Reserve Board of Governors, *Finance and Economic Discussion Series*, January 2002.

[9] Navarro, Peter. *If It's Raining in Brazil, Buy Starbucks* (New York: McGraw-Hill), 2002.

[10] Friedman, Milton, *Inflation: Causes and Consequences* (Bombay, India: Asia Publishing House, 1963); reprinted in Milton Friedman, *Dollars and Deficits* (Englewood Cliffs, N.J.: Prentice-Hall, 1968), p. 39.

CHAPTER 7

Filling the Gaps on Value Investing

I dunno, she's got gaps, I got gaps, together we fill gaps.

—Rocky Balboa, *Rocky*, 1976

One of the many appeals of top-down investing is that it is a very inclusive and dynamic approach to investing. It is different from other approaches, which are often quite rigid. Proponents of these other approaches actually laud their rigidity, believing that rigidity is what is necessary in order to both preserve capital and discover investment opportunities. I concur, as every investment approach requires a heavy dose of discipline. After all, if you don't follow your investment blueprint, you'll build a portfolio that looks a lot different from what your blueprint is designed to build, and it will become unmanageable. It won't fit your style. This is why I believe that the best investment approach is one that requires discipline but is also dynamic and flexible. This is a philosophy that I wish were applied more by those who embrace value investing, which is a terrific approach to investing, but which in today's more efficient, integrated, and fast-moving world may not be expansive enough to help investors maximize their profit potential.

Although I hope to make converts of followers of value investing and other investment approaches, there are many who for whatever reason won't give up their way of investing and enter the realm of top-down investing. For those of you in this camp, you will find in this chapter a number of ways in which the methods used by top-down investors can augment your investment approach. For everybody else, this chapter will help you see how top-down can be blended with other investment approaches to produce a powerful new investing style.

STRENGTHENING THE PILLARS OF VALUE INVESTING

Value investing is an investment approach that involves the selection of stocks in companies trading at levels deemed to be below their intrinsic value, which is determined by comparing a company's share price to its future cash flows. Fair enough. It takes a lot of work to go obtain the information just described, and it might not be for you, which is an idea we discuss later in this chapter. For now, we focus on how to apply tools from the top-down investment approach to value investing, and along the way you will see ways they can be applied in reverse.

There are many pillars upon which the value investing crowd draws comfort. The most important of these are drawn from Benjamin Graham who, along with David Dodd in 1934, produced the groundbreaking classic book *Security Analysis*. Graham would later write another classic, *The Intelligent Investor* in 1949, still considered one of the most important investment books ever written, especially to his disciple, Warren Buffett, who said that the book was "By far the best book on investing ever written."[1] So influential was Graham in Buffett's life that he chose Graham as the middle name for one of his two sons (Howard Graham Buffett).

The two most important pillars upon which value investing sit are the following:

1. *Intrinsic value*. Determine the company's intrinsic value through an analysis of its balance sheet.
2. *Margin of safety*. Purchase only those stocks that provide a "margin of safety." A margin of safety exists on stocks that trade at a discount to their intrinsic value.

These are both very sound principles that really can't steer you wrong. Purchasing stocks below their intrinsic value certainly seems likely to keep you from getting caught up in the latest craze and irrationally exuberant markets, and you stand a good chance of picking winners with this approach. It certainly worked for Warren Buffett.

As sound as these principles are, they can be strengthened by the principles that guide top-down investing. Let's begin by looking at how to enhance the process of determining a company's intrinsic value. Once you have determined a company's intrinsic value, compare it to the company's stock price. If the stock is trading at a discount to its intrinsic value, add it to your list of potential buys.

Keep in mind that the goal here is not to poke holes in value investing; I prefer to think that I am filling gaps. For those of you who are already value investors or will be among those who move on to adopt the principles of value investing, you could say that the advice here will help fill gaps in top-down investing. Whichever investment approach you choose as your primary approach, I am sure that if you combine the two, you will be armed with a powerful system.

Seven Steps toward a More Accurate Determination of a Company's Intrinsic Value

There are many ways to determine a company's intrinsic value, and no two investors follow the same methodology. Nevertheless, value investors, particularly disciples of Graham, have settled on a set of exercises for determining intrinsic value. The list is rather long, but I have settled on exercises that I believe fit well with the top-down investing approach.

1. *Value the company's assets.* In any analysis of a company's assets, there is plenty of room for top-down, macro principles. For example, if your task is to value the real estate assets on a company's books, wouldn't it be helpful to know a thing or two about the macroeconomic condition of the real estate environment? The answer is an unequivocal yes! It is one thing for a company to declare a value to its assets, but it is your job to take that valuation with a grain of salt and dig a bit deeper. In the case of commercial real estate assets, for example, a few top-down questions you might ask that would have relevance for the future value of the assets would include: What is the vacancy rate for commercial property? In what regions of the country are the assets held, and what is the condition

of both the economy and the real estate market in that area? What is the condition of the economy on the whole, and what impact might it have on the demand for office space? And so on. If instead your task is to value the inventories on a company's books, might it not be useful to know whether the inventories held are in either in abundance or in short supply economywide? Certainly. You can do this by tracking the government's monthly data on business inventories, focusing in on inventory-to-sales ratios. If financial assets are on the books of a company you are analyzing, might it not be a good idea to know a few facts about the macro trends that underpin the price movement in those assets? It certainly would have been a good idea in 2007 and 2008 when many companies were holding mortgage-related securities on their books at values that were a poor reflection of what they could actually be sold for in the marketplace.

Many other assets reported on company balance sheets can be put into better context using tools of the top-down approach. For example, fixed assets such as factories and capital equipment, while valuable to a company when they are being used to capacity, have much less value when they are underused. A change in the economic climate, particularly in the industry in question, can easily bring this about, making an asset more of a liability. Data on capacity utilization rates throughout the economy are available monthly from the Federal Reserve and are easily found on the Fed's Web site, Federalreserve.gov.

2. *Determine how liquid the company is.* Value investors find it extremely important to determine a company's *liquidity*, which is the company's ability to raise cash in a short period of time. There are a couple of ways in which macro variables can play an important role in this determination. For starters, don't just look at the list of short-term financial assets on a company's books and then take what you see at face value. It would be better to consider how the value of those assets might be subject to adverse impact, as was the case with many money market instruments in 2007 and 2008 when their values

plummeted. In addition to the impact on asset values, adverse conditions in the money market made it difficult for companies to refinance their short-term liabilities, as credit had dried up. The 2007–2008 credit crisis also showed the importance of understanding the macro climate for raising short-term capital. Many companies that previously were able to obtain short-term financing on a steady basis were suddenly forced from the market. Can this happen to the company you are buying?

3. *Determine the company's long-term financial health.* As with any analysis you make of a company's short-term liabilities, if you are to enhance your bottom-up analysis of a company's long-term debt situation, it would be a good idea to have a bead on the condition of the long-term funding markets. For example, if the company you are analyzing needs to tap the corporate bond market for credit and issue, say, 5- and 10-year notes, you should know a few things about the market for these securities. For example, are issuers being forced to pay more for credit for any reason (such as the 2007–2008 credit crisis)? What are issuers of a similar credit rating being forced to pay? Are issuers of a similar credit rating being shut out entirely, and might this not impair the company's ability to operate and pay its obligations and expand its profits? If the company has issued bonds denominated in foreign currencies, are there currency risks that have the potential to affect the company's future cash flows? Finally, what do you know about the interest-rate climate that has the potential to affect future cash flows? Answering these and many other top-down questions will significantly enhance any analysis you make of a company's long-term debt situation.

4. *Analyze the growth trends in the company's revenues and/or sales.* The first thing that you need to do is analyze the source of the company's revenues to determine where the company is having success and where it isn't. This will help tell you whether the company is more or less diverse than what the aggregate figures suggest. The next step is to apply a few top-down principles and scrutinize what it is

that the company is selling. For example, if the company has seen strong growth in sales of medical products that because of favorable demographics looks likely to continue, you will then have a stronger basis for making assumptions about futures sales than if you looked at past trends alone. Past performance is no guarantee of future returns, as they say. There might also be macro factors that could render a company's products obsolete. The balance sheet can't tell you that.

5. *Analyze the company's cost of goods sold.* Included in the costs that a company incurs when producing the products that it sells are many costs that are subject to macroeconomic influences. For example, raw material costs are significantly affected by macroeconomic factors from around the globe. Crude oil is an obvious example of this. Numerous other industrial materials prices are influenced by global factors that fall under the guise of top-down investing. One of these is obvious: the pace of global economic activity. Another is not so obvious, except to top-down investors: the cost of shipping goods across waters. Figure 7.1 shows the strong relationship that exists between global shipping rates and industrial materials

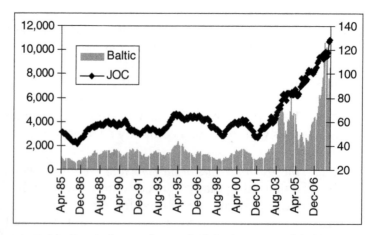

Figure 7.1 Baltic Dry index vs. Journal of Commerce index (Baltic on left axis; JOC on right axis).

Sources: Baltic Dry index: Baltic Exchange; Journal of Commerce index: JOC-ECRI.

prices. There are other costs that fall under the umbrella of "cost of goods sold" that can be put into better context with a little bit of knowledge about the macro influences that they are subject to. These include labor costs, foreign exchange rates, economy-wide inventory levels, and transportation-related factors.

6. *Analyze the company's net profit margin.* Value investors believe that by tracking trends in a company's profit margin, which is the percentage of each dollar of revenue received that is turned into a net profit, you will spot important trends that are both specific to the company you are analyzing and to the company's industry. With respect to trends specific to a company, its balance sheet will be revealing when it is put in the context of the balance sheets of other companies within the same industry. With respect to industry-wide trends in net profit margins, these will also be apparent after scanning company balance sheets within the industry. The problem, though, is that the factors driving profit margins for the industry of the company you are analyzing are likely to be macro factors, which means that it is critically important to know what these are. For example, in the toy industry, profit margins have been shrinking for many years, which in the early stages of the decline would have been obvious in company balance sheets for reasons that might have gotten lost upon those who were fixated on balance sheets. It would have been better to pair balance sheet data with top-down information such as the idea that Wal-Mart and other fast-growing discount chains had entered the toy-selling business, creating substantial economies of scale and immense downward pressure on pricing. In addition, the outsourcing of toy production to China also put sharp downward pressure on pricing.

7. *Determine the outlook for the company's sales and pricing power.* Sales forecasts that are based on a company's sales trends alone seem to me to lack depth. To be sure, how a company has fared against its competition and penetrated its market could tell you a great deal about the company's prospects for the future. But then again it might not. For all

you know, sales of the company's products will begin faltering for any number of macro reasons, whether it is product obsolescence, the shifting of production overseas, or a forthcoming change in demographics. Pricing power is also an issue that extends well beyond a company's balance sheet and into the realm of the macro environment into issues such as the relative supply of labor both domestically and internationally, international trade agreements (more trade equals more competition and lower prices, generally), the imposition or reduction of trade tariffs, supply disruptions, and fads (think destroyed jeans!).

It is difficult to challenge the idea that investors who take these seven steps will increase their chances of picking stocks that are winners and avoid picking duds. At the same time it is difficult to challenge the idea that applying top-down principles to some or all of these exercises will improve the chances at success even more, especially in light of the increased pull from macro forces from throughout the world. Determining a company's intrinsic value is not as easy as it once was because in today's complex world there are significantly more variables (for those of you who follow media stocks, do you remember when there were just six or seven television channels to choose from?), and they are more fluid than ever.

OTHER AREAS WHERE VALUE AND TOP-DOWN INVESTING CAN COMBINE

There are many elements to value investing beyond determining a company's intrinsic value and seeking a margin of safety. Most of these are meant to provide additional safety for investors. Nevertheless, there are gaps in these other elements that I believe can be filled by applying top-down investment principles. Let's rattle off a few of these.

Diversification

Investors are always in search of the final frontier; Markowitz's "Efficient Frontier," that is.[2] See Figure 7.2. Along the Efficient Frontier there rests a set of investments that diversifies a portfolio in

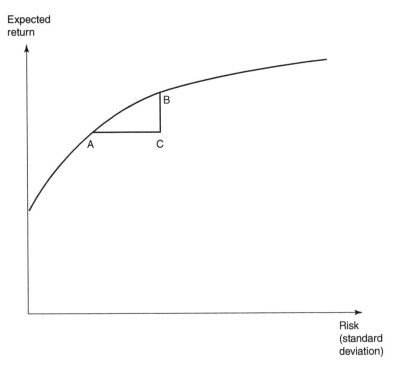

Figure 7-2 An efficient frontier, showing the location of three portfolios.
Source: From: http://www.bos.frb.org/economic/neer/neer1999/neer699b.pdf, page 3.

a manner that optimizes its returns. Finding this kind of diversification is an elusive task to many investors, often because they have
a tendency to put their eggs in one basket, hoping for home runs
that never happen. Value investors are particularly interested in
diversification, partly because of their tendency toward methods
that seek to reduce risk.

There is a certain comfort that comes with having a diverse
portfolio. On any given day a few of your investments might be
down, but if your choices have been good, then most of what you
own will be up and you won't sweat the stocks that are down.
Conversely, if you own just a few concentrated positions, every little wiggle in the market becomes gut-wrenching, often leading to
emotionally driven investment decisions, which are the worst kind.
You become whipsawed, moving in and out of positions, unable to
look past a horizon of even a few minutes on investments meant to
be held for the long term. It wrecks your original game plan. Rarely

does one feel this way with a diversified portfolio, where losses for individual positions tend to be small.

Value investors recognize the benefits of diversification, which is why they typically invest in a fairly large number of securities within their portfolio, spreading their money across many asset classes. Diversification provides value investors with the "margin of safety" urged by Graham, who warned, however, that even if a margin of safety exists on a security when it is purchased, it might not be a profitable investment:

> For the margin guarantees only that he has a better chance for profit than for loss—not that it is impossible. But as the number of commitments is increased, the more certain does it become that the aggregate of the profits will exceed the aggregate of the losses. That is the simple basis of the insurance underwriting business.[3]

If the goal, then, is to diversify a portfolio, what constitutes the best possible diversification that minimizes losses and maximizes gains? Just because a portfolio contains a large number of investments spanning numerous industries does not by itself mean that it is diversified optimally. I would argue that a portfolio constructed using solely the principles of value investing can't in the modern era be diversified optimally. It can't because as an investment approach it is no longer capable of capturing the plethora of investment opportunities that are now best spotted using top-down investment principles. For example, value investors are unlikely to latch onto the multitude of themes standing a great chance of leading to vast numbers of investment opportunities both domestically and internationally for many years to come. Moreover, given the concept that a well-diversified portfolio is one that contains investments spread across industries, investors are best served by utilizing a top-down approach to investing, where macroeconomic principles will aid the formulation of weightings for sectors and for asset classes (i.e., stocks versus bonds, commodities, etc.). It is much riskier to diversify solely from the bottom up, where many macro influences could be missed. It is also possible that bottom-up investors, seeking out "value" in companies abroad, will miss the forest for the trees and miss out on glaring opportunities in countries that appear to provide little or no margin of safety. Ever since the fall of communism, there have been many situations like this, and only top-down investors were there for the ride. Value investors missed it because of the margin of safety issue that made investments in countries like China, India, and Russia look too risky.

While I fully concur with the idea that avoiding what appear to be risky situations each time they arise will help preserve capital, the massive miscalculation made by many value investors over the past decade in avoiding the emerging markets exposes a serious flaw in value investing, particularly in what constitutes diversification. Today, diversification includes investments in asset classes once considered risky but which are now mainstream. This includes asset classes such as high-yield bonds, commodities, and the emerging markets. Investments in each of these asset classes may not provide a margin of safety by its classic definition, but when viewed from the macro perspective, the margin of safety looks gigantic, hardly the moat that Warren Buffett seeks for his investments—more like an ocean! For example, China's vast sovereign wealth fund, which stood at $1.68 trillion in April 2008, provides a colossal margin of safety against economic weakness. Granted, this may not stop the country's equity prices from falling hard given the massive run-up they have had, but it is certainly a backstop for good companies participating in the growth of China's economy. This is why value investors should not hesitate to take advantage of declines in share prices that occur in China.

What I am arguing here is that true diversification can be achieved only if a portfolio contains investments that not only are large in number and spread across industries and asset classes, but also contain investments in situations that are based on compelling top-down fundamentals, as has been the case in China for a number of years. Value investors must redefine what constitutes "margin of safety" if they are to capitalize on emerging situations where the traditional definition for margin of safety fails to record the same level of safety as can be found through an analysis from the top down.

MACRO MAVENS RUN MARATHONS TOO

It is often said about investing that it is a marathon, not a sprint. This certainly is a philosophy that applies to value investing, where patience is a virtue. Top-down investing is also a very patient investment approach, one that gives you the confidence to sit back and watch events play out as the top-down influences suggest that they inevitably will. For example, an investment in an exchange traded fund (ETF) for water infrastructure is one that does not depend upon the events of today, tomorrow, next week, or next month. Rather, it is a story that will play out over the course of years—centuries for that matter, because water is of course a very basic need of human existence.

As with value investing, the compelling premise behind each top-down investment provides a strong basis to stay invested rather than move in and out of the markets. Investing in this way is extremely important because many studies show that large portions of the gains made by stocks occur over brief intervals of time. Browne[4] cites a study by Sanford Bernstein & Company showing that from 1926 to 1993 the returns reaped in the period's best 60 months averaged 11 percent. In other words, the best returns achieved during the period occurred over just 7 percent of the 67-year span. In the remaining 93 percent of the months, returns averaged just 1/100 of a percent!

WHO OWNS THE ASSETS?

Searching for ideas, value investors span information showing the largest holders of stocks. One problem with doing this is that if other value investors have already caught onto the idea, the window of opportunity might already be closed or is closing. Another problem is that it is far too one-dimensional compared to the way in which top-down investors track the largest holders of stocks and other asset classes.

To augment any analysis of the holders of companies, you need aggregate data on the types of entities that own the asset you are invested in. These data are available in the Federal Reserve's flow of funds accounts, which are produced quarterly and are available on the Fed's Web site, federalreserve.gov. Look specifically in the tables called "levels tables." There you will find tables on all of the major financial securities outstanding and the entities that hold the securities. These tables are also shown in reverse, indicating the financial assets held by the entities. An example of one of these is shown in Table 7.1, the table on holders of Treasury securities. As the table shows, the biggest holder of Treasuries by

TABLE 7.1

Excerpt from the Fed's Flow of Funds Report

	2005	2006				2007			
		Q1	Q2	Q3	Q4	Q1	Q2	Q3	Q4
1 Total liabilities	4678.0	4834.4	4750.6	4805.2	4861.7	5014.3	4904.0	5010.0	5000.2
2 Savings bonds	205.1	205.9	205.2	203.6	202.4	200.3	198.6	197.1	196.4
3 Other Treasury issues	4472.9	4628.5	4554.4	4599.6	4659.4	4814.0	4705.4	4812.9	4902.8
4 Total assets	4678.0	4834.4	4750.6	4803.2	4801.7	5014.3	4904.0	5010.0	5099.2
5 Household sector	549.7	666.9	625.2	586.2	490.2	466.4	420.6	396.4	308.8
6 Savings bonds	205.1	205.9	205.2	203.6	202.4	200.3	198.6	197.1	196.4
7 Other Treasury issues	344.6	461.0	420.1	382.6	287.8	266.1	222.0	199.4	112.4
8 Nonfinancial corporate business	50.7	47.5	42.6	42.5	44.4	52.7	45.2	51.1	50.7
9 Nonfirm noncorporate business	56.2	58.3	59.8	61.6	63.3	65.1	67.1	69.6	69.3
10 State and local governments	463.2	465.7	476.7	478.2	497.7	524.6	549.2	535.8	524.9
11 Rest of the world	1984.4	2019.2	2026.5	2066.2	2115.0	2192.6	2193.9	2217.1	2324.0
12 Monetary authority	744.2	758.5	766.4	768.9	778.9	780.9	790.5	779.6	740.6
13 Commercial banking	97.1	97.0	101.7	98.1	95.2	105.6	95.9	103.3	112.5
14 U.S.-chartered commercial banks	64.2	66.1	68.1	62.3	61.9	70.2	68.5	70.0	73.0
15 Foreign banking offices in U.S.	27.9	24.2	27.3	30.2	27.1	31.5	23.5	30.3	30.6
16 Bank holding companies	1.1	2.7	2.6	2.3	2.5	0.7	0.8	0.7	7.1
17 Banks in U.S.-affiliated areas	3.9	4.0	3.7	3.3	3.7	3.1	3.2	2.2	1.8

(continued)

TABLE 7.1

(Continued)

	2005	2006				2007			
		Q1	Q2	Q3	Q4	Q1	Q2	Q3	Q4
18 Savings institutions	12.3	10.3	7.9	7.9	12.4	7.6	7.4	8.0	7.0
19 Credit utilities	7.7	8.0	7.7	7.8	7.4	7.0	7.3	7.1	7.0
20 Property-casualty insurance companies	69.2	71.1	72.8	74.1	75.8	76.6	77.3	78.1	78.3
21 Life insurance companies	91.2	90.2	88.5	86.5	83.2	84.2	84.9	86.3	86.1
22 Private pension funds	92.7	93.0	93.8	94.9	96.3	98.0	100.8	100.3	99.2
23 State and local govt. retirement funds	153.8	153.0	150.9	151.6	153.0	155.1	156.1	161.4	161.9
24 Federal government retirement funds	68.4	60.9	74.4	76.2	76.7	80.4	81.3	85.5	88.1

Source: Federal Reserve. From: http://www.federalreserve.gov/releases/z1/Current/z1r-4.pdf, page 30 of March 6 report.

far is foreign investors. This is a simple example, perhaps a fact you already knew, but what I mean to do here is to show you this terrific tool.

Having a sense of who it is that holds the securities you hold is important because it can lead to many conclusions. For example, in the case of Treasuries, knowing that foreign investors are the major holders can help you to have a better sense as to the types of developments that might cause foreign investors to adjust their holdings. Basically, you can know their pressure points better. Another way to use the data is by considering how there might be ripple effects onto your assets from developments occurring in securities you do not own. For example, it was important in 2007 to have a sense of the amount of mortgage-backed securities held by major banking institutions. At that time, the Fed's flow of funds report indicated that banks had large amounts of exposure, which meant that they were likely to report news that would generate anxiety throughout the financial markets, as they surely did. It was also important in 2007 to have a sense of the amount of exposure that money market funds had to the commercial paper market, which was under substantial strain. The sharp contraction of the commercial paper market nearly led money market funds to do the unthinkable: break the buck (this happens when the net asset value of money market funds fall below $1).

There is another top-down way to examine the holders of securities of great value. Each Friday at around 3:30 p.m., the Commodity Futures Trading Commission (CFTC) releases its so-called commitments of traders report, which details the types of traders that are long and short all the futures regulated by the CFTC, which is just about everything under the sun, including futures for the S&P 500, U.S. Treasuries, gold, silver, corn, wheat, the U.S. dollar, and crude oil, among many others. You get the point. When these data are released, I scan them as quickly as I can searching for clues to the amount of speculative fervor that exists in each contract, looking in particular for signs of extreme bullish or bearish sentiment. The information on holders is divided into two camps: commercial traders and noncommercial traders. Commercial traders are those who buy and sell futures to hedge risks associated with their business enterprise. Commercial oil traders, for example, would include oil producers, while noncommercial traders would be traders speculating for their own account in the oil trading pit. Commercial traders are considered smart money. Noncommercial traders, well, you can say that they are dumb money because they tend to bring their positions to extremes at major peaks and bottoms in the market, holding large long positions at the top and large short positions at the bottom.

Data on positions held by noncommercial traders therefore provide valuable clues to whether extreme sentiment exists in a wide variety of markets. The information can then be taken a few steps further to provide clues to investor sentiment toward a variety of important topics that relate to the economy and the financial markets. From there, those who use the data can more easily spot excesses (or the lack thereof) in their investments. Even a straitlaced stock investor who does not dabble beyond stocks can benefit. For example, investors who hold energy stocks can benefit from knowing whether there is excess sentiment driving the price of oil higher. If there is, then the chances of a decline in the price of oil should be viewed as high, which, if it leads to a drop in the price of oil, could put downward pressure on oil stocks.

Gaming the Business Cycle

Value investors love to buy downtrodden stocks that have fallen out of favor and into territory that makes them compelling on a valuation basis. This is particularly true of investments in cyclical industries, which because of fluctuations in the business cycle eventually wind up on the value investor's list of stocks to buy. A risk for value investors who ignore the macroeconomic climate is that they will buy too early. I do not mean to suggest that investors should try to pick the bottom and wait until the economy is deep into recession to buy shares. Rather, investors should endeavor to know enough about the macroeconomic climate that they can enter and exit their investment positions in a more timely manner, whether in stocks, bonds, commodities, or whatever. No, this is not market timing. It's just a smarter way of handling your investments.

Fisher (2007), the astute money manager and author, provides a good game plan for timely entries and exits from the stock market, as shown in Figure 7-3.[5]

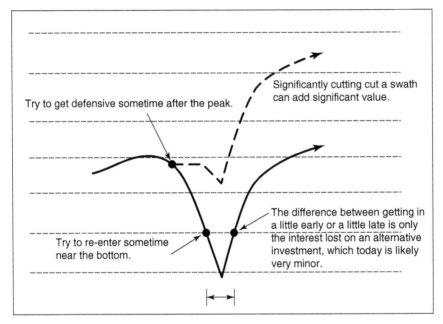

Figure 7.3 Game plan for entries and exits from the stock market.

Source: From Ken Fisher, *The Only Three Questions That Count* (Wiley, 2007).

Fisher's chart supports the idea that investors needn't catch the bottom in order to time the market well. The main idea is to be cognizant enough of the cycle in order to know when to get in and when to get out. The same rule applies to the timing of decisions about which stock sectors you should put your money in. As a general rule, Figure 6-3 in the previous chapter provides some guidance.

Following the business cycle is something that makes many value investors cringe, but the increased efficiency of the markets implores value investors to seek new ways to enhance their investment returns. I am not suggesting that value investors should abandon their methods, just that they augment them. Value investors should continue to seek out investments that meet their criteria while also considering the impact that the macroeconomic climate might have on their investments and the investments they are considering. Value investors must also consider the fact that economic and market cycles now affect a wider variety of investments now in the mainstream.

In other words, ignoring today's cycles means ignoring a swath of investment possibilities in areas such as commodities, foreign currencies, and the equities and debt markets of both developed countries and the emerging markets. For example, there will probably be corrections in the large upswings that have occurred in commodities prices and in the emerging markets, where secular forces have created strong underpinnings for many more years of strength. Top-down indicators such as those that reflect upon the vast fiscal might of sovereign states make this obvious. Bottom-up investors could miss it entirely if they stay too focused on the margin of safety issue and ignore the compelling top-down arguments that create a greater margin of safety than is readily apparent in the individual investments value investors might consider. A sense of supercycles, or secular trends, is what is needed here.

Finding Even More Excitement in Boring Industries

Value investors take pride in finding companies in boring, underappreciated industries. Top-down investors get that same feeling although probably more so, because they find opportunities not only in the stock market but also in other asset classes and in all parts of the world. For example, a profitable top-down idea in recent years has been to invest in companies involved in the production of ethanol, where production has soared as a result of high gasoline prices, as is shown in Figure 7.4. There have been many companies throughout the world that have benefited from the surge in ethanol production, including many in Brazil, where sugar production increased by roughly 50 percent in the five years ended February 2008 (Figure 7.5). While it is possible that value investors could have spotted some of the companies benefiting from the ethanol boom, many of these companies would not have had the margin of safety that value investors demand, which meant that they rejected many of the best opportunities. Value investors who have warmed up to the concept have been too late to the party, as this was an idea that developed several years ago when the price of crude oil started to surge. It has now become a somewhat crowded trade, with more speculative fervor than existed a few years ago. There are still opportunities, but they require greater scrutiny and must be continuously reassessed to see if the macro forces driving ethanol demand higher

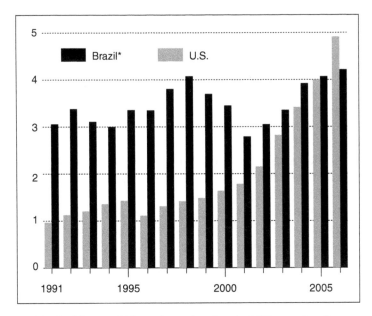

Figure 7.4 Biofuel boom. Ethanol production in billions of gallons.

* Brazil data are for harvest seasons through 2005–2006.

Sources: Wall Street Journal, UNICA, Renewable Fuels Association.

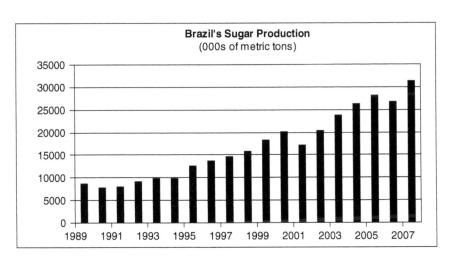

Figure 7.5 Sweet opportunities the value players missed!

Source: U.S. Department of Agriculture.

remain in place. Here is a situation in which many of the key principles of value investing can be very useful, as they can help identify
situations where speculation is particularly high.

The investment opportunities that developed from the surge
in ethanol production went well beyond investments in shares of
companies involved in the production. Top-down investors caught
this in the same way that they catch so many opportunities, since
they are naturally inclined to consider every possible investment
possibility that arises from a set of macro factors. Value investors
are not so inclined, and their investment approach will tend to miss
situations that develop quickly, chiefly because companies that
stand to benefit from emerging situations are not apt to meet the
value investor's set of criteria, especially with respect to the margin
of safety issue. Top-down investors will see it differently, believing
that the macro forces underpinning certain companies create a
powerful margin of safety.

Amid the surge in ethanol production, one investment that
top-down investors caught but value investors missed was the
sugar trade—the commodity itself. Figure 7.6 shows the surge in
the price of sugar that has taken place recently. Value investors tend
to avoid investments such as direct bets on commodities, which

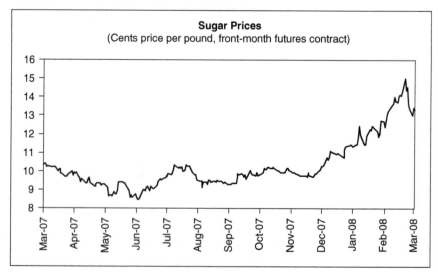

Figure 7.6 Sugar prices, March 2007–March 2008.

means they have missed out on one of the most important investment concepts of the new century—surging commodities prices. Top-down investors also knew to invest in the currencies and bonds of countries benefiting from surging commodity prices. For example, Brazil's currency doubled in value against the U.S. dollar in the five years ended February 2008. A great trade.

In this wonderful age of spreading market capitalism, investments of all kinds can be found in the world's most intriguing places. Investing has never been so exciting, at least for top-down investors.

The View from the Top Down: Three Must Approaches for the Macro Maven

Value investors who combine their basic approach with a solid dose of top-down investing are likely to become very successful investors.

1. *Embrace value investing, but augment its principles.* Value investing is a terrific approach to investing, but it is not without its failings. There are many ways in which top-down investing can augment the principles of value investing and fill in some of the gaps, as is shown throughout this chapter. Embrace the disciplined approach that drives value investing, but open up to new forms of flexibility by integrating the top-down approach to investing.

2. *Consider the margin of safety provided by powerful macro influences.* Value investors prudently seek a margin of safety in the investments they make, but they fail to take into account the margin of safety that today's powerful macro influences provide. Seek a margin of safety, but reassess how to define it.

3. *Take boring to a new level, and look beyond value stocks.* You want boring? Go beyond value stocks and span the globe. There are plenty of "boring" opportunities just about everywhere and in asset classes that value investors tend to ignore, which is a huge mistake in this age of spreading market capitalism.

THE GOLDEN COMPASSES:
THE TOP TOP-DOWN INDICATORS

- *Business inventories.* For decades, the ups and downs of the business cycle were connected in one way or another to fluctuations in the level of business inventories. This powerful indicator continues to be among the most important that helps in determining the risks that exist to economic expansion and the prospect for economic rebounds. For value investors, aggregate data can aid in the assessment of a company's inventories by giving clues about the macro climate in which the inventories must eventually be sold.

- *CFTC commitments of traders report.* One of the best ways to judge whether markets have become excessively bullish or bearish is to check the positioning of speculative traders. The CFTC's report contains data on the positioning of noncommercial traders in a wide variety of futures contracts, including foods, metals, energy, foreign currencies, and financials, for example.

- *Sovereign wealth funds.* One of the best ways to spot opportunities throughout the world is to consider those countries that are building up vast amounts of money in their sovereign wealth funds, which are basically savings accounts for sovereign nations. Wealthy countries are likely to see sustained periods of economic growth and experience only short downturns. Invest there and monitor closely where these funds are putting there money. Value investors seeking a margin of safety should view sovereign wealth funds as a major source of comfort.

- *Flow of funds report; holders section.* The Fed's flow of funds report contains vast amounts of information on all the major financial instruments, including the holders of these instruments. It is helpful to know who holds the financial assets you own because you will have a better understanding of what presses their buttons, so to speak. In addition, the data can be used in reverse by revealing the types of entities affected by changes in the value of financial instruments.

Notes

[1] Graham, Benjamin, and Jason Zweig, *The Intelligent Investor*. With a preface and appendix by Warren E. Buffett (HarperCollins, 2003), front cover.

[2] Markowitz, Harry M., "Portfolio Selection," *Journal of Finance*, vol. 7, no. 1, 1952, pp. 77–91.

[3] Graham and Zweig (2003), p. 282.

[4] Browne, Christopher. *The Little Book of Value Investing*. (Wiley, 2007).

[5] Fisher, Ken, *The Only Three Questions That Count* (Wiley, 2007).

CHAPTER 8

Diversifying Your Portfolio from the Top Down

To cut portfolio risks, embrace traditional portfolio theories but recognize that today a well-diversified portfolio includes diversity not just between and within asset classes, but also between themes and macro ideas.

A number of events combined in the early 2000s to signal that the traditional definition of a well-diversified portfolio has changed drastically, making it necessary for investors to rethink what they think is risky, what they think is safe, and how to offset risks between investments. Investors must now create portfolios that are more dynamic than ever before, giving weighting to macro themes, which is a new idea. This means that investments tied to major macro themes have their *own* coefficients. In other words, the correlation that is relevant to such investments is between ideas, not the asset classes used to express the ideas, although the historical correlation between and within asset classes remains a potent factor.

DIVERSIFICATION IN THE CLASSICAL SENSE

For over a half century, investors have endeavored to construct portfolios that produce an optimal balance between risk and return, and while millions of investors have been able to do so using the so-called *modern portfolio theory* introduced by Markowitz in 1952,[1] the notion that classical portfolio theories can be considered "modern" is beginning to lose credibility because of the increased integration of the global financial system and the spread of market capitalism.

Modern portfolio theory uses optimization techniques and historical data on the returns, risks, and correlations of available securities to construct a portfolio with the lowest possible risk for a given level of return.[2] The theory has been applied by all sorts of investors, particularly the more sophisticated, including pension funds, insurance companies, and mutual funds, for example. In relatively recent times individual investors have increasingly adopted its principles, often not knowingly, thanks to the availability of financial products such as mutual funds and exchange-traded funds, which make it easy to invest in a wide swath of investments across and within asset classes.

The basic premise behind portfolio theory relates to the idea that investors seek to maximize their portfolio returns while taking the least possible amount of risk. The most efficient of these portfolios sits on Markowitz's so-called Efficient Frontier, which consists of portfolios that have optimized their mix of assets to produce the highest possible expected return for the risks taken. Figure 7.2 in the previous chapter illustrates an efficient frontier. As the chart shows, portfolios A and B sit on the efficient frontier, with portfolio A offering the prospect of lower risk and lower return than portfolio B. Portfolios above the efficient frontier in theory cannot exist. For example, it would be impossible for portfolios to achieve high rates of return while taking little or no risk. Portfolios that sit below the curve are inefficient because they could earn higher returns for the same amount of risk taken. In other words, it is possible for portfolio C to earn a higher return without increasing risk.

Achieving a Portfolio That Optimizes Return Relative to Risk Using Modern Portfolio Theory

In modern portfolio theory, the best way to construct a portfolio that optimizes return relative to risk is to invest in assets that correlate as little as possible with each other. For example, a portfolio that holds shares in automobile companies, tire companies, and automobile parts companies could hardly be considered optimal, since each of these companies correlates—they are in the same industry. This means that when the automobile industry experiences weakness, shares in companies in each of these industries would likely fall, all else being equal. Conversely, a portfolio consisting of shares in automobile companies, pharmaceuticals, and consumer staples would likely perform relatively better in a case in which only the automobile sector weakened.

It is important to keep in mind that when constructing an efficient portfolio, portfolio theory dictates that an asset's prospective contribution to a portfolio's risk and return profile be foremost. In other words, the contribution made by either the asset's return or its overall risk should not be considered in isolation; their combined impact on the risk/return profile of the portfolio must be considered. For example, a mutual fund that tends to have relatively low returns might seem ideally suited to be combined with a portfolio that includes mutual funds that tend to have relatively higher returns, but if the low-returning mutual fund tends to be positively correlated with the other funds, it would add no diversification benefit to the overall portfolio. Hence, under modern portfolio theory the low-returning mutual fund should be rejected.

The Sharpe Ratio

As I said, focusing on either an asset's return or its risk (variance) alone will fail to optimize a portfolio's risk/return profile, and it can lead to poor judgments on the contribution that an asset is making to a portfolio's overall return. It is therefore crucial to assess the risk/return profile of an asset. One way to supplement this is to find its *Sharpe ratio*, or reward-to-variability ratio, as it was originally called. The Sharpe ratio was developed by Nobel Laureate William F. Sharpe in 1966 to measure the performance of mutual funds.[3] Through the use of a relatively simple formula, the ratio measures the amount of excess return, or risk premium, that can be attributed to an asset's risk attributes. The higher the Sharpe ratio or an asset or a portfolio of assets, the better its risk/return profile is. In other words, a high Sharpe ratio indicates that an asset is able to achieve relatively higher returns relative to the risks taken. A low Sharpe ratio indicates that the returns provided by an asset or a portfolio of assets are resulting more from increased risk-taking than compared to assets with higher Sharpe ratios.

Figure 7.2 in the preceding chapter shows the formula for the Sharpe ratio along with an example comparing two mutual funds. Note how although portfolio B achieves a higher rate of return than portfolio A, it does so by taking on greater risk, as can be seen in the comparison of risk premiums, standard deviations, and Sharpe ratios.

It is crucial to note that collecting a portfolio of investments with high Sharpe ratios will not necessarily result in an efficient portfolio that maximizes the risk/return ratio. Sharpe noted as much in the summary remarks from his 1994 study revising his original work:

> Whatever the application, it is essential to remember that the Sharpe Ratio does not take correlations into account. When a choice may affect important correlations with other assets in an investor's portfolio, such information should be used to supplement comparisons based on Sharpe Ratios.

All the same, the ratio of expected added return per unit of added risk provides a convenient summary of two important aspects of any strategy involving the difference between the return of a fund and that of a relevant benchmark. The Sharpe Ratio is designed to provide such a measure. Properly used, it can improve the process of managing investments.[4]

What Sharpe is saying is that his ratio should not be used as the only means of constructing a diversified portfolio because the ratio does not take into account the correlation that exists between securities within a portfolio. For example, a portfolio consisting of securities with relatively high Sharpe ratios might contain securities that are highly correlated, which will hurt the portfolio's risk/return profile—the portfolio would not be diverse. Sharp attention—no pun intended—must therefore be paid to the correlation between the investments contained in a portfolio, not just the risk/return profile of individual securities.

FLAWS IN APPLYING MODERN PORTFOLIO THEORY AND WHERE TOP-DOWN INVESTING FITS IN

Constructing a diversified, efficient portfolio is challenging to say the least, especially for individual investors. The task has been made easier by the advent of securities such as mutual funds and exchange-traded funds, which let investors invest more broadly both across and within asset classes. Nevertheless, there remain formidable challenges, not the least of which is the idea that a portfolio containing lots of securities may not necessarily be diversified, as I suggested earlier in focusing on the fact that while individual securities may themselves have good risk/return profiles, collectively they might not.

One compelling argument in favor of constructing portfolios with fewer securities is the idea that doing so enables investors to focus with greater intensity on the assets that they own. Warren Buffett said as much in 1993 in a letter to shareholders in which he discussed the fact that his company tended to focus on owning a relatively small number of businesses.

> Many pundits would therefore say the strategy must be riskier than that employed by more conventional investors. We disagree. We believe that a policy of portfolio concentration may well decrease risk if it raises, as it should, both the intensity with which an investor thinks about a business and the comfort level he must feel with its economic characteristics before buying into it.[5]

Backing up Buffett's contention is a study by Van Nieuwerburgh and VeldKamp, who studied the idea that most theories of portfolio allocation make certain assumptions about the degree of knowledge that investors have about the investments that they own.[6] Most intriguing was the researchers' conclusion that risk-averse and knowledgeable investors have a tendency to construct larger portfolios that are less diversified:

> Since risk-averse investors prefer to take larger positions in assets they are better-informed about, high-capacity investors hold larger "learning portfolios," causing their total portfolio to be less diversified.

Nieuwerburgh and VeldKamp's work serves as a warning to investors to avoid constructing portfolios that contain large numbers of assets that lean too heavily toward one's area of knowledge. Such a portfolio is not likely to be diverse even though it contains a large number of investments, because the portfolio will be filled with investments that investors specialize in, which does not add to a portfolio's efficiency.

Another potential challenge posed by portfolio theory that makes it difficult for investors to construct a diverse portfolio is the idea that the correlation assumed between investments is based on historical information. As Sharpe (1994) put it:

> Most performance measures are *computed* using historic data but *justified* on the basis of predicted relationships. Practical implementations use ex post results while theoretical discussions focus on ex ante values. Implicitly or explicitly, it is assumed that historic results have at least some predictive ability.[7]

I would argue that in a dynamic environment such as the present the historical correlation between assets is weaker than it was in the past and therefore can't be used as a predictor of the amount of correlation that will exist between assets in the future. I am not saying that the basic rules of economics and finance have changed, but rather that there are many more variables now that have changed the way that assets correlate with each other. For example, in years past a significant decline in U.S. economic growth and U.S. stock prices correlated strongly with the performance of asset prices in emerging markets such as those in Asia and Latin America. We have seen, however, a *decoupling* of that relationship in recent times, such as was the case in 2007 in Brazil, for example, when the country's benchmark equity index, the Bovespa, gained 44 percent despite a paltry rise of only 3.5 percent for the S&P 500 and very anxious markets generally. In past years, such conditions would likely have caused sharp underperformance of stock and bond prices in Brazil and in other emerging markets. Obviously, something has changed. The correlation between the emerging markets and U.S. markets has fallen, although cyclical influences are likely to boost the correlation between these markets now and then. Strict observers of modern portfolio theory failed to recognize these changes, mostly because of their heavy emphasis on the historical data they use to predict correlation between assets. This means that throughout the early 2000s many U.S. investors shied away from the emerging markets, believing that the strong historical correlation between U.S. markets and the emerging markets disqualified the emerging markets as an asset class to be held in significant quantities in their portfolios.

Simons agrees with this idea, concluding that more emphasis on recent observations may be necessary in order to more accurately predict future correlation:

> Observations in the past may not be as relevant as the more recent observations in estimating expected returns, volatilities, and correlations, especially since structural changes in the economy and financial markets could make the past less meaningful.[8]

Simons's argument falls right into my hands, as I believe that investors using top-down investment principles are in a better position than other investors are to spot emerging opportunities, assign these opportunities high margins of safety, and hence construct more diversified portfolios. Top-down investors would, for example, have looked past the tight correlation that existed historically between markets in the United States and Latin America when considering Latin America as an investment in the early 2000s. The top-down investor would have been compelled to consider how major macro influences were altering the equation. For example, many Latin American countries went from last to first, so to speak, by bringing down their budget deficits and by improving their external balances on trade, which moved toward substantial surplus partly on the heels of an increase in commodity prices. Economic growth was also much stronger. All of this required that the rule books be tossed. In other words, more weight on the most recent observations was what was needed in order to more accurately estimate correlations between investments and to construct diverse portfolios.

INTERNATIONAL DIVERSIFICATION IS MORE CHALLENGED WHEN THE FED RAISES RATES

It has long been felt that markets much smaller than those in the United States are affected greatly by the behavior of U.S. markets. Plenty of research exists to support this idea. The *decoupling* argument, which suggests that foreign markets will diverge from U.S. markets, is compelling for many reasons such as the shrinking portion of U.S. growth relative to the global economy, the ascension of China and India, the strengthened fiscal and economic positions of Latin America, the spread of market capitalism into Eastern Europe and Africa, the advent of the euro, and massive growth in the world's sovereign wealth funds.

Investors are hence likely to be best served by believing in the decoupling argument and assigning lower correlations to investments abroad. They should do so especially in cases where the top-down fundamentals are powerful in countries outside the United States. For example, investors tracking demographics in India will find that the number of people likely to seek the help of financial services companies is extraordinarily high, which makes a case for investing in financial services companies in India. Such an investment should be viewed as having a low correlation to U.S. markets, making it ideal for investors seeking to diversify their portfolios.

As compelling as the decoupling theory is, there is a limit to the amount of decoupling that can take place against the United States, which accounts for about 20 percent of global economic activity. Powerful cyclical forces that arise in the United States are likely to push back secular forces now and then. In particular, during periods when the Federal Reserve is raising interest rates, it is possible that the correlation between U.S. and international markets might increase, which is a very bad scenario for investors hoping that their investments abroad will shield their portfolios from declines. Guidolin and Hyde researched this idea by focusing on the correlation between the stock markets in Ireland, the United States, and the United Kingdom, finding that in bear markets Ireland's stock market, which performed exceptionally during the 1990s, performed "the worst across the three markets while Irish equity returns are highly correlated with foreign ones when the benefits of diversification ought to pay off, during bear markets."[9] In light of this finding, the researchers looked at whether it would be better during bear markets to switch out of Irish stocks and into U.S. and U.K. stocks, concluding that changing portfolio weights improved portfolio returns, especially when short sales and riskless investments are allowed.

Guidolin and Hyde make note of the fact that Ireland's Sharpe ratio is high, further underscoring the idea that high Sharpe ratios by themselves do not qualify assets as the best possible picks for the construction of a well-diversified portfolio.

Ireland's stock market makes a good case study because it represents a small open economy, the type of which has sprung up throughout the globe since the end of the Cold War and amid Asia's ascension. The takeaway is that investors must be careful to avoid the presumption that their investments will be shielded from the ups and downs of markets in industrialized economies.

DIVERSIFYING BY MAKING BETS ON EQUITIES USING PURCHASING POWER PARITY AS THE FOUNDATION

One very intriguing strategy involves the diversification of portfolios through investments in foreign markets based on apparent deviations from *purchasing power parity*, a theory that states that currencies will appreciate in countries where prices on goods and services are measurably below prices for the same goods and services in other countries. The idea is that by selecting investments in countries whose currencies seem likely to appreciate and avoiding investments in countries whose currencies seem likely to depreciate, investors can achieve both diversification benefits and additional return on their money. Pinfold, Qui, and Rose note that about half of long-term deviations from purchasing power parity tend to be reversed over a three- to five-year period. Therefore, it is best to avoid countries likely to see their currencies fall because they are overvalued on a purchasing power parity basis.[10] In their study, the researchers looked at seven countries with mature equity markets and free floating currencies for the period 1986 to 2003. A strategy was devised whereby portfolios where held containing the market index of each of the seven markets for which the exchange rate was expected to increase or hold steady using as a predictor the three-year cumulative deviation from purchasing power parity. Currencies that were expected to fall in value were excluded from the portfolio. The home market was always included in the portfolios, and the portfolios were held for three years. Each quarter a new portfolio was formed using the purchasing power rule. This means that at any one time there were 12 overlapping portfolios in place.

The results for the 12 portfolios were averaged, and they showed that the strategy resulted in a 2.1 to 3.6 percent increase per year in higher returns than were achieved in portfolios invested in an equal-weighted global portfolio of equities in six of the

TABLE 8.1

Correlation Coefficients of US$ Returns of National Stock Markets*

	AUS	CAN	GERM	JAP	NZ	SW	UK
CAN	0.602						
GERM	0.622	0.722					
JAP	0.375	0.418	0.398				
NZ	0.787	0.499	0.432	0.357			
SW	0.625	0.644	0.769	0.401	0.425		
UK	0.695	0.679	0.742	0.384	0.527	0.792	
US	0.677	0.780	0.734	0.471	0.518	0.727	0.794

*The coefficients are estimated on quarterly stock market return data in terms of US dollar returns, realized between 1991: Q1 and 2004:Q4 All the coefficients are significant at 5 percent level.

Source: Pinfold, John, Mei, and Lawrence Rose. "*A Superior International Asset Allocation Strategy Condition on Currency Prices.*" Department of Commerce, Massey University-Albany. Auckland, New Zealand, June 2005.

countries. For top-down investors the results further add to the allure of top-down investing, mainly because the notion of purchasing power parity is a top-down affair and also because investing in countries abroad requires a good sense for the global macroeconomic situation. Keep in mind Table 8.1, which shows that although the correlation between most of the seven countries is fairly high, because the correlation is below 1.0, there remains room for diversification between the countries.

DROP YOUR HOME BIAS

Empirical findings nearly universally show that investors have a strong preference to invest in their home country. Few dispute this notion. The bias has nonetheless weakened in recent years, with capital flowing more freely across borders. It is notable, for example, that U.S. residents held $5.6 trillion of foreign stocks and bonds at the end of 2006, up from $2.1 trillion five years earlier. In addition, foreign investors held $8 trillion of U.S. long-term securities, double what they held in 2001.[11] Further reinforcing this idea is the recent surge in cross-border deposits, which represent monies deposited across borders by a variety of entities. Cross-border deposits stood at $30 trillion at the end of June 2007, an increase of 22 percent compared to the previous year and an increase of $17.5 trillion compared to five years earlier.[12]

These figures are powerful indicators telling us that the world is now more integrated than ever before. It is a trend that appears likely to continue in the years to come thanks to the ease with which money can be sent across borders, increased harmonization of international banking laws, the expansion of free trade, and the spread of market capitalism. There remains plenty of room for U.S. investors to send money abroad, too, given that U.S. ownership of international equities is well below the international equity market's share of the world's market capitalization, which is close to 50 percent. At the start of this decade, the share of foreign equities in U.S. portfolios was only 13 percent, and the share of U.S. equities in foreigners' portfolios was similarly low (Figure 8.1). The figures have obviously gone up since then, and it is also necessary to consider another element: many investors gain exposure to markets abroad through their investments at home, as I discuss in the next section.

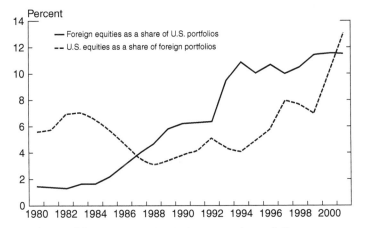

Figure 8.1 Share of foreign equities in investors' portfolios.

Source: Federal Reserve.

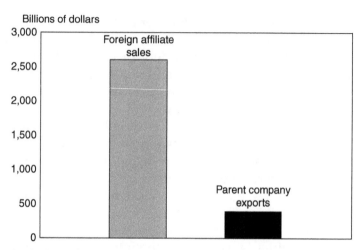

Figure 8.2 U.S. multinational goods sales through foreign affiliates and exports, 2004 (U.S. multinationals serve foreign markets mainly through their foreign affiliates).

Source: Department of Commerce (Bureau of Economic Analysis).

Buying "Foreign" Stocks at Home

U.S. companies were exporting about $155 billion in goods per month in the middle of 2008, and they had a vast global footprint. Data from the U.S. Bureau of Economic Analysis show that although U.S. multinational companies represented less than 1 percent of U.S. firms, they employed 9 million workers abroad at the end of 2004. Moreover, the combined value-added output of multinationals was $3.04 trillion in 2004.[13] (See Figure 8.2.) These impressively large numbers underscore the idea that U.S.-based investors can easily diversify their portfolios through ownership of U.S. multinational companies.

Cai and Warnock investigated the idea that U.S. investors might have much more exposure to foreign markets than is evident by their ownership of foreign shares alone.[14] They found that when ownership in shares of companies that are themselves diversified internationally is included, the percentage of exposure that U.S. investors have to foreign markets roughly doubles.

For those of you who are worried that buying shares in U.S. companies cannot possibly give you the kind of coverage you are

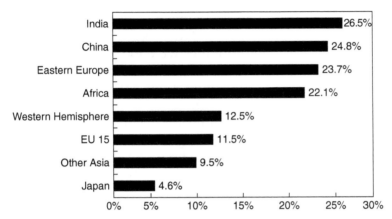

Figure 8.3 Average annualized growth in U.S. exports to trading partners, 2003–2006.

Note: "EU 15" refers to the 15 countries that were members of the European Union as of December 31, 2003. "Other Asia" excludes Mainland China, Japan, and India.

Source: International Monetary Fund, Direction of Trade Statistics, adapted from The Economic Report of the President to the Congress of the United States, February 2008.

looking for compared to big-growth stories such as China and India, take a look at Figure 8.3, which shows that U.S. exports to India, China, and countries in Eastern Europe grew at about a 25 percent annual pace between 2003 and 2006, outpacing exports to all other countries. With growth rates like that, it is easy to see how investors who have a home bias can participate in the economic success stories playing out abroad. An investor need only decide upon which countries to allocate exposure to and then find companies with major footholds in those countries. Companies that derive a heavy percentage of their revenues from abroad are the best candidates for this situation, particularly because of the diversification benefits.

DIVERSIFY BY INVESTING IN IDEAS WITH UNMISTAKABLE TOP-DOWN IMPLICATIONS

In Chapter 7, we discuss the concept that there are a great number of investments whose so-called margin of safety is much greater than what can be found on a balance sheet. This is why value investing has become ill-suited for today's fast-changing, integrated

world. Value investors missed numerous opportunities to participate in growth stories in the Eastern Bloc, Asia, and Latin America
simply because the opportunities were too fresh to have reached
corporate balance sheets and provide a basis for investing. Top-
down investors saw it differently. They saw that there were compelling stories providing a much larger margin of safety than was
readily apparent from any number crunching that could be done.
Top-down investors were investing in ideas.

The implications behind the top-down ideas that spurred big
moves in world markets in the early 2000s were unmistakable. To
name a few of the biggest: the spread of market capitalism in
Eastern Europe, Latin America's tackling of its domestic and external imbalances, the decline in trade barriers worldwide, and China
and India's rapid economic growth, particularly beginning when
China entered the World Trade Organization in 2002. These were
momentous occurrences. They were ideas, yet they were not
viewed as important by those who remained encapsulated in their
old-fashioned investment approaches.

One of the ideas I just mentioned is free trade, which has been
expanding massively throughout the world in part because of the
many free-trade agreements (FTAs) put in place since the 1990s.
Numerous studies show that when countries engage in free-trade
agreements, trade between the two countries accelerates. It is
important for top-down investors to note that the benefits of free-
trade agreements last for many years and in fact accelerate over
time. This means that when two countries engage in a free-trade
agreement, you have plenty of time to get in on investments that
stand to benefit from the FTA. The facts on this are compelling.
Recent research shows that after 5 years the average FTA increased
trade between bilateral trading partners by 32 percent, and after 10
years the increase bolted to 73 percent. After 15 years the increase
moves to 114 percent. After that the average FTA has little impact on
trade growth.[15] Part of the reason why the benefits accelerate over
time is that for many FTAs the removal of tariffs and other trade
barriers is phased in, usually over 5-year phases, and it often takes
as long as 15 years before the changes are fully implemented.

Recent FTAs involving the United States call for relatively
early implementation, which means that the bulk of benefits from
recent FTAs are likely to be seen within the next 5 to 10 years. In

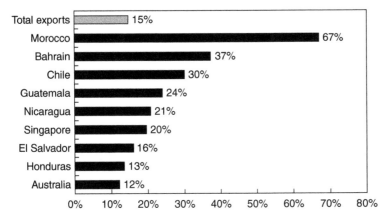

Figure 8.4 Growth of U.S. goods exports to free-trade agreement partners, 2005–2006.

Note: This group is restricted to U.S. trading partners with free-trade agreements that were both signed and entered into force from 2001 to 2006.

Source: The Economic Report of the President to the Congress of the United States, February 2008, Department of Commerce, Census Bureau.

total, the United States has negotiated free-trade agreements with 17 countries, 14 of which were negotiated during the presidency of George W. Bush. Three of these had not yet received approval in the early part of 2008. You therefore have a lot of time to select investments that stand to benefit from the FTAs recently signed with the United States (Peru is the most recent) and the three that await Congressional approval: Colombia, Panama, and South Korea.

The growth of U.S. exports to countries that enter into free-trade agreements with the United States is substantial. Figure 8.4 underscores this powerful top-down concept.

Thematic Investing Provides Diversification Benefits

In Chapter 4 we discuss thematic investing, which is a powerful form of investing in its own right, but which can also be used as a basis for diversifying a portfolio. As we said, thematic investing is a form of top-down investing that develops investment ideas based on major trends, changes in government regulatory and tax laws, and global influences on economies and markets that are powerful enough to override numerous other factors as considerations in the investment decision-making process. With thematic investing, you embrace ideas first and then invest in the specific investments the ideas lead to. In today's more integrated world, economic and financial systems are harmonizing, making it more likely than ever that trends occurring in a single country or industry will be seen elsewhere. Investors can therefore latch onto themes that are likely to cut across industries and countries.

When diversifying from the top down, it is important to find themes that are likely to be sustained. Often this means that you have to search for themes that have entrenched secular attributes strong enough to overwhelm most cyclical forces that could come along. For example, the compelling data I mention earlier on free trade makes it likely that there would be diversification benefits from investments made in response to the signing of FTAs, mainly because the FTA overrides most cyclical influences.

Another example would be the water theme and other situations like it where there is a compelling basis for believing that no amount of cyclical pressure would likely alter the imperative behind the theme. With water, for example, all countries are being pressured to substantially increase the supply of clean water owing to growth in the world's population. Demands on the world's water infrastructure will increase significantly regardless of the ups and downs of the business cycle. This is the kind of top-down investment that has strong diversification appeal.

Diversifying between and within Asset Classes from the Top Down

Diversifying a portfolio between and within asset classes using top-down investing principles is fairly straightforward because top-down investing gives investors ample tools to select investments that are likely to have minimal correlation with each other and hence add diversification benefits. For example, top-down investing principles are instructive in terms of choosing the proper allocation of stocks and bonds or within stock sectors or bond segments (Treasuries versus corporate bonds, for example). What is needed mostly is a sense for the economic climate, which is something that is much easier to understand using top-down investing principles than is possible using bottom-up approaches.

Here's an example. Let's say that the combined indicators point to a sharp weakening of economic activity. In the bond market, there is a wide variety of trades that should be implemented under this scenario, and there are many things to expect and respond to. In each case, some consideration would be given to how best to fit what is expected into the construction of a diversified portfolio. Keep in mind that there are many additional varieties of trades that can be implemented for each of the strategies shown:

- Bet on Fed rate cuts using federal funds and eurodollar futures.
- Bet on a steepening of the Treasury yield curve once the Fed starts cutting.
- Expect the U.S. budget deficit to increase, thus boosting issuance.
- Expect agency securities to underperform Treasury securities.
- Expect investment-grade bonds to underperform Treasuries.
- Expect junk bonds to significantly underperform Treasuries.
- Expect loan securities to underperform Treasuries.
- Expect corporate default rates to rise.
- Expect low-coupon mortgage securities to underperform high coupons.
- Expect credit default swap rates to rise.
- Expect interest rates to fall in Europe, although less than in the United States.

When deciding between asset classes, what you should look for in every macro scenario such as those above are those assets that are likely to either outperform or underperform; it is as simple as that. At that point you can determine how best to allocate your money, whether it be 60 percent stocks, 20 percent bonds, 10 percent international, and 10 percent commodities, or whatever. In a strengthening economic environment, a few obvious actions and expectations would be in order, although I emphasize that every cycle is different, and therefore you must keep your eyes glued to the indicators:

- Expect equities to outperform bonds.
- Expect commodities to rally.

- Expect emerging markets to outperform industrialized countries (in the years ahead this will probably be the case no matter what the economic climate is like, except during market corrections, which will likely occur mostly when economic growth decelerates).
- Expect the possibility that U.S. dollar's decline will be interrupted.
- Expect global shipping rates to rise.
- Expect real estate to stabilize.
- Expect lending standards to loosen.
- Expect an increase in innovations and new technologies.
- Beware of bubbles!

As you can see, from a simple concept many trading scenarios arise and each one is dependable. Such is the allure of top-down trading.

The View from the Top Down: Three Musts for the Macro Maven

In this era of globalization, portfolio diversification depends heavily upon top-down investing.

1. *Embrace portfolio theory, but enhance it from the top down.* At over 50 years old, modern portfolio theory needs a makeover. Modern portfolio theory does not allow enough room for recent observations to influence the decision about which investments to choose when developing a diversified portfolio. Top-down investing places more emphasis on the big picture, recent observations, and the compelling macro themes that common sense alone tells us makes certain investments appealing from a diversification standpoint.

2. *Drop your home bias.* One of the least-disputed arguments regarding international investing is the idea that investors tend to stay invested mostly in their home country. From a diversification standpoint, this is a mistake. Moreover, investors with a home bias stand to miss out on the terrific opportunities that have developed abroad.

3. *Diversify using top-down ideas with unmistakable implications.* Quantitative analyses that provide statistical data on the correlation between assets are nice, but they are not the only means of finding the right mix of assets to optimize a portfolio's risk/return profile. Investors should also consider concepts and themes that are big enough to cut across industries, countries, and cycles and therefore provide diversification benefits.

THE GOLDEN COMPASSES: THE TOP TOP-DOWN INDICATORS

- *Treasury international capital data.* Each month, the U.S. Treasury department details the net foreign purchases made by foreign investors in U.S. financial assets. The data give clear indications on investor sentiment abroad toward the major U.S. asset classes, including Treasuries, corporate and agency securities, and U.S. equities. These data are helpful for helping to round out views on preferences for these major asset classes. The data are also important in terms of their implications for the ability of the United States to finance its trade and budget deficits.

- *Free-trade agreements.* When countries engage in free-trade agreements (FTAs), a surge in trade between the countries follows. Importantly, because FTAs are implemented over a stretch of as long as 15 years, the benefits of FTAs tend to stretch out just as long, with significant benefits occurring between 5 and 10 years after the agreements are signed. This means that top-down investors have plenty of time to select investments that stand to benefit from FTAs.

Notes

[1] Markowitz, Harry M., "Portfolio Selection," *Journal of Finance*, vol. 7, no. 1, 1952, pp. 77–91.

[2] Simons, Katerina. "Should U.S. Investors Invest Overseas?" Federal Reserve Bank of Kansas City, *New England Economic Review*, November/December 1999.

[3] Sharpe, William F. "Mutual Fund Performance." *Journal of Business*, (vol. 39), 1966 pp. 119–138.

[4] Sharpe, William F., "The Sharpe Ratio," Stanford University, *The Journal of Portfolio Management*, 1994.

[5] From comments by Warren Buffett in Berkshire Hathaway's 1993 letter to shareholders.

[6] Van Nieuwerburgh, Stijn, and Laura VeldKamp, "Information Acquisition and Portfolio Under-Diversification," New York University, paper presented at USC FBE Macroeconomics and International Finance Workshop, November 2004.

[7] Sharpe (1994).

[8] Simons (1999).

[9] Guidolin, Massimo, and Stuart Hyde, "Equity Portfolio Diversification under Time-Varying Predictability and Comovements: Evidence from Ireland, the U.S., and the U.K.," Federal Reserve Bank of St. Louis, Working Paper Series, January 2008.

[10] Pinfold, John, Mei Qui, and Lawrence Rose, "Improving International Portfolio Returns by Incorporating Foreign Currency Predictions," Paper. Department of Commerce, Massey University–Albany, Auckland, New Zealand, June 2005.

[11] U.S. Treasury Department, Report on International Capital Flows, 2007.

[12] Data from the Bank for International Settlements, Quarterly Banking Report, December 2007.

[13] Economic Report of the President of the United States, 2007.

[14] Cai, Fang, and Francis Warnock, "International Diversification at Home and Abroad." Federal Reserve Board of Governors, International Finance Discussion Papers, Number 793, February 2004.

[15] Economic Report of the President of the United States, 2008.

CHAPTER 9

Do the Math!

The whole is more than the sum of its parts.

The mathematical sciences particularly exhibit order, symmetry, and limitation; and these are the greatest forms of the beautiful.

—Aristotle (384–322 BC)

People hate math. In a poll of U.S. adults conducted in 2005 by the Associated Press and America Online, by far the subject that respondents said they hated most while they were in school was math (Figure 9.1).[1] Unfortunately, this means that there are an awful lot of investors out there who will do whatever it takes to steer clear of math, especially complex math and anything that has to do with those babbling, boring balance sheets. There is of course no escaping the use of math when it comes to investing, so you can't get away from it completely. What I can tell you, though, is that with top-down investing the amount of math that you need to do is not beyond either your capabilities or your patience and that the math you do will bring you comfort. I feel especially confident in saying this now, given how miserable things turned out for the so-called whizzes who lured people into complex structured products and other math-heavy instruments that cost investors hundreds of billions of dollars worldwide in 2007 and 2008. So leave the misery of such things to others and stick with things you can understand; there is plenty of it in top-down investing.

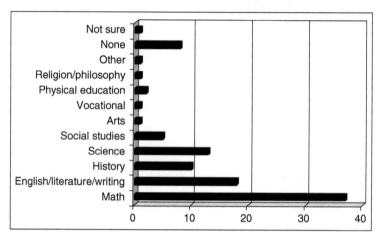

Figure 9.1 The subject that respondents said they hated most while they were in school.

Source: Associated Press/American Online poll conducted August 2005.

YOU CAN DO THE MATH, SO DO IT! FOLLOW YOUR NUMBERS

As I said, investors can't escape using math completely; numbers are what make the financial world go around. What astounds me, though, is that people so loathe math that they often avoid it almost completely, failing to do the math on big-picture ideas that in concept carry much more weight than the numbers do. Mind you, I am not talking about complex math, and often no math is needed at all for investment ideas whose premise is so powerful that no number crunching is needed. With top-down investing, there is a great deal of calculating that you can literally do on the back of an envelope. You really don't need much more than that, but you must do these things in order to judge where important numbers will be going. By "important numbers" I am referring to the simple idea that just like numbers on a roulette table, there are certain numbers that you need to see in order to win—to see your investments become profitable. The only way to know whether the numbers will turn your way is to follow them.

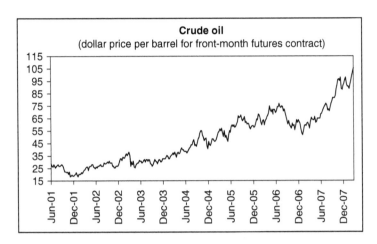

Figure 9.2
Source: New York Mercantile Exchange.

The Market's Miscalculation on Oil: The View from the Top Down

A glaring example of the failure by very large numbers of market participants to "do the math" occurred in the early 2000s when energy prices began to soar (Figure 9.2). It was said about the surge, which began in 2003 and 2004 that consumers would buckle, be hamstrung, or otherwise strained to such an extent that they would almost certainly stop spending on everything else and the economy would henceforth stop expanding. Investors were particularly nervous when oil moved toward $40 per barrel (we'd certainly take that price today!) in the middle of 2004. This idea proved wrong until the end of 2007 when a renewed surge in energy costs combined with the weak housing market, the credit crisis, and other factors produced a sharp slowing in economic activity. This means that investors who failed to do the math were wrong for years. Such was not the case for top-down investors, however, as they had the simple tools needed to avoid this trap, a trap that let top-down traders win investment dollars from the crowd.

Let's take a closer look at the top-down math that made it obvious that the paranoia about oil was related more to human tendencies toward anxiety and fear than to any sense of reality. Figure 9.3 contains the most important elements in the equation. Take note of the

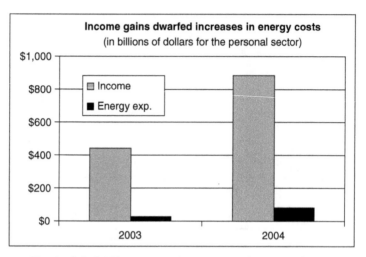

Figure 9.3 Do the Math! Things aren't so scary when you do.
Sources: U.S. Bureau of Economic Analysis, U.S. Department of Commerce.

fact that there are only two categories of numbers there. This is the kind of thing that I come across all the time in my top-down realm. It's as much as you need. Of course, if you want to take the analysis deeper and throw in other variables, go right ahead, but this is all that is needed for this part of the analysis.

As Figure 9.3 shows, the aggregate increase in energy expenses was far below the aggregate increase in personal income. You tell me, if you saw these numbers, what else would you think but to conclude the market had it wrong? Even with a little more slicing and dicing, the conclusion remained the same and actually looked even better. For example, some of the increased energy expenditures wound up as income for many corporations, meaning that estimations of the impact of higher energy expenditures rightfully should have been cut by the impact that the oil price rise had on corporate profits. Moreover, shareholders of publicly traded oil companies saw large gains, none of which is included in the income figures, except for dividend income.

This example highlights the usefulness of personal income figures, which in the middle of 2008 were running at a $12.1 trillion annual pace. Data on personal income can be used as a basis for making a wide variety of judgments and decisions. The personal income data make a terrific foundation to launch many analyses. For example, whenever you are faced with a question of whether a particular factor will have a meaningful impact on the consumer, simply compare the dollar figure to the income figures, focusing in particular on the monthly and yearly increases that are occurring. So the next time you hear people whining about something that they think is important but looks puny relative to income growth, tell them you know better and won't be brought into the realm of the worrywarts.

Curb Your Selective Reasoning

I am always amazed at how the financial markets often tend to see things one way, particularly at extremes when no amount of information can change things. I actually chomp at the bit for situations like this, where investors seem to have their blinders on because when the markets disregard reason and begin tossing out important numbers, opportunities to take contrary bets inevitably develop. At the root of what compels people to cast aside reason is of course human nature. Psychologists like to refer to this behavior as *selective reasoning, motivated reasoning,* or *confirmation bias,* among other things. Selective reasoning (or whatever you want to call it) refers to the tendency of people to seek out or interpret new information in a way that confirms their own thoughts about a particular subject matter and avoid information and opinions that contradict their own. This happens every day in the financial markets, and the best investors know how to spot it.

Providing substantial support to the idea that people engage in thinking that the part of their brains normally engaged in reasoning is blocked out is the focus of a study conducted by researchers at Emory University in 2006.[2] The researchers used functional neuroimaging (fMRI) to study people who were dedicated Democrats and Republicans in the three months prior to the 2004 U.S. presidential election. Each was given a reasoning task about the candidate they favored and they underwent fMRI to see what parts of the brain were active. The people in the study were given all sorts of information, including information that seemed to contradict their beliefs. The amazing finding was that there was no increase in activation of the parts of the brain that were normally engaged during reasoning. Instead, a network of emotional circuits lit up, including those thought to be involved in regulating emotion. Yep, that's just like what happens every day in the financial markets!

As difficult as it is to avoid selective reasoning, it is simply something you've got to do if you are going to be a successful investor. This means that when situations arise in which the conventional wisdom seems to have become entrenched and devoid of any reasoning, that is the time to wake up and do the math. Check and see if the conventional wisdom might be wrong, because it often is.

DON'T IGNORE OBVIOUS NUMBERS

A tendency I have seen repeatedly is the way that most people tend to ignore data that are right in front of their face. When this happens, they make very bad bets on market-moving statistics. Here's an example. Fairly often, the nation's automobile manufacturers adjust their production schedules in ways that have a significant impact on the economy. Amplifying the impact on financial markets is the fact that the economic calendar is dominated by factory statistics despite the fact that the U.S. economy is predominantly service-oriented. Take special note of what I just said. Although the U.S. economy is a service-oriented economy, the economic calendar is laden with factory statistics. Shall I say it again? I can't stress enough how important this concept is for investors to remember. It is the economic calendar that dictates how people feel about the economy. Sure, there are plenty of other economic indicators available, many of which appear in this book, but these are not the ones that people are collectively focused on and obsessed with. Without question it is fair to say that data on the monthly calendar tend to have a hypnotic effect on the financial markets.

Okay, now that I made that important point, let me get back to my example on automobile production and how people tend to ignore data that are right in front of them. As I said, now and then automobile production schedules are either increased or decreased in response to changes in demand. Sometimes, the production changes are significant enough that they can either add or subtract as much as a percentage point or more from the nation's gross domestic product (GDP) during a particular quarter on a seasonally adjusted annualized basis. That's a big deal when you consider that GDP tends to increase at a 3 percent pace each year.

When automobile production schedules are either ramped up or cut sharply enough to have the kind of impact I mentioned, the economic calendar practically lights up from the impact of the automobile sector because, as I said, the calendar is laden with factory statistics. Just to rattle off a few, the automobile sector affects all these monthly statistics: durable goods orders, factory orders, the Chicago purchasing managers index, the Philadelphia Fed business outlook survey, the Institute for Supply Management's purchasing managers index, industrial production, capacity utilization, jobless claims, and personal income among a few others that are affected indirectly. That's pretty much the entire economic calendar, or certainly the bulk of data that move markets each month, save for inflation data. To top it off, when quarterly figures on GDP are released, the automobile sector's reach grows even more, as GDP data tend to spur sharp movement.

The funny thing is that despite the glaring impact that the automobile sector has on economic data and by extension the way in which changes in automobile production schedules shape perceptions about the economy, people tend to overlook them. (Data on production schedules can be obtained each month from automobile manufacturers, and the impact on GDP can be computed from the monthly figures on industrial production released by the Federal Reserve; conversely seek data from Wards Automotive, from the economic departments of most major Wall Street firms, or from economic research firms such as Stone & McCarthy, which is one of the best on the Street)

This is just one of many examples that I have seen repeated over and over much to my delight because it creates opportunity. There are many other obvious numbers out there, some of which come by at random, so you have to spot them when they fall on your doorstep. Just don't ignore them, and do the math.

DON'T LISTEN TO THE CONSENSUS;
THE CONSENSUS IS ALWAYS WRONG

When I first started making my own forecasts on economic data in the early 1990s, I was a bit worried when my forecasts seemed far away from the consensus on the street. How could it be that my estimations were so different from everyone else's, and how was it possible that I could come up with such outliers so often? It wasn't because I was coming up with inaccurate forecasts. In fact, much to my surprise my outlier forecasts were "right on the screws" as they say on Wall Street, and I hit number after number. I soon realized that what was happening was that Wall Street's supposed titans were all clustered around each other for a reason: if each analyst were to miss, he or she would have plenty of company and all would feel shielded from having missed. If, on the other hand, the forecasters were to individually miss on forecasts that were far different from the consensus, they would feel more open to criticism because their miss would stand out. I'd rather think that if I am right, I would stand out, although my forecasts are never based on a desire to stand out; they are based on numbers, a sense of the data, and intuition.

In many ways, the uncourageous behavior shown by most economic forecasters is similar to the reticence shown by equity analysts before the financial bubble burst in 2000. At that time, equity analysts stood by rosy forecasts on stocks that had no realistic growth and earnings prospects, and they were reluctant to issue sell recommendations when the environment clearly called for it. It is a well-known fact that less than 1 percent of analysts' stock recommendations were sells at that time. This is a shocking statistic that underscores the tendency among analysts and forecasters to cluster together. I say let them cluster while you and I let numbers guide us; numbers do not lie, and I always believe in them and stick by them, not the consensus.

Where the Consensus Is Wrong Today

Hardly a day goes by that I am not thinking in one way or another of Ronald Reagan's famous line from the 1980 presidential debates: "There you go again." Although the circumstances change, many patterns in the financial markets repeat themselves time and time again. One of these is people's constant failure to do the math on issues that have heavy influence on market prices. So where is the calculus wrong today? Here are a few on my list:

- *Subprime mortgage defaults.* Major credit default swap indexes are priced for defaults on subprime mortgages to reach as high as 40 percent. This is despite the fact subprime delinquencies would first have to move substantially higher than they have been (Figure 9.4) and the fact that subprime

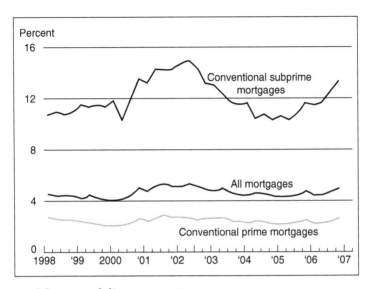

Figure 9.4 Mortgage delinquency rates.

Note: The Delinquencies are for mortgages that are 30, 60, and 90 days past due.

Source: Federal Reserve and Mortgage Bankers Association.

foreclosures haven't moved above 10 percent in the past (Figure 9.5). Yes, this situation is different, but even allowing for that, the efforts being undertaken by the Federal Reserve, Congress, the White House, bank regulators, federal agencies, and the private sector to this glaringly obvious problem will likely reduce the problem's size. Fixing the mortgage problem has become a national imperative, and this spells the beginning of the end of the problem. With this issue there also has been a lot of double-counting, with market participants counting up losses beginning with the mortgages themselves, the securities within which the loans are held, and the losses chalked up at financial institutions. This has led many to estimate eventual subprime losses as high as $500 billion or more.

The actual number of defaults is likely to be considerably less. The Federal Reserve has indicated that approximately 14 percent of all of the nation's approximately $10 trillion of first-lien mortgages are subprime mortgages, which

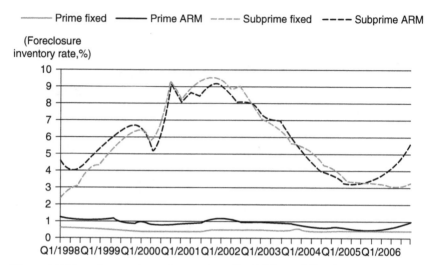

Figure 9.5 Foreclosure inventory rate; adjustable and fixed rate.

Source: Mortgage Bankers Association National Delinquency Survey; Standard & Poors.

amounts to 7.5 million loans totaling about $1.4 trillion.[3] With these numbers in mind, if 50 percent of subprime mortgages were to enter foreclosure, which seems highly unlikely for the reasons I indicated, this means that there would be $700 billion of foreclosures. Recovery on the loans would likely amount to at least 50 percent, which means that defaults even under a worst-case scenario would not likely exceed $350 billion, a massive tally but below what the market is priced for.

- *Construction drag.* Here is a situation in which people clearly are not doing the math and are engaging in selective reasoning, seeing only what fits their views. Market participants seem to think that the economic drag from declining home construction activity will go on in perpetuity. Housing has indeed been a drag on the U.S. economy, subtracting about a percentage point from GDP on an annualized basis in 2006 and 2007. During that time, housing starts have fallen from a peak of 2.292 million in January 2006 to about 1.0 million in the first half of 2008. Here's where a little math can go a long way: considering the fact that approximately 200,000 of the 1.0 million starts are actually restarts (tear-downs and rebuilds and such), this means that only 800,000 new dwellings are being built. Still too many, you say, given the massive number of unsold homes? Well, consider the fact that approximately 1.2 million new households form each year because of increases in the population. This means that builders are currently building *too few* homes relative to what is needed and that even after accounting for the excess amount of supply on the market, housing starts can't fall much more from current levels. Yes, maybe they fall a bit more, but obviously they can't fall as much as they already have because they can't fall below zero.

- *The cushion provided by sovereign wealth funds.* Vast numbers of investors fail to realize the monumental growth in wealth that many countries have experienced in the early 2000s and what it means for the stability of the global economy for at least the next decade. Although some of what has happened is the result of transference of wealth from relatively wealthier nations such as the United States and other industrialized nations to commodity-rich nations, particularly those that are rich in oil, a great deal of what has happened is the result of the spread of market capitalism, better central banking, economic reforms, and innovation, among many other factors. This means that the changes are more structural than cyclical and will likely last. Therefore, with money in the bank, countries that have vast amounts of money in their sovereign wealth funds have a significant backstop against economic downturns. Even countries such as Argentina and Russia, which defaulted on their debt obligations in 2001 and 1998, respectively, find themselves with large amounts of reserves (Russia in particular). It seems that in the next 20 years, the number of countries likely to experience at least one serious bout of banking problems will be far fewer than the 125 countries that experienced such problems over the past 20 years, and far fewer than the 70 developing-country cases whose banking systems became essentially insolvent over the past 20 years.[4] With growth well-supported abroad, there is virtually no basis to believe that U.S. economic weakness will have lasting impact on economies abroad.

- *No collapse in U.S. dollar.* I have been on the side of the
  thinking that has expected the dollar to decline over the
  years, but I have never entirely bought into the doom and
  gloom camp expecting the dollar to experience an abrupt,
  substantial decline that sparks a crisis and removes its
  status as the world's reserve asset. The reasons I feel this
  way are too long to write about in depth in this book, but a
  few of the reasons to bet against such a major call include:
  the tendency in Europe, whose currency is the only
  possible substitute for the dollar as the world's reserve
  currency, to adopt policies that prohibit vigorous economic
  expansion; relatively illiquid and fragmented corporate
  bond markets in Europe and elsewhere; U.S. military
  might; continued innovation in the United States; mature
  U.S. legal and financial infrastructures, especially in
  comparison to those of developing countries; the ability of
  the American people to force change through their robust
  U.S. political system; and the vast U.S. corporate footprint
  abroad, among many other factors. To add to this, there is
  a growing disparity between prices in the United States
  and prices abroad, which is lowering the U.S. trade deficit.
  The influence of this so-called purchasing power parity
  will likely overtake the influence at some point, probably
  when the U.S. economy starts performing better relative to
  its trading partners.
- *Fiscal stimulus works.* I love this one. There are those out
  there who think that when Americans are given tax rebate
  checks, only a fraction of the money, say about 25 percent,
  will get spent. Give me a break! We all know that
  Americans spend every penny put in their pockets!
  Americans love to spend and with good reason given all
  the cool products that are available to buy. It is human
  nature to try to enjoy life to the fullest, especially in the
  United States. It may be that when American households
  receive rebate checks, some of the money will be targeted
  at that moment toward paying a bill or a being deposited
  in a savings account, but eventually the money gets spent.
  Figure 9.6 shows the savings rate for the household sector.
  The top-down view wins on this one. Enough said.

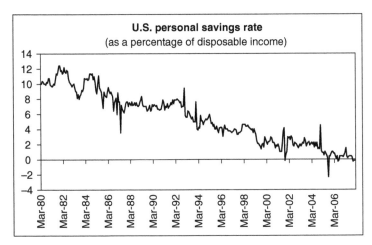

Figure 9.6 Top-down fact: Americans love to spend!
Source: Bureau of Economic Analysis.

ESTABLISH YOUR BASE NUMBERS

When investing from the top down, it is crucial that you have a strong set of numbers to use as a base for making snap judgments. For example, in the example I cited earlier in the chapter, I referenced the figures on personal income. Those are the kinds of figures that help give perspective on many others, enabling you to make faster, more accurate assessments about what the numbers may mean to the economy and the financial markets. Everyone will have a different set of numbers that are kept as base numbers, but there are a few that I believe are essential and that are needed often in the top-down realm. They are shown in Table 9.1.

BOTTOM UP OR TOP DOWN, CHOOSE YOUR MATH POISON

If you are going to be a successful investor, you have to do math no matter which investment approach you choose to follow. You can either choose the bottom-up approach and crunch numbers off globs of company balance sheets (pardon me while I take a nap), or you can look at the world from the top down where numbers

TABLE   9.1

Establish Your Base Numbers; Context Is Crucial When Analyzing New Information

Statistic	Base number	Possible uses
Personal income	$11.933 trillion annually, as of Jan. 2008	Compare hits (i.e., oil) against income growth
Gross domestic product	$14.084 trillion annually, as of Dec. 2007	Compare just about everything to GDP and gain big perspective
Barrels of oil consumed per day	20.7 million in 2007; 20.74 million in 2008 (est.)	Use this to calculate impact on U.S. of oil price changes
Number of households; growth per year	114.3 million in 2006; growing 1.2 percent per year	Calculate absorption rate for excess home supply; many other uses
Total payroll employment • In goods sector • In service sector	138 million Feb. 2008 21.8 million 116.16 million	Never forget what really drives the economy
Long-run U.S. budget deficit as percentage of GDP	Averaged 2.2 percent from 1968 to 2007	Calculate dollar potential for fiscal stimulus; keeps budget data in perspective
Japanese and Chinese holdings of U.S. Treasuries	Japan: $571 billion (Jan. 2008) China: $406 billion (Jan. 2008)	Much needed perspective on constant talking point
Size of U.S. bond market	$29.6 trillion (Dec. 2007)	Puts developments in bond segments into perspective
Household net worth	$57.7 trillion (Dec 2007)	Adds perspective on wealth, income changes
Value of U.S. equity market	$22.4 trillion (Dec. 2007)	Calculate changes in wealth, impact on economy

Sources: Personal income: U.S. Department of Commerce; gross domestic product: U.S. Bureau of Economic Analysis; oil consumption: U.S. Department of Energy; number of U.S. households: U.S. Census Bureau; Total payroll employment: U.S. Bureau of Labor Statistics; budget deficit: U.S. Treasury Department; Foreign holdings of Treasuries: U.S. Treasury Department; Size of U.S. bond market: SIFMA; Household net worth: Federal Reserve Flow of Funds; Value of U.S. equities: Federal Reserve Flow of Funds.

enhance the exciting concepts they back. Obviously I am biased in favor of the top-down approach, but I truly believe that it is what is best for vast numbers of investors who find that they simply do not have the time or patience to invest any other way, particularly because of the amount of number crunching involved in other approaches. Aristotle, who is quoted at the start of this chapter, had it right when he said that the whole is more than of the sum of its parts. Math, if it brings order and clarity, truly is a thing of beauty, as long as we don't get too much of it, that is.

The View from the Top Down: Three Musts for the Macro Maven

When you do the math, emotion gets put aside.

1. *Curb your selective reasoning.* There is now scientific evidence indicating that the part of the brain associated with reasoning is inactive when people are given information that conflicts with their own thoughts about a particular subject. In place of reason, people seek out information and opinions that confirm their own views. This is destructive behavior in any walk of life including the investment world. For you, it is a good thing if you recognize this because it means that while you are doing the math and making rational judgments, others are looking the wrong way, creating opportunities for you to exploit. Look for situations in which selective reasoning is blinding the markets from reality, and nail it.

2. *Don't listen to the consensus.* The consensus is nothing more than a cluster of people too afraid to think outside the box, which is where you need to be very often if you are going to make any real money. Don't stay away from the consensus for the sake of doing so, but part ways with the consensus whenever the numbers tell you that you should. It is the consensus that you will be winning money from.

3. *Establish base numbers.* With a relatively small and manageable set of major numbers in hand such as data on personal income, the total of number of households, household wealth, nominal GDP, and international reserves, you can quickly and accurately make judgments about the economy and the financial markets. Base numbers provide perspective on other data, and they can make you look downright smart whenever you're faced with issues regarding the big picture.

THE GOLDEN COMPASSES: THE TOP
TOP-DOWN INDICATORS

- *Personal income.* Each day in the financial markets there are issues concerning the potential impact that a certain factor will have on U.S. consumers. If you are to make accurate judgments about how these influences will play out, then you must have a sense for both the aggregate level of personal income and its growth rate. With these numbers in hand you can more readily answer questions such as: How will rising energy costs affect consumers? From there you can make important judgments and invest accordingly.

- *Automobile production schedules.* Despite being a smaller part of the U.S. economy than it was in past years, the automobile sector continues to make a major splash on the U.S. economic calendar, mainly because the calendar is stuck in the past and filled with factory-related statistics. This means that the auto sector can substantially influence the way that investors view the economic situation. In addition, there are times when the automobile sector either adds or subtracts as much as a percentage point from GDP on a quarterly annualized basis, compounding the sector's impact on the financial markets.

- *Flow of funds; household balance sheets.* There are numerous base numbers that you can obtain from the Fed's flow of funds report regarding the household sector, including household net worth; a breakdown of household assets such as holdings in stocks, bonds, and real estate; and a breakdown on liabilities, most prominently mortgage debt and consumer credit (credit cards, car loans, and such). From these data you can make terrific judgments about a wide variety of situations affecting the household sector.

Notes

[1] Poll conducted by the Associated Press and America Online, August 2005, http://wid.ap.org/polls/050816school/index.html.

[2] Westen, Drew, Pavel S. Blagov, Keith Harenski, Clint Kilts, and Stephan Hamann. "Neural Bases of Motivated Reasoning: An fMRI Study of Emotional Constraints on Partisan Political Judgment in the 2004 U.S.

Presidential Election, Emory University. *Journal of Cognitive Neuroscience*, 2006, Volume 18, Number 11, pp. 1947–1958.

[3] Bernanke, Ben, "The Subprime Mortgage Market," from a speech delivered at the Federal Reserve Bank of Chicago's 43rd Annual Conference on Bank Structure and Competition, Chicago, Illinois, May 17, 2007.

[4] Happen, Charles, "Why the International Financial Structure Matters, Including to the United States, in Safeguarding Prosperity in a Global Financial System," report of an Independent Task Force Sponsored by the Council on Foreign Relations, 1999, p. 27.

CHAPTER 10

Other Reasons to Invest from the Top Down

We are facing a great change in civilization, and the responsibility, I think, for what we do with our leisure time is a very great responsibility for all of us who have intellectual interests.

—Eleanor Roosevelt, the District of Columbia Library Association Dinner, April 1, 1936

Our time on earth is precious, and in recognition of this, human beings have always endeavored to optimize the use of their time to achieve the maximum fulfillment of their lives. Work has always been a feature, whether it was creating fire, building the Roman Empire, engaging in mercantilist trading, building the British Empire, or the development and production of iPods. Leisure has always been a feature, too, of course, and it has become an even larger feature of our lives over the past century. This trend has accelerated in recent decades, and it is unlikely to change in the decades ahead because the desire for increased fulfillment is an innate part of human existence. Moreover, centuries of productivity gains have reduced the amount of labor needed to produce the essential elements of society as well as personal goods and services. These are obviously top-down ideas.

YOU DON'T HAVE TIME TO INVEST ANY OTHER WAY

The idea that people are working less and spending increasing amounts of time on leisure is well documented. In a recent study, the amount of time that Americans work each year was found to have fallen by 550 hours from 1900 to 2005.[1] In another study covering the period of 1965 to 2003, the amount of time that men spent on leisure was found to have increased by 7.9 hours per week; for women the amount of time spent on leisure increased by 6.0 hours.[2] Figure 10.1 illustrates these results. Predictably, studies on the amount of time that people spend on leisure as they get older indicate that people allocate increasing amounts of time to leisure as they age (Figure 10.2).

Armed with these figures on leisure time and the idea that people everywhere endeavor to increase their leisure time in order to live fuller lives, it is hardly a leap of faith to assume that vast amounts of investors are also inclined to spend more time being leisurely. This means that they are devoting less and less time to investing. This is creating a need for a new style of investing that requires as little of our time as possible. There is no sense in fighting this reality; there's 100 years of proof, and, with the way we are

Changes in weekly hours (1965–2003)	All	Men	Women
Total market work (paid work, commute, breaks, meals)	–3.2	–11.6	3.4
Total nonmarket work (housework, time obtaining goods and services, other)	–4.6	3.7	–11.1
Total work (total market + total nonmarket)	**–7.8**	**–7.9**	**–7.7**
Leisure 1 (socializing, relaxing, recreation)	5.1	6.3	3.8
Leisure 2 (Leisure 1 + sleeping, eating, personal care)	5.6	6.4	4.9
Leisure 3 (Leisure 2 + primary and educational child care)	6.9	7.9	6.0
Leisure 4 (total hours possible minus total work)	7.8	7.9	7.7

Figure 10.1 Working hard or hardly working?

Source: The Federal Reserve Bank of St. Louis, The Regional Economist, January 2007, adapted from a study by Mark Aguiar and Erik Hurst, "Trends in Leisure: The Allocation of Time over Five Decades," Federal Reserve Bank of Boston, Working Paper Series, No. 06-2, February 2006.

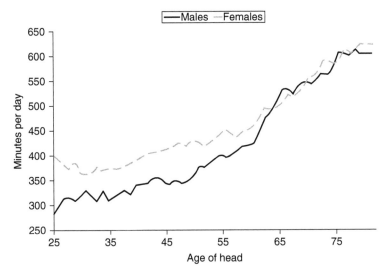

Figure 10.2 Time allocation over the life cycle; leisure time increases with age.*

*Series depict minutes per day allocated in total home production, shopping, and leisure for household in the 2003 American Time Use Survey conducted by the Bureau of Labor Statistics.

Source: Aguiar, Mark, and Erik Hurst. "Measuring Trends in Leisure: The Allocation of Time over Five Decades." Federal Reserve Bank of Boston, Working Paper Series, No. 06-2, February 2006.

multitasking these days, it is imperative that we find as many ways as possible to be efficient with our time. Moreover, the aging of the population (Figure 10.3) is sure to boost further the desire for more leisure time.

Top-down investing is ideally suited to today's investors, whose crammed lifestyles and desire for additional leisure time mean that they don't have the time to invest any other way. It is an efficient approach to investing, not only because today's invest-ment climate is ideally suited for macrostyle investing, but also because it depends more on ideas than on number crunching. As a result, a top-down investor can formulate an investment strategy in a car, on a plane, on the subway, while shopping, on a treadmill, or wherever.

I am stretching this a bit because ideas don't pop out of thin air, and both background work and follow-up work are going to be needed no matter how you slice it. My point, though, is that because top-down investing depends on very big ideas, many of

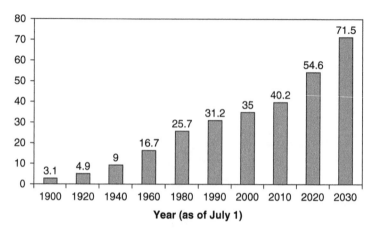

Figure 10.3 Number of persons aged 65 and up, 1900–2030 (numbers in millions)

Note: Increments in years are uneven.

Sources: Projections of the population by age are taken from the January 2004 census Internet release. Historical data are taken from "65+ in the United States," current population reports, Special Studies, P23-190. Data for 2000 are from the 2000 census, and 2004 data are taken from the census estimates for 2004.

these will be readily apparent and can be arrived intuitively. For example, with a little bit of background knowledge on a few demographic trends such as those that relate to the baby boom years of 1946–1964, a wide variety of ideas can be generated, whether on investments in health-care stocks, financial services, housing, vacationing, real estate, or whatever. Another thought might come to mind while pulling up to the gas pump and realizing the global implications of the massive shift in wealth that has taken place and the implications that higher energy prices are having on a variety of industries in the United States and abroad.

Buying Ideas Is Easier Than Buying Companies

Once ideas are generated and checked out, putting them in place is faster with top-down investing than with other investment approaches that depend upon close scrutiny of company balance sheets or other analyses because you are buying an idea, not a company. There are of course many situations in which you absolutely must pay very close attention to company-specific details, but with top-down investing it isn't necessary because you can invest in exchange-traded funds and mutual funds and numerous asset classes such as commodities, currencies, government bonds, and real assets. Moreover, even in cases where a top-down idea leads you to buying and selling companies, in most cases you can depend upon the scrutiny that others have given the company you are looking at. I am not saying that you should take their word for it, especially given the difficulties that the major rating agencies had in recent times with respect to assigning ratings that accurately reflect credit conditions, but the margin of safety that major top-down ideas provide will help you to minimize the amount of follow-up work you need to do. That said, I suggest that you try to pick the company perceived to be the best in its field in order to increase your margin of safety even more. Remember, though, what will carry you is the big-picture concept that you have embraced, which should mean that the assets you invest in will be pulled along for the ride, assuming of course that you steered clear of assets that were at the bottom of the heap in your investment concept.

With Top-Down Investing, You More Quickly Narrow Down Your Investment Checklist

Another time saver with top-down investing is that it narrows down your investment choices very efficiently, especially compared to investment approaches that require scrutiny of literally hundreds of companies when you're trying to develop an investment idea. For example, if, by analyzing your top top-down indicators, you decide that investing in farmland companies in Brazil is a good idea, then you need only look at the pick of the litter in that category. With other investment approaches finding such companies might take the weeding through of a very large number of companies from the bottom up. Spare me! Moreover, in many cases other investment approaches won't pick up the ideas generated by using the top-down approach because these other approaches are too rigid, especially in today's opportunity-filled world. With top-down investing, a perusal of the top top-down indicators—the golden compasses—can quickly generate ideas for outright investments, portfolio diversification, hedging, and shifting between asset classes. Not so with other investment approaches, which for starters are ill-suited to making decisions about which asset classes to invest in and which also are too laborious to keep up with as much as is required to follow such investment approaches effectively. I should add that because top-down investing tends to develop ideas with staying power, it leads to many buy-and-hold ideas. It is therefore a minimally intensive approach to investing as compared to strategies that tend to result in greater portfolio turnover.

Women: Where Do You Find the Time?

Women of course have very special demands upon their time compared to men, especially women who have children. It is a responsibility that transcends time and that has become more difficult to manage in recent decades, as many women have entered the workforce. Interestingly, while the entry by women into the workforce is well documented, women have also somehow found the time to obtain much deserved leisure time. As I noted at the start of the chapter, women have increased their time spent on leisure by 6.0 hours between 1965 and 2003. Importantly, this has happened even as women have increased their amount of work and while—listen up men—continuing to outpace men in the amount of work done outside the home on household chores, preparing meals, shopping, and obtaining goods and services. Where have women found the time? By decreasing the amount of time spent on work outside the home, which means that men and women are spending less time in this area. For example, in 1965 both men and women were spending 14.4 hours on food preparation and indoor household chores. In 2003 the figure had dropped to 8.1 hours. This is additional evidence of the substantial time constraints that households face these days. This leaves very little time to spend on investing, which is yet another reason to choose top-down investing over other approaches.

EVERYBODY ELSE IS DOING IT

Join the revolution! Millions of investors are already investing from the top down. Investors increasingly are buying ideas first and then the assets. For example, these days many investors have shied away from buying shares directly in companies that produce precious metals. Instead, investors are buying shares in exchange-traded funds and mutual funds that either invest in companies that produce precious metals or in the precious metals themselves. This is an opportunity that did not exist even a few years ago, and new products seem to develop almost every day, giving investors new ways of investing in the basis of macro ideas that depend less and less on scrutiny of company balance sheets. Investors who choose this route are also getting diversification benefits.

People Are Buying Indexes, Not the Underlying Stocks, and Looking Abroad

ETFs and index mutual funds held $1.1 trillion in assets at the end of 2006, accounting for 10 percent of the total amount of assets managed by all registered investment companies, data from the Investment Company Institute show.[3] Assets in these indexed products have increased tenfold over the past decade, mostly in funds that track broad market indexes. ICI's data also show that at the end of 2006, ETFs and index mutual funds that track large-blend domestic equity indexes, such as the S&P 500, managed 40 percent of all assets invested in mutual funds and ETFs that focus on large-blend domestic stocks. These data are further proof of the shift away from direct ownership of stocks and into groups of stocks that in essence represent investments in ideas and concepts. Table 10.1 shows the sharp increase that has occurred in recent years in the total amount of assets held in index mutual funds.

Investments in mutual funds have grown sharply throughout the world. ICI data show that the total amount of assets held in mutual funds worldwide was $21.765 trillion at the end of 2006, an increase of about $10 trillion compared to five years earlier. The tally almost certainly has increased further given the strength of the world's equity markets in 2007 and the shift away from direct ownership of shares and into index funds and ETFs. There are now thousands of U.S. mutual funds that invest internationally, a gigantic increase compared to 1980 when there were fewer than 20.[4] To underscore the degree to which money is flowing overseas, it is notable that at the end of 2006, U.S. residents held about $5.6 trillion in foreign stocks and bonds versus $2.1 trillion five years earlier.[5] For their part, foreign investors held about $8 trillion of U.S. stocks and bonds, double the amount held five years earlier.

TABLE 10.1

Net Assets of Index Mutual Funds (*Millions of Dollars, 1993–2006*)

			Investment objective			
Year	Total	S & P 500	Other domestic equity	Global/ international equity	Hybrid	Bond
1993	$ 28,691	$ 19,241	$ 4,959	$ 1,095	$ 856	$ 2,540
1994	33,299	21,883	5,736	1,818	1,008	2,855
1995	58,377	40,037	9,517	2,642	1,561	4,620
1996	99,622	70,787	16,213	3,932	2,540	6,151
1997	172,971	124,392	29,276	5,177	4,050	10,077
1998	268,728	193,998	46,209	7,813	5,036	15,672
1999	392,402	273,910	78,641	12,777	7,152	19,922
2000	388,878	261,147	87,590	12,218	4,096	23,827
2001	374,982	238,210	88,382	10,656	4,229	33,505
2002	331,296	191,722	81,360	10,649	4,314	43,251
2003	460,849	260,173	130,319	17,709	5,829	46,819
2004	560,146	300,844	170,163	27,133	7,357	54,649
2005	625,046	315,047	196,673	41,082	8,047	64,197
2006	748,823	354,679	248,807	61,923	8,930	74,484

Source: Investment Company Institute Factbook.

In most cases, money flowing into international funds is done on the basis of a top-down idea, not from an inspection of a company in a foreign country. The effort required to learn about foreign companies is even more tedious than the effort required for finding out about domestic companies partly because the process is complicated by language and cultural differences, which limit the amount of information than can be obtained from sources outside the companies themselves and thus reduces the margin of safety. In such cases it is far better to own a group of stocks managed by portfolio managers who have expertise in the area of interest.

I am not saying that buying groups of foreign stocks is the only way to go; in fact, a top-down analysis might generate an idea that requires investment in a specific company because no ETF or mutual fund exists in the area. For example, we show in Chapter 8 that when the United States enters into trade agreements with other countries, trade between the United States and the counterparty in the agreement increases substantially. One top-down idea would be to buy into a broad index that would benefit from the increased economic activity in the foreign country. A second idea would require drilling down a bit more to find specific companies in either the United States or the foreign country that would likely see a disproportionate share of the increased business between the two countries. This means that you would have to do a bit of checking and find companies that not only fit this mold but are also considered strong players in their field and that have stable balance sheets.

YOU DON'T KNOW BALANCE SHEETS

In the 2004–2005 school year, 312,000 bachelor's degrees were awarded to U.S. students in the field of business, which was 22 percent of all bachelor's degrees conferred by degree-granting institutions and roughly double the second most popular category, social sciences and history (Figure 10.4). When coupled with

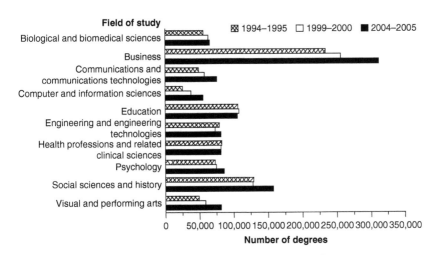

Figure 10.4 Trends in bachelor's degrees conferred by degree-granting institutions in selected fields of study: 1994–1995, 1999–2000, and 2004–2005.

Source: Institute of Educations Sciences, National Center for Education Services, U.S. Department of Education.

the fact that less than 20 percent of U.S. residents aged 25 and older have received a college degree, this means that the percentage of the population with specialized knowledge of business subject matter is rather low. Taking this a step further, even those who do have a college degree in business may lack the skills necessary to take on investment approaches that require close scrutiny of company balance sheets. Of course, there are many who choose to take on these approaches and build up their ability to dissect balance sheets, which is certainly a worthwhile endeavor, but I would prefer that such knowledge be combined with the top-down approach. As I have emphasized throughout this book, I do not believe that forming ideas from the bottom up is the right approach for this era of expanding market capitalism and today's more integrated world.

The View from the Top Down: Three Musts for the Macro Maven

An investment philosophy that makes you money and saves your time? Who would have thought!

1. *Recognize that you simply do not have the time to invest any way but from the top down.* Our time on earth is precious, and people have been striving for centuries to spend more of their time on leisure to maximize their time for enjoyment. This means that we are spending less and less time on work both in our occupations and at home. Moreover, in our endeavors we are multitasking, spreading ourselves even thinner. This is why we need to approach investing with an eye to being as efficient as possible, recognizing that we should not get caught up in investment approaches that require substantial allotments of time.

2. *As you age, your leisure time will increase, as will your time spent on investing.* There is a natural tendency to work less as we age, and this goes for work in our occupations and at home. With large numbers of Americans entering age brackets where the tendency to work is lower, there will be an even greater tendency toward activities that have

less to do with work. This will push investors toward
big-picture investment strategies and products that fit
their lifestyles. Stay abreast of this trend, as it is sure to
affect market prices. Moreover, you too are likely to be
part of this trend.

3. *Relax; you don't have to learn about balance sheets.* You're not
the only one; few people have a deep understanding of
company balance sheets. Relax. You don't need that
knowledge to be a successful investor. You can develop
magnificent investment ideas by investing from the top
down. Get back to your leisure time.

THE GOLDEN COMPASSES: THE TOP TOP-DOWN INDICATORS

- *Demographics and life cycles.* There are many life cycles that
  can be drawn into analyses of all sorts of trends. In this
  chapter I highlight the life cycle as it pertains to the use of
  time. One of the more useful life cycle patterns for
  investors to track pertains to consumption patterns. The
  fact is that people consume more or less of certain
  products at different points along their life cycles. This is a
  very basic concept whose top-down implications become
  obvious with a little thought.
- *Publicly funded research—diamonds in the rough.* Talk to
  people at the Federal Reserve, and they will boast, as Alan
  Greenspan once did to me, that the Fed employs about 200
  Ph.D.s. The Federal Reserve has every right to be proud of
  its researchers, whose collection of work are the most
  remarkable and relevant materials available. The Fed's
  research is spread out among the Fed's 12 Reserve Banks,
  but the best way to search for research on a topic you are
  interested in is through *Fed in Print*, which is available on
  the San Francisco Fed's Web site. Other diamonds in the
  rough include data and research on Web sites for the
  Census Bureau, the Bank for International Settlements, the
  International Monetary Fund, and, believe it or not, the

Central Intelligence Agency (the *World Factbook*). Two of the notes for this chapter reference research from the Federal Reserve. There are many more references throughout the book.

Notes

[1] Ramey, Valerie A., and Neville Francis, "A Century of Work and Leisure," manuscript, University of California, May 2006.

[2] Aguiar, Mark, and Erik Hurst, "Measuring Trends in Leisure: The Allocation of Time over Five Decades," Federal Reserve Bank of Boston, Working Paper Series, No. 06-2, February 2006.

[3] Data from the *2007 Investment Company Factbook*.

[4] Patro, Dilip, "International Mutual Fund Flows." Rutgers Business School, January 2005. Paper. Available at http://www.fma.org/Chicago/Papers/imf-flows.pdf

[5] Bertaut, Carol, and Ralph Tryon, "Monthly Estimates of U.S. Cross-Border Securities Positions," Federal Reserve Board of Governors, International Finance Discussion Papers, Number 910, November 2007.

CHAPTER 11

Sector Performance
Is King*

Narrow down your investment choices by beginning with sector selections.

A key premise of this book is the idea that by applying the principles of top-down investing, an investor can formulate a portfolio strategy whereby assets are selected primarily on the basis of broad concepts, with the specific choices being picked secondarily. In this chapter we analyze this premise specifically with respect to the importance of selecting stock sectors over specific stocks. We look at some of representative studies that have examined this idea and dig a little deeper to help you to gain a better understanding of how best to choose the optimal asset allocation, specifically with respect to choosing a sector that fits your overall portfolio strategy. We strive to convince you further that beginning the investment decision-making process with an idea or a concept is an extraordinarily appealing and effective way to invest.

CHOOSE THE BEST SECTORS TO OPTIMIZE
YOUR ASSET ALLOCATION

The goal of asset allocation is to find the optimal mix of assets from asset classes such as stocks, bonds, real estate, currencies, commodities, and so forth and allocating a portfolio's capital

---

*This chapter was contributed by Dan Greenhaus, an analyst and trader in the Equity Strategy Group at Miller Tabak + Co. Dan previously worked for Credit Suisse First Boston in its high-yield research department. Mr. Greenhaus obtained his MBA from Baruch College in 2006 and is currently a CFA candidate.

across these asset classes. Top-down investing takes this idea and drills deeper in each of the asset classes. For example, in the corporate bond market, in a weak economic climate, by using top-down principles, an investor would choose to not only allocate money previously allocated to corporate bonds into cash instead, but also within the corporate bond market the investor would choose to move up the credit quality scale by selecting higher-quality bonds.

For equities, which are the focus of this chapter, top-down investors look at the world from afar, investing in broad themes, beginning with concepts first and looking at numbers and companies second. The goal is to identify an industry or a sector that looks likely to outperform others because of the concepts in focus, and then invest in the sectors by some means, whether it is an exchange-traded fund (ETF) or a specific company stock. This is in contrast to more traditional styles of investing, particularly bottom-up investing, where the jumping-off point is a specific company, followed by further analysis of the company's balance sheet, cash flow statements, financial statements, and lots of other fun stuff.

To begin the process of selecting stock sectors, we must first examine how to approach investments from a top-down vantage point. Let's use the price of oil as an example. At the outset, one can intuitively assume that the price of oil has an effect on the earnings of oil companies, as well as consumer spending. We saw this in 2007 when the soaring price of gasoline climbed rapidly relative to income growth. This hurt the earnings performance of retail companies as well as retail share prices. Taking this a step further, one can intuitively assume that the price of oil affects the enthusiasm for investing in alternative energy, as well as sentiment toward agricultural products affected by demand for ethanol, and so on and so forth. There is much more drilling down that one can do, but our point is clear: from a top-down influence, numerous sector choices develop, along with ideas about how to allocate assets. Keep in mind that one can further assume that many of the companies within the sectors mentioned are to one degree or another exposed to many other top-down influences, which makes it important to determine which of the influences will win out in order to plan accordingly.

EMPIRICAL STUDIES ON ASSET ALLOCATION

In their oft-cited 1986 study titled "Determinants of Portfolio Performance,"[1] Brinson, Hood, and Beebower examined over 90 pension plans from 1974–1983 and determined that approximately 93.6 percent of the total variation of quarterly returns could be explained by a portfolio's asset allocation policy. The study's subsequent 1991 update, using later time frames, showed that 91.5 percent of the variation of quarterly returns could be explained by asset allocation. Whichever numbers you choose, they send the same resounding message, with the researchers demonstrating that the vast majority of gains earned by investment in a particular asset are determined more by the asset classes chosen than by any other factor.

Of course, this landmark study is not without its critics. Some contend that the use of original study's use of *r* squared in the original study[2] puts the focus on volatility in the short term rather than longer-term returns.[3] Others, such as William Jahnke, assert that the study is flawed, noting that Brinson, Hood, and Beebower, "define "variation" as the *variance* of quarterly returns. In fact, the most appropriate measure is *the standard deviation* of quarterly returns, which operates in the same units of measurement as return. That is why portfolio risk is reported in terms of standard deviation, not variance." Jahnke's main contention with the Beebower study is that researchers "focus on explaining portfolio volatility rather than portfolio returns." Even so, one of Jahnke's studies found that "when using the more appropriate standard deviation, asset allocation policy explains only 79 percent of the variation of quarterly returns."[4] Whatever the level—whether 79 percent, 91.5 percent, or 93.6 percent—and irrespective of an investor's understanding of the intricacies of the academic studies on asset allocation, the empirical evidence is in: an investor's asset allocation policy goes a long way toward explaining portfolio returns. Extrapolating from these studies, minus the mumbo jumbo statistical analyses of course, we can apply the findings to stock investing by focusing on picking the best possible sectors for a portfolio. In conjunction with timely entry points, which can often be determined by an assessment of the macroeconomic climate, investors can therefore maximize their returns not necessarily by choosing the best companies, but by choosing the best sectors of the broader market. This is a core principle of top-down investing, of course. Many investors have yet to catch onto this idea, which is one that not only maximizes one's return, but is also easy to understand and apply.

A GOLDEN EXAMPLE OF THE IMPORTANCE OF SECTORS

We show earlier how from a simple variable such as the price of oil an investor could easily conjure up a number of ideas about which sectors to choose when allocating capital in a portfolio. Another easy-to-understand example can be taken from the events of 2007 when the Federal Reserve began cutting interest rates in response slowing economic growth and the impact of the subprime mortgage crisis. There were many people in late 2007 and early 2008 who speculated that the Fed's rate cuts would have its traditional effect on the U.S. dollar and cause it to weaken, hence pushing up the price of gold in its usual way. Taking this a step further, these investors reasoned that if gold were to rally, so would shares in gold-producing companies. A simple premise behind the expectation for higher gold prices was that gold would be viewed in its historical context as a store of value and hence be favored as a hedge against inflation, which would be expected to accelerate as a result of the Fed's actions. As simple as this may sound, top-down investing naturally leads to such conclusions. In our example, should investors choose to drill down even further, they could either identify a gold-mining company in which they'd like to invest, or perhaps purchase an ETF that is directly linked to the price of gold. Alternatively, investors could simply go out into the marketplace and buy gold coins! In each situation, equity investors begin their investing approach with the thesis that gold stands to benefit without knowing what specific company or other investment they would invest in.

INSULATING YOUR PORTFOLIO AGAINST RISK THROUGH SECTOR SELECTION

Despite what many brokerage firms and investment banks will tell you, one thing I think we can all agree on is that most individual investors do not have the time, nor the tools to properly educate themselves on all of the intricacies of the marketplace, particularly the specifics of individual companies and their balance sheets. If "Wall Street's finest"—the name applied to Wall Street analysts following the bursting of the financial bubble of the late 1990s because of their inability to foresee it—could not have uncovered the shenanigans associated with Enron's balance sheet, can we really expect just anyone on the street to do so? Of course we cannot. More importantly, as individual investors many of us are not trained to do so nor do we have the time to learn how. Dissecting balance sheets and determining the sustainability of operating cash flow is a laborious, time-consuming process best left to those more familiar with it. Particularly with the explosion of ETFs, investors now have many more choices of securities to choose from that enable them to avoid many of the pitfalls associated with individual stock evaluation and stock picking.

Assessing Risk

Before turning toward an examination of some of the lessons of the bursting of the financial bubble in 2000, let's first look at the academic backdrop, beginning with a brief discussion of risk.

A stock's share price volatility is measured by its *beta*. The market as a whole has a beta of 1; a beta over 1 is applied to stocks that are relatively riskier than the overall market; betas under 1 are applied to stocks that are relatively less risky than the overall market. Essentially, beta measures the amount an individual stock will move in relation to a benchmark. For example, if the benchmark S&P 500 index is up or down by 1 percent, a stock with a beta of 1.5 can be expected to move 50 percent more than the benchmark. This is not an absolute relationship of course, but being aware of a stock's beta is an important step in understanding its relative risk and how investing in sectors can partially insulate investors from risk.

When investing in a single stock, an investor is exposed to the entire variability of that stock over the holding period and thus the stock's individual risk profile. Without getting very deep into modern portfolio theory, adding even one additional stock constitutes a *portfolio*, and with that, a "portfolio beta." The portfolio beta is simply the average of the individual betas in the portfolio, adjusted for the weightings of the companies within the portfolio. For example, in a portfolio holding 100 shares of company A with a beta of 1.5, and 100 shares of company B with a beta of 0.5, the portfolio's beta is 1, the same as the broad market (i.e., the S&P 500).

When investors buy stock, they obviously take a gamble on the company's financial future. In exchange for the theoretical possibility of unlimited gains (there is no ceiling on a stock price), investors accept the fact that their investment might be entirely lost. In light of this risk, investors can add another stock to their portfolio to reduce the risk that they could lose all their capital. Obviously the probability of going broke from selecting two companies in a portfolio that eventually go belly up are lower than the odds of it happening when only one company is in a portfolio.

Perhaps you are now asking what this discussion of betas and such has to do with sector investing. Well, if we take the discussion further to include a broad range of stocks—a sector of stocks, for example—we can infer that the broad range of stocks is going to have a beta that is less than many of the individual stocks that make up that sector, and thus investing in that sector rather than one individual company would constitute a strategy that is inherently less risky. Figure 11.1 illustrates an example of how diversification through sectors can protect investors.

As Figure 11.1 shows, the technology sector of the S&P 500 declined by over 50 percent while the energy sector was essentially flat. During the same period, there were of course a number of

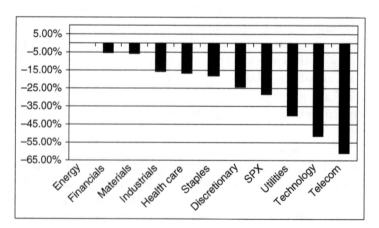

Figure 11.1 Sector returns, 1999–2002.

Sources: Miller Tabak + Co., LLC; Bloomberg.

individual stocks that fell substantially, including Enron Corp. and Sun Microsystems Inc., which declined by 100 percent and 95 percent from their highs, respectively. Choosing to invest in either Enron or Sun Microsystems, which was not a ridiculous notion not too long ago as both were highly respected companies prior to 2000, would have yielded a much greater loss than if one had been invested in the sectors that drew them to the individual names in the technology and energy sector. Obviously, this example is a bit extreme, but it is certainly illustrative. The individual risk profiles for the two companies were, or became, higher than the benchmark risk.

Continuing with our very brief foray into modern portfolio theory, while ignoring all the pesky formulas, one can further reduce risk by investing in sectors that are affected inversely by the same external factor. For example, as oil prices move higher, shares in energy companies typically gain. Conversely, shares in consumer discretionary companies are often hurt when energy prices rise because consumers tend to spend fewer dollars on "discretionary" items—those they have control over—when they are paying more for energy. When the price of oil surged in 2007 and breached $140 per barrel in the summer of 2008, this pattern would again assert itself both in the real economy and in the financial markets. One need only look at the results of any of the major consumer confidence surveys released in 2008 to see that consumers were in no mood to engage in big-ticket purchases. The weak level of automobile sales in 2008 provides proof, and the weakness undoubtedly was due in no small part to the rise in energy prices. Crafting an asset allocation that considers such factors and their wide-ranging impact—both the good and the bad—insulates investors from risk and boosts returns.

GAINING CYCLICAL EXPOSURE THROUGH SECTOR INVESTING

Money managers are often (at least they should be) in tune with the business cycle and where the economy is within the cycle. Understanding the business cycle and the sectors of the economy that traditionally perform better or worse during its various stages is a very important part of top-down investing. Table 11.1 illustrates the various stages that occur in a normal business cycle, along with many of the industries that tend to fair well at these various stages.

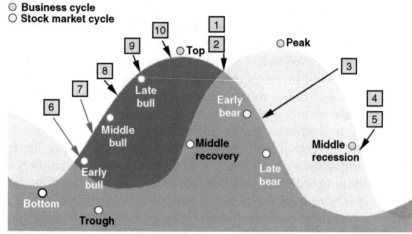

1. Consumer noncyclicals (e.g., food, drugs, cosmetics)
2. Health care
3. Utilities
4. Consumer cyclicals (e.g., autos, housing)
5. Financials
6. Transportation
7. Technology
8. Capital goods
9. Basic Industry (e.g., aluminum, chemicals, paper, steel)
10. Energy

Figure 11.2 The business cycle and the stock market cycle.

Source: Peter Navarro, *If It's Raining in Brazil, This Must Be Starbucks*, McGraw-Hill, 2002.

As Figure 11.2 illustrates, the typical business cycle moves through four phases: expansion, peak, contraction, and trough (or trough, middle recovery, and middle recession as indicated in the figure). While the names and labels for these various stages may vary, the ideas behind them are the same, and an investor's approach to investing should be the same for each phase regardless of its designation. Referring back to the figure, we see, for example, that consumer cyclical companies tend to fair well early in the business cycle, as shown by box number four, the point just after the middle of recession has passed. Cyclical industries are those that tend to move in tandem with the business cycle. Examples include the housing, automotive, and retail industries. Companies in these industries traditionally do well as the economy expands. Conversely, the consumer staples sector, which includes companies such as Hershey Co., Campbell Soup, Procter & Gamble, and

Coca-Cola, tends to outperform in a slower growth environment, as consumers are less likely to alter their spending patterns on items they consider necessary. Shares in these industries tend to perform better than shares in cyclical industries after the peak of the business cycle has been reached.

History has shown that using the business-cycle approach as a means of selecting investments can play an important role in the investment decision-making process. By using this approach, an investor can identify capital gains opportunities and find sectors that can help insulate a portfolio against the powerful cyclical forces that tend to affect both the real economy and stock prices. For example, consider the impact of economic recession on the housing sector. The events of 2007 are illustrative in this regard, as anything and everything housing was affected. Conversely, companies with exposure to the resilient global economy fared better, as did companies in both the consumer staples and health-care sectors. With the advent of ETFs, such diversification tactics have broadened to include a much wider variety of industries and asset classes, including international markets, for example.

GAINING DIVERSIFICATION BENEFITS BY INVESTING IN SECTORS ABROAD

As we've noted, there are many more opportunities these days to achieve diversification by investing abroad, and investors are taking advantage of this in large numbers, as evidenced by flows into international mutual funds and ETFs, as well as by the large amount of cross-border capital flows. These forays enable investors to diversify into sectors that in today's integrated global economy can be optimized only by gaining sector exposure on an international scale. For example, gaining exposure to the automobile sector would be optimized by investing not only in North America, but also abroad, in Europe, for example.

One word that we hear quite a bit about these days is *globalization*, which we discuss in depth in Chapter 3. Globalization is a term often used to describe today's more integrated world, particularly with respect to economic activity, financial markets, and the spread of market capitalism. The impact of globalization and its benefits to global trade are evident in economic data for the United States, which account for about a fifth of global economic activity.

For example, it is notable that the United States exported $144 bil-
lion of goods and services in December 2007, a $63 billion increase
compared to five years earlier and a massive tally on a 12-month
basis. One implication of this is that U.S. residents can gain exposure to the global economy simply by investing in companies in sectors that are benefiting from the export boom.

Another implication of the increase in global trade is the disproportionate number of benefits occurring in some countries.
China stands out. For example, in 2007, the United States imported
approximately $320 billion of goods from China, up sharply from
the $120 billion of goods the United States bought from China five
years earlier.[5] China's economy grew sharply during the period,
expanding at a double-digit pace. Not surprisingly, China's stock
market soared, increasing several times in value.

Investors wanting exposure to China's growing economic
prominence can invest in the iShares FTSE/Xinhua China 25 index
fund, a widely traded product offered by iShares, which gears its
index to achieve results that correspond generally to the price and
yield performance (before fees and expenses) of the FTSE/Xinhua
China 25 index. Figure 11.3 shows the positive correlation that
exists between the iShares FTST/Xinhua China 25 index fund and
the Shanghai composite. Global ETFs such as the China 25 index
funds have made it increasingly easy for investors to take positions

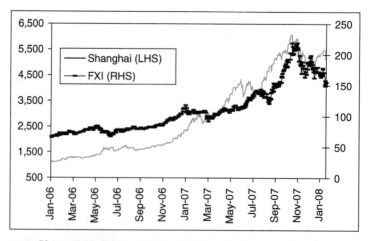

Figure 11.3 China ETF (FXI) versus the Shanghai composite.

Source: Bloomberg

with an investment thesis that begins with an idea and then works its way down to individual sectors and companies. It is the exposure to sectors on a global scale that is one of the more exciting in today's environment, as the only way to efficiently achieve sector exposures in the past was to invest in domestic sectors.

THE BOTTOM LINE

Sector investing provides an additional means for investors to allocate their capital in ways that are both effective and a small burden on their time. Who, after all, wants to sift through company balance sheets on an ongoing basis when empirical evidence suggests that the proper selection of sectors is a better route to choosing the best types of companies and industries to invest in? Managing one's personal life is challenging enough. Sector investing is ideal for investors who lack financial expertise, as it is an approach that depends more on concepts than on the minutia associated with bottom-up investing. Investors can thus leave the number crunching to those with specialized knowledge of corporate accounting and industry dynamics. While there is perhaps no substitute for the advice and input of professional money managers, investing from the top down can help empower investors to make their own choices using sector selections as a basis. The proliferation of mutual funds and ETFs certainly gives investors far more opportunities to invest this way than was the case just a few years ago.

The View from the Top Down: Three Musts for the Macro Maven

You will miss enormous opportunities if you fail to make changes to your investment portfolio during the various points along the business cycle. "Letting it ride" is a copout and far too old-fashioned for today's times.

1. *Choose sectors first and then stocks within the sectors.* Empirical studies and a casual observation of the performance of the major sectors of the stock market strongly support the idea that the performance of a particular stock depends significantly on the performance of the sector it is in.

2. *Insulate your portfolio by focusing on how sectors perform at different points in the economic cycle.* It is a simple fact that a sector's performance both in the real economy and in the financial markets is materially affected by the economic cycle. It makes sense, then, to select sectors accordingly to fit with where the economy is along the economic cycle.

3. *Augment the diversification benefits of sector investing by looking abroad.* An enormous opportunity has recently developed to add additional diversification benefits to a portfolio by broadening a portfolio's sector selections to include investments in similar sectors abroad. It is also a means of hedging against major influences such as inflation (by investing in oil interests abroad, for example).

THE GOLDEN COMPASSES: THE TOP TOP-DOWN INDICATORS

• *The business cycle.* Where an economy is along the business cycle can materially affect a wide variety of asset prices, and there is plenty of historical evidence to prove it. Even though the so-called "great moderation" has smoothed the business cycle, the human proclivity to shift from fear to greed and back again and the general tendency toward excesses will keep the business cycle rolling along for as far as the eye can see.

Notes

[1] Brinson, Gary P., L. Randolph Hood, and Gilbert L. Beebower, "Determinants of Portfolio Performance," *The Financial Analysts Journal,* July-August 1986.

[2] R-squared is a tool used in regression analysis that helps explain how well a regression line approximates its data points.

[3] Surz, Ronald L., Dale Stevens, and Mark Wimer, "Investment Policy Explains All," *Journal of Performance Measurement,* Summer 1999.

[4] Jahnke, William, "The Asset Allocation Hoax," *Journal of Financial Planning,* February 1997.

[5] U.S. Census Bureau.

CHAPTER 12

Market Sentiment Is a Top-Down Affair

You make your fortunes when the market is down.

Top-down investors have a major advantage over other investors when it comes to maximizing their portfolio returns because they pay closer attention to market sentiment, which is a top-down affair. Tracking market sentiment is one of the most reliable ways to forecast price changes in stocks, bonds, commodities, tulips—you name it. Extreme bullishness and bearishness have foretold key turning points in asset prices literally for centuries. Market history is strewn with periods in which attention to market sentiment proved to be wise. You need look no further than the bursting of the housing bubble of the early 2000s and the financial bubble of the late 1990s for proof.

In this chapter we examine some of the best top-down tools for tracking market sentiment and at what strategies work best when market sentiment reaches extremes, looking beyond pure directional bets toward strategies that you can adopt within asset classes.

WHAT STOCKS ARE AFFECTED MOST BY EXTREME MARKET SENTIMENT

Market prices will occasionally deviate from fair market value prices because speculators tend to be more aggressive than buy-and-hold investors when setting market prices. Buy-and-hold investors tend to be a lot less forceful about bringing prices closer to where fundamentals suggest they should be. The types of assets

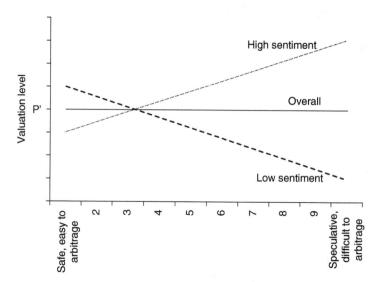

Figure 12.1 Cross-sectional effects of investor sentiment. Stocks that are speculative and difficult to value and arbitrage will have higher relative valuations when sentiment is high.

Source: Malcom Baker of Harvard Business School and NBER, and Jeffrey Wurgler of New York University's Stern School of Business. "Investor Sentiment and the Cross-Section of Stock Returns," *Negotiations, Organizations and Markets Research Papers, Number 03-53*, November 2003.

most prone to speculation include those whose valuations are open to a greater amount of subjectivity than other assets. For example, when sentiment appears to be high, stocks that are likely to be relatively attractive to optimists and speculators and at the same time unattractive candidates for arbitrage—young stocks, small stocks, unprofitable stocks, nondividend-paying stocks, high-volatility stocks, extreme-growth stocks, and distressed stocks—experience low future returns relative to other stocks.[1] In contrast, stocks of well-established firms with lengthy track record of publicly releasing their earnings are likely to be less prone to impact from speculators. This tendency is illustrated in Figure 12.1.

A FEW BASICS ON MARKET SENTIMENT

It is easy to understand why extremes in investor sentiment create excellent opportunities to place bets on reversals in prices. Basically, if the preponderance of investors is either very bullish or very bearish, market prices are less likely to continue moving in the direction they are currently moving because they already reflect underlying fundamentals. For example, if the stock market moves continuously lower in anticipation of economic recession, then when data confirm recession, there is no new reason to push prices still lower unless the recession is deeper than what the market is priced for. This helps to explain why the stock market tends to reverse price declines that occur ahead of economic recessions— roughly in the middle of them. Savvy investors know to adjust their investment strategies when investor sentiment reaches an extreme.

I note in Chapter 9 the idea research indicating that human beings tend to engage in selective reasoning when confronted with a set of facts that conflict with their personal views and how the portion of the brain involved in reasoning is inactive during such times. It is obviously human nature to do this, as we have seen for centuries, with investors letting their emotions get the better of them. A classic example of this was the great tulip mania that occurred in Holland in 1634–1637. During that time, horticultural experiments created new exotic tulips that common people in Holland sought both for their beauty and their status. Eventually, these motives gave way to immense speculative fervor. At the height of the mania, tulip bulbs were trading for valuable amounts of land, livestock, food, and much more. In 1635, a sale of 40 bulbs was recorded for 100,000 Dutch florins, which was much more than the 150 florins that the Dutch people were earning on average in a year. Single bulbs such as the Viseroij (Figure 12.2) sold for between 3,000 and 4,200 florins, an amount equal to 15 to 20 times a year's salary for school craftsman.[2]

The fact that in today's more sophisticated era bubbles continue to occur clearly illustrates the powerful role that human nature has on market prices. This happens because people put excessive weight on their most recent experiences and irrationally extrapolate from recent price trends what they think will happen to prices in the future. The tendency of markets to reach extreme valuations will exist as long as humans are making the investment decisions. It's human nature for investors to fall victim to fear and greed and for emotions to therefore play an important role in the behavior of the markets. It would be extremely naïve to think that this will end anytime soon.

Figure 12.2 Viseroij: The $2 million tulip; priced during tulip mania in 1637.
Source: The Special Collections of Wageningen UR Library adapted from the tulip book of P. Cos, 1637.

Bottom-up investors tend to ignore the powerful influence of market sentiment, but I can't imagine investing without assessing it. After all, a forecast on the direction of market prices is essentially a forecast on the behavior of people. It is therefore crucial to incorporate the human element into the formulation of investment strategies. You will spot more risks and opportunities in the process. The advantage of using the top-down approach over the bottom-up approach is that it captures big, influential changes in market sentiment, including bubbles, abrupt market moves, and patterns that repeat with great frequency. Unlike the bottom-up approach, tracking market sentiment from the top down is much simpler and intuitive.

Key Gauges of Stock Market Sentiment

There are many ways to track market sentiment, but I have found that it is best to look at the indicators collectively rather than in isolation, although now and then individual gauges make a strong case, too. A few of the most widely followed top-down gauges of stock market sentiment include:

- Mutual fund flows
- Investor surveys
- Surveys of market newsletters (Investors Intelligence, for example)
- Trading volume
- Initial public offerings
- Positions held by noncommercial futures traders
- Implied volatility on options
- Equity issuance as a percentage of total equity and debt issues by all corporations
- Trading by corporate insiders
- Investor moods shaped by events and seasonal tendencies

Key Gauges of Bond Market Sentiment

The 2008 credit crisis has proven that market sentiment reaches extremes in the credit market too. Investors were practically throwing their money at the credit markets, into credits thought to be AAA-rated when in fact they were nothing of the kind. The problem was that no one thought to look under the hood; they had selective reasoning. Luckily, spotting the kinds of excesses experienced recently will be easier in the time ahead, because investors have basically closed the door on anything but a sure thing. For example, the market for subprime mortgages has evaporated, which will improve the crop of mortgage securities as time goes on. Moreover, corporate credits with questionable assets and cash flows have also been shut out. Excess pessimism is likely to be the next extreme in the credit markets, which will become obvious in the yields on corporate, agency, and mortgage securities relative to Treasuries. What is most likely to happen is what has happened many times before: the market will price itself for a much higher default rate than actually occurs, particularly for subprime mortgages. The signal to buy in such circumstances is when pessimism on the economy is very high and credit spreads stop responding to bad news.

Although an efficient market, the Treasury market is often affected by excessively bullish and bearish sentiment. The difference with Treasuries, though, is that the excesses are often a reflection of excesses in other markets, since Treasuries are bought and sold in response to events in other asset classes. A benefit of tracking sentiment in Treasuries is that Treasuries encapsulate sentiment on so many fronts, which means that you can obtain a very broad synopsis of investor sentiment in general just by tracking Treasuries, particularly because Treasuries trade so efficiently compared to other asset classes. The Treasury market is the most liquid market in the world, trading $650 billion on a daily basis in March 2008.[3] The idea is that because the Treasury market tends to be influenced strongly by expectations in the economy and from other macro factors, when sentiment in the Treasury market reaches an extreme, that extreme is likely to reflect extremes in other markets, too.

A few of the best ways that I have found to track sentiment in the Treasury market include:

1. The yield spread between two-year Treasury notes and the federal funds rate
2. Surveys of aggregate portfolio duration levels
3. Put/call ratios on Treasury note futures
4. The Commodity Futures Trading Commission's (CFTC) commitments of traders report

Let's take a quick look at each of these.

1. *Yield spread between two-year Treasury notes and fed funds.*
   Over the past 20 years, the yield on two-year Treasury
   notes has closely tracked the federal funds rate, falling
   below the funds rate on only five occasions, each time
   ahead of interest-rate cuts by the Federal Reserve. The close
   relationship between the two-year note and the fed funds
   rate is why the two-year is such a good gauge of sentiment.
   What you want to look for here are signs that sentiment
   toward the Fed might be excessive relative to your own
   expectations (assuming you are thinking rationally while
   the market is going batty). Extreme expectations about Fed
   rate actions are an excellent gauge of sentiment on issues
   plaguing the markets. On the flip side, when two-year
   notes trade well above the funds rate, by showing high
   levels of anxieties about Fed rate hikes, two-year notes can
   signal excessive optimism on the economy. No other
   maturity on the yield curve has proven to be as reliable as
   the two-year, largely because of its proximity to the fed
   funds rate.
2. *Surveys of aggregate duration levels.* Okay, bear with me on
   this. Bond geeks know what I mean. For the rest of you,
   suffice it to say that the *duration* on a bond or portfolio
   essentially gauges its maturity length. Aggregate duration
   surveys such as the weekly survey conducted by Stone &
   McCarthy, a top economic research firm whose survey I
   have found to be the most reliable, capture the average
   duration level among the portfolio managers surveyed.
   What you want to look for is the degree to which fixed-
   income portfolio managers are either long or short relative
   to their benchmark index, which is often the Lehman
   index. For example, a reading of 98 percent would indicate
   that on average, portfolios had duration levels that were 98
   percent of their benchmark indexes, which would make
   them short relative to their benchmarks. Over time, I have
   found that portfolio durations tend to fluctuate in a range
   of between 96 and 104 percent, with movements outside of
   that range very extreme. Figure 12.3 illustrates the long-
   term pattern.

3. *Put/call ratios on Treasury note futures.* This is a popular gauge also used in the stock market. It is simply a measure of daily trading volume in put options compared with the daily trading volume in call options. Since puts are a bearish bet on the future direction of Treasury prices and calls are a bullish bet, extreme volume in either one is a sign of excess sentiment. Put volume tends to exceed call volume for a variety of reasons, meaning that the put/call ratio tends to be above 1.0. Extremes tend to begin at readings of 0.75 and 1.75 for options on 10-year Treasury note futures. The average reading was 1.36 in the three years ended June 2008.

4. *The CFTC's commitments of traders report.* Data within the CFTC's weekly commitments of traders report, which is released every Friday afternoon at about 3:30 p.m. ET, yield extremely powerful clues about the amount of speculation that resides in all U.S. futures, encompassing all the major asset classes, including Treasuries. The CFTC separates the holders of futures into two groups: commercial traders and noncommercial traders. Commercial traders are known as "smart money," the true end users of the contracts. Market tops and bottoms frequently have been foreshadowed by extreme positions taken by noncommercial traders, who trade with a herd mentality and are apt to change their positions relatively more frequently than commercial traders.

Using Futures to Gather Market Intelligence

The futures market contains an abundance of information on market sentiment. There are four main indicators of market sentiment that can be found in the futures market, the last two of which we have already touched upon:

- Open interest
- Futures trading volume
- Options on futures trading volume
- The Commodity Futures Trading Commission's commitments of traders report

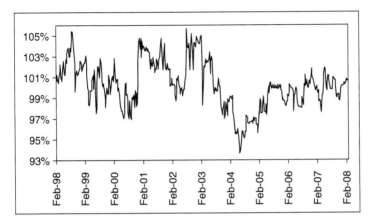

Figure 12.3 Aggregate duration of bond portfolio managers (expressed as percent of target duration).
Source: Stone & McCarthy Research Associates.

Open interest is a measure of the total number of futures positions that remain open, or outstanding, at a specific time. For each open contract there's a long position and a short position held by two different parties. Open interest is used as a way of gauging the quality of a move in the market by comparing the daily changes in open interest that occur for a specific futures contract with the direction of its price changes. In general, when open interest increases on a day when prices rally, this is seen as indicating that new long positions were behind the rally, not short covering, or the closing of short positions. It is looked at as a sign that market participants are confident that prices will continue to rise. Conversely, when open interest falls when prices are rising, this is seen as a sign that the gains are occurring from short covering, meaning that the rally is less likely to be sustained. See Table 12.1 for a useful reference on the conventional interpretation of changes in open interest.

Futures Trading Volume

Trading volume is an important gauge in most asset classes. It is used as a way of judging the degree of participation in a price trend. A price move occurring on strong volume helps validate the move and suggests that it probably will continue, but a price move that

T A B L E   12.1

Interpretation of Changes in Open Interest

Price Direction	Open Interest Change	Interpretation	Reason
Rising prices	Increasing	Bullish	Pattern suggests new longs entered the market
Rising prices	Decreasing	Bearish	Pattern suggests rally due to short covering rather than new long positions
Falling prices	Increasing	Bearish	Pattern suggests new short positions established
Falling prices	Decreasing	Bullish	Pattern suggests selloff due to long liquidations that eventually will be exhausted

occurs on light volume suggests that there is very little sponsorship for the price move and that it will therefore be difficult to sustain. It is especially important to track volume when a price trend is well established. For example, diminishing volume could be a red flag for a reversal of a particular trend.

GAMING SENTIMENT TO BEAT, BUY, AND HOLD

Aggressive investors should consider using market-timing tools such as market sentiment in place of buy-and-hold strategies. Empirical evidence on the benefits of using market-timing tools, which include indirect measures of market sentiment such as price-to-earnings ratios and dividend yields, and direct measures such as bullish sentiment indexes, are contained in a study by Fisher and Statman.[4] In their intriguing study, the researchers compared historical returns that would have been achieved using various trading rules for each of the sentiment indicators as compared to the returns achieved using the buy-and-hold approach. For example, using the price-to-earnings ratio (P/E), one rule was to switch from Treasury bills (T-bills) to stocks when the P/E fell below its median, and then back into T-bills when the P/E moved above its median. Applying this rule resulted in the accumulation of $36.45 for each dollar invested beginning in 1964 to the end of 2002 compared to $43.88 for the buy-and-hold approach. Interestingly, the result was even better for the market-timing rule that dictated a switch from T-bills to stocks whenever the Investors Intelligence bullish sentiment index moved below its median, and then back into T-bills when the index moved above its median. The accumulation of $1 beginning in 1964 to the end of 2002 was $48.29 using this rule. The researchers emphasize, however, that the use of market sentiment for market timing requires predictions of future sentiment, which is difficult to predict.

Numerous other studies support the thesis that extreme investor sentiment significantly affects market prices and that recognition of this impact can be used as a means of forecasting the future behavior of market prices. One of these is a study by Brown and Cliff, which found robust evidence of the linkage between extreme market sentiment and the ability to predict future returns, concluding that a direct survey measure of market sentiment predicts market returns over the next one to three years.[5] Despite these and other affirmations, there remain doubters, especially those who embrace the efficient market hypothesis (EMH), which states that tradable asset prices can't be predicted because they already contain all known information and as such investors cannot consistently outperform the market using information the market already knows. The EMH, which was developed by respected academic Eugene Fama of the University of Chicago Graduate School of Business in the early 1960s, was reinforced by the random walk hypothesis forwarded by Burton Malkiel in his 1973 book, *A Random Walk Down Wall Street*.

FEAR AND GREED WILL NEVER END; RISE ABOVE IT

The decision about how to use information gleaned from sentiment indicators is one that every investor must consider on his or her own, but I suggest that at the very minimum sentiment indicators be used as a means of deciding upon the best possible entry and exit points for your portfolio positions and as an important element to consider when deciding upon whether to hedge your portfolio. I strongly believe that market sentiment is a top-down tool worth utilizing given the long history on the impact the human element has

had on markets of all kinds, even tulips. Rare will it be that fear and
greed are suppressed as influences in the market dynamic, and in
light of this and the many tools available to gauge market sentiment,
there is no reason why you can't pluck yourself away from the camp
of unreasonable humans to be the investing machine you want to be.

The View from the Top-Down: Three Musts for the Macro Maven

From tulips to dot.com stocks to home prices, it is clear that no
amount of technological advances can stop investor sentiment
from moving to extremes.

1. *Be aware of the types of stocks most prone to be affected by
   extreme market sentiment.* Stocks that are most prone to
   speculation and the impact of extreme market sentiment
   include those whose valuations are open to a greater
   amount of subjectivity than other stocks. In particular,
   these include young stocks, small stocks, unprofitable
   stocks, nondividend-paying stocks, high-volatility stocks,
   extreme-growth stocks, and distressed stocks. Avoid them
   when sentiment is unusually bullish, and stick with
   companies whose lengthier track records make them
   unattractive to speculators.

2. *Always say "dot-com bubble" and "tulip bubble" in the same
   breath.* It is worth remembering for all time the traps that
   investors inevitably find themselves in as a result of the
   human condition. While bubbles are not an everyday affair,
   many ups and downs in the markets will reflect the human
   condition enough for you to take advantage of them.

3. *Seek out a wide variety of sentiment gauges.* Studies differ on
   the effectiveness of adapting rule-based trading strategies
   that dictate trading in and out of assets when investor
   sentiment reaches certain levels. There nonetheless is
   significant empirical backing to the idea that the use of
   rule-based strategies that depend on market sentiment
   can produce higher returns than the buy-and-hold
   approach. Therefore, track as many gauges as possible to
   most accurately gauge whether excesses exist and act
   upon these gauges accordingly.

THE GOLDEN COMPASSES: THE TOP TOP-DOWN INDICATORS

- *Two-year Treasuries to fed funds; market sentiment.* In Chapter 6 we discuss the usefulness of the two-year Treasury as a gauge on Fed expectations. In this chapter we take a slightly different approach, showing the two-year's ability to capture sentiment on a variety of fronts among investors in many asset classes.
- *Market sentiment.* Well, we talk about this all chapter, so there is not much more to add except to emphasize again the power of this golden compass. We have seen in our investing lifetime a couple of large bubbles, the equity market bubble of the late 1990s and the housing and credit bubbles of the early 2000s. Situations like these where making money seems easy obviously should be avoided. Commodities are beginning to behave in this way.

Notes

[1] Baker, Malcolm, and Jeffrey Wurgler, "Investor Sentiment and the Cross-Section of Stock Returns," Negotiations, Organizations and Markets Research Papers, Number 03-53, November 2003.

[2] Numerous publications make references to data such as these. See articles on "tulip mania" found at www.wikipedia.org, for example.

[3] Federal Reserve Bank of New York Web site.

[4] Fisher, Kenneth, and Meir Statman, "Market Timing in Regressions and Reality." *The Journal of Financial Research*, vol. XXIX, no. 3, Fall 2006, pp. 293–304.

[5] Brown, Gregory, and Michael Cliff, "Investor Sentiment and Asset Valuation," *Journal of Business* 78, pp. 405–440, 2005.

CHAPTER 13

A Golden Age for Macroeconomics Has Arrived

Each age brings its own opportunities; this one is magnificent.

In January 2008, the inflation rate in Zimbabwe surpassed an astronomic 100,000 percent compared to a year earlier, according to Zimbabwe's state central statistical office. No, this is not a misprint—the rate was one hundred thousand percent! Zimbabwe's hyperinflation, which has existed since the beginning of the 2000s, harkens back to an era now past. At the root of Zimbabwe's problems lie policies that have been discredited since the great inflation of the 1970s. It was an era shaped by Keynesian economic policies, which were cheered by influential economists such as John Kenneth Galbraith, who supported policies that became anathema to both policymakers and to the private sector beginning particularly when Ronald Reagan became president of the United States in 1982. Since that time, the global economy has moved increasingly toward a market-based system overseen but left largely to the devices of capitalists. What has emerged is nothing short of an economic renaissance that has restored the world's economic system to the golden eras that led to the economic and innovative miracles of the late nineteenth and early twentieth centuries, as well as the lengthy periods of economic expansion seen throughout history, most recently from the mid-1940s until the late 1960s. Investors, rejoice! The era promises abundant investment opportunities, with more predictable outcomes.

MACROECONOMIC POLICY HAS
BEEN REAPPRAISED

Zimbabwe's present difficulties have been brought about by old-school economic policies that are the antithesis of what is at the root of the global resurgence in economic activity. The Zimbabwe government seized control of private, commercial farms in 2000, spurring violence and putting control of commercial decisions into the hands of government. This caused a sharp outflow of investment from the country, driving up Zimbabwe's current account deficit and stripping the country of its capital. Naturally, Zimbabwe's budget deficit soared, and the country's central bank monetized the deficit—repeatedly—spurring hyperinflation. Meanwhile, the rest of the world has since the 1980s and particularly over the past decade reappraised its economic policies, with economic activity becoming vibrant thanks to the following:

- Promarket policies
- Smaller government
- Lower tax rates
- Reduced regulations
- Reduced welfare states
- More flexible labor markets and increased "creative destruction," the process of new industries taking the place of dying ones.
- Reduced trade barriers
- Adherence to capital standards agreed to under Basel I and Basel II, the frameworks that guide the world's banking system.
- Increased coordination among the world's central banks
- More integrated and transparent financial markets
- Increased cross-border capital flows
- Increased legal protection for property owners
- The Internet
- More sophisticated and efficient transportation systems
- Vastly improved inventory controls

- Increased incentives to innovate
- A productivity boom brought on by technological advances in and incentives to invest in capital equipment

With governments everywhere encouraging the above, the economic processes that historically have been at the heart of past expansions are now in place, and these virtuous features are likely to self-feed and last a while. With such strong underpinnings, the global economic story has all the characteristics of a secular upswing that looks likely to stay in place for at least another decade. The worst-case scenario is for an occasional cyclical bump or two. An even lengthier period of strong economic growth is possible; much depends on the ability of policymakers to keep growth on an even keel and avoid excesses. Prudent monetary policy and bank oversight will be needed in particular, as will a buildup of legal and financial structures in countries relatively new to market capitalism; Russia stands out. Without a strengthening of the rule of law in these countries, especially toward property ownership, the global economic story will weaken.

For now, the world economy is in the midst of a golden era where populism has been uprooted from the government sector and taken root in the private sector. The populous now sees capitalism as the best route toward personal gain, a change from the late 1960s and the 1970s when the consensus was toward heavy government involvement. More than ever, the public recognizes that there are limitations to what demand-management policies can achieve; hence, Keynesian economic policies have been minimized and are now sought only as short-term stabilizers rather than as central elements of economic policymaking. In 2008, for example, with the U.S. economy experiencing deep weakness, lawmakers in Washington decided upon $170 billion of short-term economic stimulus. Absent were any meaningful spending initiatives, new public programs, or any public outcry for such things. Even with respect to the subprime mortgage crisis, no substantive involvement by government occurred. Government largely stood on the sidelines, thinking up ways to make the system better on the other side of the crisis. Such is the role that government now plays in the private sector; more as a guardrail, letting the private sector pave the road.

Like Vintage Wine, Policymaking Gets Better with Age

I often think that one of the reasons why the world economy had such difficulties and that there was so much crime in the 1970s was because of an important top-down influence: the median age of the world's population was much younger than it is today. For example, today the median age in the United States is about 36, far higher than it was in 1970 when it was about 27 years of age, which was the lowest since the 1930s.[1] As some of you readers may know, a lot happens between age 27 and 36, and it is a statistical fact that crime rates among age groups tend to decline when people enter their 30s. It therefore makes sense, for example, that the crime rate in New York City has fallen significantly over the past 20 years. Greater maturity among its population is almost certainly behind the drop, as well as New York's excellent police force, which has been able to use its past experiences to craft more effective polices.

Policymakers have also benefited from past experiences, having witnessed the failed policies that led up to the great inflation and the economic malaise of that era. Central banks also had to relearn what worked, with Federal Reserve chairman Paul Volcker implementing the tight monetary policy prescription that his predecessors Arthur Burns (February 1970 to January 1978) and George William Miller (March 1978 to August 1979) rejected. Volcker's predecessors believed in the Keynesian idea that inflation could "prime the pump" of the economy and would at some point self-correct. Miller, with no background in economics or on Wall Street, was even rejected by his peers, being outvoted in 1979 by his colleagues on the Federal Open Market Committee, who voted in favor of an increase in the discount rate, a hike Miller opposed. It is difficult to fathom such a thing happening today.

POLICY COORDINATION IS INCREASING, AS IT MUST

Not only have countries reappraised their own economic policies, but they are also coordinating their policies more with other nations. This has been a long process, having its beginnings near the end of World War II with the signing by 44 allied nations of the Bretton Woods agreement in July 1944. The Bretton Woods agreement established a framework for monetary policy coordination, particularly with respect to exchange rates, and it created two institutions that since their creation have played an important role in maintaining stability in the world economy: the International Monetary Fund (IMF) and the International Bank for Reconstruction and Development (IBRD), which is now part of the World Bank.

Attempts at coordinating monetary policy have largely fallen flat over the years, and it was very rare indeed that interest rates were intentionally raised or lowered simultaneously in order to achieve a particular outcome for the global economy. Instead, central banks have had only a quasi link to one another, responding to domestic conditions as their first priority, which at times had their roots in the global economic situation. Only very recently, in response to the credit crisis of 2007–2008, have central banks taken more aggressive coordinated actions, although the coordinated actions remained limited to liquidity provisions, not adjustments in interest rates (for example, the European Central Bank had not lowered interests at all while the Federal Reserve cut rates 325 basis points between September 2007 and April 2008). Still, even the agreements on liquidity provisions can be considered extraordinary cooperation when viewed in the historical context.

More important than recent coordination of monetary policy is the world's embrace of market capitalism and the many factors I cited earlier. In many cases, the embrace is by nations that had shared experiences and had to relearn and reestablish what worked. Also extremely important is the increased degree of cooperation among bank regulators, particularly under the auspices of Basel I (implemented in 1988) and Basel II (implemented in 2007), both of which provide a framework for establishing standards on bank capital. Federal Reserve chairman Ben Bernanke described Basel II well in a speech he delivered in 2006:[2]

> Basel II is a comprehensive framework for improving bank safety and soundness by more closely linking regulatory capital requirements with bank risk, by improving the ability of supervisors and financial markets to assess capital adequacy, and by giving banking organizations stronger incentives to improve risk measurement and management. The framework encompasses three elements: risk-focused regulatory capital requirements, supervisory review, and market discipline. These are the so-called three pillars of Basel II.

Given the events that took place in the world's financial markets in 2007 and 2008, the basis for cooperation between nations is now stronger than ever, as we have seen the flipside of the integration of the world's financial system. We have learned what human beings have known for years, which is that in many ways we depend on each other more than we sometimes realize. This concept was one that I recognized more than ever through an unusual personal experience I subjected myself to when I rode a bicycle over 100 miles through the scorching heat in Death Valley. I was completely alone in the vast desert at times, which for New Yorkers like me is something that we never really experience—there's always someone nearby; there's a whole system of support behind every element of our lives, from our communications networks, our transportation systems, food stores, emergency services, to passersby. Through this unusual experience, my sense of the importance of how it is that people and societies work together to further the human experience was fortified.

In applying this idea to the need for closer coordination of financial matters, particularly for bank oversight, it is clear to me that if the world is to be more prosperous, it must continue to establish frameworks for prudent banking so that enough capital is available for people everywhere to plant seeds that bear fruit that remains.

Notes

[1] U.S. Administration on Aging; www.aoa.gov.

[2] Bernanke, Ben, "Basel II: It's Promises and Its Challenges," speech delivered at the Federal Reserve Bank of Chicago's 42nd Annual Conference on Bank Structure and Competition, Chicago, Illinois, May 18, 2006.

CHAPTER 14

The Top 40 Top-Down Indicators

Note: These 40 indicators, or golden compasses as I call them, are in no particular order. This is because the relative importance of economic indicators constantly changes and because it is best to track all of the indicators when formulating winning investment strategies.

GOLDEN COMPASS 1: THE COMMODITY FUTURES TRADING COMMISSION'S COMMITMENTS OF TRADERS REPORT

Its Power: It will tell you how much speculative fervor exists in every futures contract tracked by the CFTC, from financials to foods, metals, oil, currencies, and much more. Use it as a contrary indicator.

Where to Get It: Go to cftc.gov and click the link to Commitments of Traders reports.

The View from the Top Down: From tulip mania in Holland in the 1600s to the dot-com and real estate bubbles of the past decade, the history of markets has always been to move toward excess in a rolling fashion, which is to say that excesses tend to move from one corner of the financial markets to the next. For example, after the bursting of the financial bubble, speculative capital moved to the real estate market. From there, speculative capital moved to the commodities markets. One of the better ways to track the amount of speculative fervor in any market (long or short) is to monitor the positions held by noncommercial traders in the futures contracts trading on

U.S. futures exchanges. Noncommercial traders are speculators, as opposed to commercial traders, who transact futures to edge their commercial businesses. For example, in crude oil, commercial traders will include the likes of major oil producers. Noncommercial traders would be those trading for no other reason but to speculate on the price—pit traders, for example. Commercial traders are considered smart money. Noncommercials? Well, dumb money.

How to Nail It: Sell futures contracts that see sudden spikes or a prolonged buildup to historic extremes when the net longs held by noncommercial traders increase. Buy when the opposite occurs. *Trade the nonfutures markets* by going into and out of stocks, bonds, currencies, and so on, that relate to the futures contract when the CFTC data hint at extreme sentiment in the futures contracts. For example, if there is extreme sentiment in the copper market, be sure to trade into and out of shares in companies that are influenced by the price of copper.

GOLDEN COMPASS 2: WEEKLY CHAIN STORE SALES

Its Power: The Tuesday weekly chain store sales figures will bring you extraordinarily close to the consumer, with a snapshot of what consumers were up to just a few days prior. With consumers accounting for almost 70 percent of the economy, use these data as a foundation for views of the economy.

Where to Get It: Go to www.icsc.org and www.johnsonred book.com. In addition, data from both services tend to be widely reported in the financial news media.

The View from the Top Down: You can't get any closer to the consumer than you are able to through the guise of weekly chain store sales data, which are released every Tuesday morning by both the International Council for Shopping Centers and Johnson Redbook Research before the U.S. stock market opens. I have found the ICSC's figures to be the most reliable at providing both an extremely useful descriptive accounting of what consumers either were or were not buying in the previous week, as well as stats on weekly and year-over-year sales trends. Focus particularly on the year-over-year figures, which tend to run at a pace of about 3.5 to 4.0 percent during economic expansions. Keep in mind that chain store sales that increase 3.0 percent or so on a year-over-year basis will translate into a reading of 50.0 or higher for the Institute for Supply Management's monthly purchasing managers index (the ISM index), which tends to be good for risk assets, including equities. With these data in hand, you can form a very wide variety of opinions about where both the economy and the financial markets are headed. The markets often miss the importance of trends that emerge in the weekly figures because they take a month or more to show up in retail sales statistics, and the impact on other economic data is not immediate. You gain an edge because of this. Use these data as a leading indicator, and rank them as among the best if not the best.

How to Nail It: With great conviction, trade aggressively on the chain store sales data. Buy equities, sell Treasuries, buy commodities, and buy the dollar (if expectations on growth are low) when the chain store sales data point to a strengthening of economic activity. Within these groups, buy shares in cyclical companies, transportation industries, basic materials, and technology companies. Favor corporate bonds over Treasuries on the basis of rising corporate cash flows. Do the opposite on weakness in store sales.

GOLDEN COMPASS 3: WEALTH EFFECTS

Its Power: Changes in household wealth reliably predict changes in consumer spending, which is the most powerful influence on the economy.

Where to Get It: Start with base statistics from the Federal Reserve's flow of funds report found on federalreserve.gov under "statistical releases." Click the most recent quarterly release and click "levels tables." There you will find on one page the household holdings of real estate and corporate equities, held both directly and indirectly through mutual funds. From there you can calculate the dollar impact on household net worth for a given percentage of change in equities prices and home values.

The View from the Top Down: The concept here is very simple and reliable. When people feel wealthier, they spend more. When their net worth falls, they spend less. Fifty years of data back this up. It is the American way, after all, to spend both earned income and wealth garnered through capital gains and other means. As with chain store sales, changes in wealth should be expected to result in substantial chain reactions that feed through the economy and foster self-reinforcing elements of economic growth. For example, if people spend more, companies will raise their output of goods and services. This boosts income growth, which in turn boosts spending, resulting in a self-reinforcing cycle of increases in production, income, and spending. This is how to view the situation qualitatively. To calculate impact from wealth effects on GDP, keep these rules of thumb in mind: for every $1 increase in stock values, expect consumer spending to change by 4 cents over an 18-month span, with the impact emerging after 3 months. The impact from home prices is a little higher than for stocks, say 8 or 9 cents, because people extract equity from their homes when they sell it, refinance or take home equity loans, liquefying events not mirrored in the stock market.

How to Nail It: Adjust your viewpoint on GDP according to the calculation shown above and plan accordingly, with an eye on consumer-related stocks in particular. For example, if equities fall by 10 percent, this will cut household wealth by about $1.5 trillion. Using the 4-cent rule, this means that consumer spending will slip by $60 billion. You must decide whether the wealth effects are enough to alter GDP enough to affect the various asset classes and the segments and sectors within these asset classes.

GOLDEN COMPASS 4: THE MORTGAGE BANKERS ASSOCIATION'S WEEKLY MORTGAGE APPLICATIONS INDEX

Its Power: Since 1990, these data have accurately portrayed conditions in the housing market, both for purchases and mortgage refinancing, two powerful indicators of economic activity, as recent events have illustrated.

Where to Get It: Every Wednesday morning, go to www.mbaa .org to obtain the indexes, which will be for the week ended the previous Friday. Alternatively, check financial Web sites such as Bloomberg.com or Marketwatch.com for stories about the indexes.

The View from the Top Down: The housing sector has a significant influence on the U.S. economy, and activity in the housing sector is often revealing with respect to the condition of the U.S. consumer. On occasion, when bankers go to excess, events in the housing sector have also affected the financial system, as was the case in the early 1990s and particularly in 2007 and 2008. Closer scrutiny, financially painful lessons, and increased regulations will likely reduce this element of the housing sector's ups and downs in the years ahead, but it will remain a formidable factor to consider when assessing the health of the financial system. Distortions appeared in the MBA's data in 2007 when prospective home buyers began having difficulty obtaining mortgages, which resulted in double filings and suggested misleading strength in the purchase index. In addition, a migration of filers from mortgage brokers, which are not counted in the index, to more traditional mortgage institutions boosted the index. These influences will wash out over time. As a cyclical sector, developments in housing will tip off activity in many cyclical sectors. Moreover, it is important to appreciate the idea that as the biggest big-ticket item, housing will be extraordinarily revealing about consumer finances, confidence, and the job market.

How to Nail It: The direct and indirect impact of housing is broad. As for sectors, when conditions improve, buy home builders, building-supply companies, furniture companies, and (in most cycles) mortgage finance companies. Typically, strong housing turnover is good for home merchandising companies. An uptick in housing will hurt the Treasury market; buy corporate bonds and agency securities, instead. The short end of the Treasury curve will perform worst on Fed fears. The key metric for the MBA index is its level relative to its one-year average.

GOLDEN COMPASS 5: THE ABC NEWS WEEKLY CONSUMER COMFORT INDEX

Its Power: This timely gauge captures the impact of very recent events on the consumer, helping you to nail turning points in the economy and the markets.

Where to Get It: On Tuesday evenings at 5 p.m. ET, go to abcnews.com and scan the site for the index.

The View from the Top Down: Consumer sentiment is indelibly linked to people's emotions, which can fluctuate for reasons unrelated to consumer fundamentals. For this reason, consumer sentiment is often a poor predictor of consumer spending. There nonetheless are effective ways of using consumer sentiment gauges to your advantage. First, use the data as a means of assessing the emotional verve toward issues important to the United States. This will help you to decide on the likely path of major policies that will affect the economy and the markets. Second, put the data, especially the weekly data, in the context of other data such as jobless claims, chain store sales, car sales, and home sales, to gauge whether any changes might be occurring in consumer spending that would alter the course of the economy. Pay particularly close attention to the personal finance component of the ABC index, which will help tell you whether the fluctuations in sentiment are occurring because of changes in consumer fundamentals or because of an emotional response to very recent events. In such instances, downgrade the sentiment index with respect to the outlook on consumer spending.

How to Nail It: When the ABC index breaks in a new direction and is backed by other factors of significance to the consumer (i.e., rising jobless claims, surging gasoline prices), see it as confirmation of a change in consumer fundamentals and adjust your portfolio accordingly. Lean toward traditional strategies on asset allocation, portfolio diversification, and risk aversion to reflect the economic situation the ABC index confirms.

GOLDEN COMPASS 6: THE TREASURY'S INFLATION-PROTECTED SECURITIES (TIPS)

Its Power: In a flash, TIPS can tell you about the inflation expectations of millions of investors, a critical element in establishing views about the Federal Reserve and the interest-rate outlook.

Where to Get It: To determine the market's inflation expectations, you must first determine whether you want the 5-year view or the 10-year view. Both are revealing, but the long-term view is what matters most because it is shaped by influences expected to last beyond short-term, cyclical ones. Compare the yield on the inflation-protected security to a conventional Treasury note of equal maturity. The yield difference indicates the market's expectation for what the consumer price index will average over the maturity span chosen. Find these yields on Bloomberg.com, in the *Wall Street Journal*, and on many financial Web sites.

The View from the Top Down: Inflation expectations are of gargantuan importance to the economy and the financial markets.

Two completely different environments are engendered when inflation expectations are either high or low. When high market interest rates will be higher, the Fed will be tighter, real economic growth will be slower, and equity valuations will be lower in response. When low, the opposite occurs, and productivity gains accelerate in response to increased business investment typically fostered in a low interest-rate environment. Inflation expectations also play a major role in the inflation process in the real economy. Boosting the importance of this indicator is the Federal Reserve's repeated references to it, which clearly show that TIPS influence the Fed's decision making on monetary policy. The Fed would prefer to see inflation closer to 2 percent, so when TIPS cross the 2.50 percent threshold, expect the Fed to show discomfort. TIPS are a relative newcomer to the scene, with issuance in the United States having begun in 1997. The market for TIPS has since grown, with $474 billion outstanding in March 2008, making its signals more reliable.

How to Nail It: Use indications on inflation expectations as a major element in your forecasts on interest rates and the Fed, and adjust your portfolio accordingly. Buy TIPS and sell Treasuries if you feel that inflation will exceed the amount of inflation embedded in TIPS; Sell TIPS and buy Treasuries if you feel that inflation will be lower than what is priced into the markets. Use TIPS also as a gauge of excessive inflation worry or complacency in the broader markets. Own TIPS as an inflation hedge in your portfolio and seek out inflation-protected securities in countries you have exposure to.

GOLDEN COMPASS NO. 7: THE BUSINESS INVENTORY-TO-SALES RATIO

Its Power: Imbalances in business inventories have played a major role in the ups and downs of the business cycle for decades. When inventories are too high or too low, look out! Big things will happen.

Where to Get It: From the U.S. Census Bureau's Web site: http://www.census.gov/mtis/www/current.html.

The View from the Top Down: Part of the reason for the so-called great moderation in economic activity has been an improvement in inventory management. No longer do firms find themselves saddled with large amounts of unwanted inventories. This is an extraordinarily important development for the economy, because excess inventories can drag the economy down for several quarters. On the other hand, when inventories are lean, any uptick that occurs in spending sparks an almost immediate increase in production. In either case, when inventory levels fluctuate, the ripple effects on the economy can be enormous because of how inventories affect the production cycle. For example, when inventories build up, companies cut output, thereby weakening income growth and spending. When spending weakens, output is cut further, spurring a self-feeding *vicious cycle* of decreases in production, income, and spending. The opposite occurs when output increases and results in a self-feeding *virtuous cycle*. This is the stuff that expansions and contractions are made of. Figure 14.1 shows the inventory-to-sales ratio dating back to the early 1980s.

How to Nail It: Always view inventory data in the context of spending data. If spending rises amid lean inventories, expect a strong economic expansion. If spending weakens amid high inventory levels, expect economic weakness. Beat the markets by focusing on how spending is faring relative to output, treating the spending figures as leading indicators over production figures, which inevitably will catch up to spending. For the inventory-to-sales ratio, any uptick should be taken seriously, as it goes against the grain of the secular downturn of the past 25+ years. A rising inventory-to-sales ratio could spell weakness for the economy;

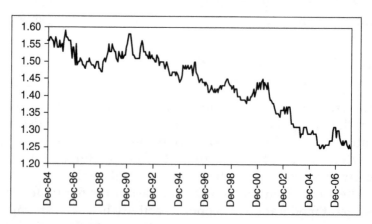

Figure 14.1 Inventory-to-sales ratio for business Inventories (in number of months).

Source: U.S. Census Bureau.

overweight Treasuries compared to risk assets such as equities and corporate bonds. Drill down further into the report for figures on which areas of the economy might have inventory imbalances of some sort. This will say a great deal about the economic strength in the various sectors and their pricing power.

GOLDEN COMPASS 8: THE CENTRAL INTELLIGENCE AGENCY'S WORLD FACTBOOK

Its Power: When you need a quick snapshot of any country, the CIA's Web site will surprise you with a bounty of information. You can use this information to develop the perspective and context you need to make good decisions about countries you might invest in. Funny, though, are the CIA's maps, which are anything but sophisticated. We know they have better!

Where to Get It: From the CIA's Web site: https://www. cia .gov/library/publications/the-world-factbook/index.html. All countries can be accessed there.

The View from the Top Down: If you are going to make good judgments about countries you are considering investing in, you need to know as much as possible about those countries. It is not enough to Google the country or to read news stories about it. You need much more. Given the CIA's vital role to the United States, we can trust that its information will be sourced extraordinarily well. In the *World Factbook*, for each country you will find a plethora of facts and vital statistics, including population statistics, climate facts, age demographics, the country's gross domestic product and its composition, and data on exports and imports. To illustrate the level of detail, note that there is also information on the country's communications system, from the number of Internet users, to radio stations, to telephones in use. In a separate section of the CIA's Web site there is information about who each country's leaders are. Armed with all this information, you can put any other information you gather on a country into the proper context and make much better investment decisions. This is of utmost importance now because so many of the best investment opportunities will be found abroad.

How to Nail It: Travel through cyberspace to any country you are considering investing in abroad. Use the Web sites of major internationally recognized organizations such as the CIA, the United

Nations, the World Bank, the International Monetary Fund, and the Bank for International Settlements to gain access to information about countries; do not depend upon the media, which could be biased or yield information that is not in the proper context.

GOLDEN COMPASS 9: THE BANK FOR INTERNATIONAL SETTLEMENTS RESEARCH AND STATISTICS

Its Power: There is no better place to find vital information about the amount of money crossing borders, both in terms of the amount of movement and where the money is going, and the size and scope of the global derivatives market. In addition, the BIS produces unparalleled research on topical matters such as carry trades, foreign exchange, monetary policy, and the world financial system in general. The statistics empower you with information to help you find hotspots throughout the world, identify risks, and obtain greater clarity on topical issues.

Where to Get It: Go the BIS Web site, www.bis.org, and scan the front page for recent papers. Put your cursor over the button titled "publications and research" in order to open up a pop-out menu that gives you access to the *BIS Quarterly Review* and to various BIS papers and other data.

The View from the Top Down: The BIS is the best source of information on cross-border deposits, which are those monies that are deposited outside of a base country into another country. At the end of the third quarter of 2007, cross-border deposits totaled $30 trillion, up by 80 percent from three years earlier. From these data you can draw several conclusions. For one, when the growth rate in cross-border deposits is strong, take it as a sign that the global economy is strong. This is because when monies are deposited offshore, it must obviously mean that the depositors have excess capital to invest, which would primarily come about when economic growth is strong. A second way to view these data is to look more specifically at which countries are making and receiving the deposits. Those countries making deposits should be considered in good health, as they have excess capital to invest. This has been the case in the oil-producing nations in recent years. Countries on the receiving end might be good places to invest because the influx of capital reduces the cost of capital in those countries, which is good for economic growth. For example, big recipients of cross-border deposits in recent years have been the emerging economies in the former Eastern Bloc. Moreover, the money flowing to such countries represents "smart money," as opposed to speculative money, and is therefore likely to stay invested. It is of course better to follow smart money than speculative money.

How to Nail It: About two months after the end of every quarter, go to the BIS site, look closely at the 100 or so pages of the *BIS Quarterly Report*, and pluck information about cross-border flows, derivatives markets, and vital topical subjects. There are often charts illustrating where monies are flowing from and flowing to. Generate ideas and perspective on these to help you with all your investments, particularly for investments outside of the United States; the data are sure to help you to drop your "home bias," the preference for staying invested in the country in which you live.

GOLDEN COMPASS 10: FEDERAL RESERVE RESEARCH

Its Power: The Federal Reserve produces the most valuable information anywhere on topics of importance and relevance to investors. Few know of this diamond in a rough, which is paid for by your tax dollars.

Where to Get It: One of the reasons so few investors know about the Fed's research is that it is not organized as well as it could be, because it is spread throughout the Fed's 12 reserve banks. There is, however, a central location for Fed research called *Fed-in-Print*. It can be found on the San Francisco Fed's Web site, www.frbsf.org. When you get there, type in a topic—any topic—and you will find an amazing number of insightful articles.

The View from the Top Down: One crisp evening on a rooftop balcony in New York City I had the privilege of meeting Federal Reserve chairman Alan Greenspan. In the short meeting I described to him how valuable the Fed's research had been to me in my 1,200 page revision to Stigum's *The Money Market*. The chairman said to me that he was not surprised because the Fed employed 200 Ph.D.s who worked together in an atmosphere as collegial as any he had ever seen, a fact that Greenspan has said surprised him in his early days at the Fed. The collegial atmosphere results in remarkable work, with each piece of research building on previous work, raising the quality of research to levels that can't be found anywhere else and above the works produced by the nation's top-ranked universities and academics. To the layperson, some of the Fed's research will seem too complex. The key, though, is to look past the math equations to the discussion. I like to look at the abstract, the first few pages (many studies are 50 pages or so), in plain English woven in between the math, the conclusion, and my favorite—the pictures! In the money market book, I took more charts from Fed research than from anywhere else, and there are also a number of charts in this book that were from the Fed. Although I ignore the math equations in the Fed's research, I am glad to see the math there because it tells me that the conclusions drawn were checked quantitatively.

How to Nail It: *Check the Fed's research regularly on all kinds of topics, and don't be afraid to go back about 10 years on the subjects chosen.* I have adapted many of the rules of thumb provided in the Fed's work. For example, in a study about a decade old on consumer sentiment, Fed researchers found that for every one-point change in the University of Michigan's consumer sentiment index, the Conference Board's index will change by two points. This stuff works! Other rules I have found include the fact that for every 100-basis-point cut in the funds rate, industrial production increases by 1 percent over two years. Also, a 25-basis-point surprise rate cut equals a 1 percent rise in stock prices. There are many more ideas like these made available from your tax dollars, so *why not take advantage of the Ph.D.s whom you employ?*

GOLDEN COMPASS 11: THE NATIONAL ASSOCIATION OF HOME BUILDERS MONTHLY HOUSING MARKET INDEX

Its Power: In recent times we have witnessed the mighty impact that the U.S. housing sector has on both economic activity and the financial markets. Few indicators capture conditions in the housing sector as well as this one.

Where to Get It: Each month on the day before the Census Bureau's release of figures on housing starts, which are generally released in the last calendar week of every month, the NAHB will release on its Web site (www.nahb.org) its monthly index. It will also be widely reported in the media.

The View from the Top Down: The lessons learned from the recent housing crisis will last a generation. As a result, in the immediate years ahead there will be near universal recognition of the housing sector's ability to exert substantial influence on both the economy and the financial markets. In some ways, this will make any market response to housing indicators more acute, boosting the importance of these indicators, which includes the NAHB's housing market index (HMI), one of the finest of them all. Since 1985, the NAHB's data have shown extremely tight correlation to the Census Bureau's monthly data on both housing starts and new home sales, as well as the National Association of Realtors' figures on existing home sales. The NAHB's data are also timely, reflecting very recent conditions seen by the roughly 400 home builders that respond to the NAHB survey. Movements in the HMI that coincide with similar movements in mortgage applications should be seen as potent evidence of a change in housing conditions. The HMI is reported as a diffusion index with a scale of zero to 100. Readings above 50 indicate that a greater percentage of builders saw improved conditions during the month; readings below 50 indicate contraction.

How to Nail It: *With great conviction, trade aggressively on changes in housing conditions in the several years ahead, because the financial markets are likely to keep housing in focus until the gigantic number of unsold homes starts moving decisively toward historic norms.* Trade financials, housing stocks, building supply companies, general merchandise companies, and other retailers with either exposure to housing or to the impact that housing has on consumers. In the bond market, overweight agency securities; if housing rebounds, underweight Treasuries. In commodities, transact in copper, which depends on the residential sector for about 40 percent of demand, and in other commodities affected by the housing sector.

GOLDEN COMPASS 12: THE YIELD SPREAD BETWEEN TWO-YEAR T-NOTES AND THE FED FUNDS TARGET

Its Power: The two-year Treasury note captures market sentiment toward the Federal Reserve better than any other actively traded maturity along the Treasury yield curve and provides an excellent means of capturing turning points in the financial markets.

Where to Get It: Treasury yields are readily obtained from a variety of sources including print and electronic ones. The fed funds target is the rate set by the Fed at its regularly scheduled FOMC meetings; find it on Federalreserve.gov in the statements that accompany the FOMC meetings, found here: http://www .federalreserve.gov/monetarypolicy/fomc.htm.

The View from the Top Down: There have been only five occasions over the past 20 years in which the two-year note has yielded less than the federal funds rate, the interest rate controlled by the Federal Reserve. On each occasion, a Fed rate cut soon followed. We saw in Figure 6.4 the very tight correlation between the two-year note and fed funds, further underscoring the idea that the two-year notes and funds are closely bound. The tight correlation is important because it suggests that market participants are valuing the two-year on the basis of their expectations of Fed policy, which can move to extremes now and then, revealing to you, the top-down investor, excessively bullish and bearish market sentiment that you can then use as a basis for taking contrary positions in not only the Treasury market and the bond market but also in other markets, where similar sentiment on the Fed is always present. A similar proxy on this kind of sentiment is fed funds futures, although they are sparsely traded beyond a six-month time horizon. Eurodollar futures are an excellent proxy, although not as simple to use as the two-year. As a rule of thumb, in a normal rate environment, the two-year will trade 50 basis points over the funds rate when it is not clear whether a rate cut or rate hike will be next. The two-year will trade 75 basis points over funds when a hike is likely within a few months, and will trade 100 basis points over when a hike is imminent. If the funds rate is low, say 2 percent, change this scale to 75 basis points for a neutral stance, 112.5 basis points for a nearby hike, and 150 over for an imminent hike

How to Nail It: In using the two-year, your main goal is to capture sentiment that may be a bit extreme relative to your own expectations toward the economy, the Fed, and the financial markets. Recognizing the top-down rule that the two-year goes below the funds rate only when a Fed rate cut is imminent and that as per Figure 6.4 the two-year trades right on top of funds, when two-years deviate from their historical relationship to funds, say well below the funds rate, treat this as a sign that there may be excessive pessimism on the economy and that there may be unrealistic hopes for future interest-rate cuts. If the two-year moves well above the funds rate (using the parameters mentioned above), it could be a sign of excess optimism on the economy, something that may be evident in equities, corporate bonds, emerging markets, commodities, and other risk assets.

GOLDEN COMPASS 13: THE TREASURY YIELD CURVE

Its Power: For decades, the Treasury yield curve has reliably fore-shadowed major events and turning points in both the economy and the financial markets, having worked its magic yet again ahead of the 2007–2008 credit crisis and the simultaneous economic slowdown.

Where to Get It: The Treasury yield curve can be viewed either in a graph or a table by comparing yield spreads. Treasury yields are available throughout the financial media; graphs on yield curves are available on Bloomberg.com.

The View from the Top Down: Substantial historical evidence exists indicating that the Treasury yield curve is one of the best fore-casting tools available. It is the closest thing to a crystal ball. It is the shape of the yield curve that acts as a predictor of future events. For example, if the yield curve is *positively sloped*, or steep, this means that short-term rates are lower than long-term rates, usually as a result of Fed rate cuts, which generally is good news for the economy and the financial markets, albeit with a time lag that can extend as far out as 18 months or more. A *negatively sloped* yield curve, or inversion, is the opposite, with long-term rates below short-term rates, generally reflecting the impact of a series of Fed rate hikes, with the economy slowing in response and long-term rates reflecting the idea that the Fed will at some point be forced to reverse its rate hikes. (It can be said that long-term rates are a bet on where short-term rates will be in the future.) Yield curve inversions tend to precede gloomy economic situations and weakness in risk assets. For example, since 1970, every inverted yield curve has been followed by a period in which Standard & Poor's (S&P) 500 earnings growth was negative. Numerous studies have found the yield curve to predict economic events roughly 12 months or more in advance, which beats the stock market's 6- to 9-month lead time.

How to Nail It: *Remember the rule of thumb: the yield curve tends to predict economic events roughly 12 months or more in advance.* You must nonetheless be careful about the timing of your entry and exits on strategies designed on the basis of changes in the economic cycle. For example, the Fed's rate cuts in 2001 took more than two years to push stock prices higher because of excessively high valuations entering the period. Similarly, bank stocks, which might normally fare well when the Fed cuts rates and the yield curve steepens, did not fare well in 2007 and early 2008 because of problems related to the mortgage crisis. Keep in mind that it takes a yield spread of about -80 basis points between 3-month T-bills and 10-year T-notes (with T-bills yielding more than 10-year notes) for the yield curve to indicate the chances of a recession are greater than 50 percent.

GOLDEN COMPASS 14: SWAP RATES

Its Power: Tallying up at $309.59 trillion at the end of December 2007, data from the Bank for International Settlements reveal a mammoth market, accounting for the largest portion of the $596 trillion derivatives market. Obligors everywhere go to this market to express their beliefs about the direction of interest rates and risk attitudes, two potent top-down elements. Use swap rates to gauge these things.

Where to Get It: These data are found each day on the Federal Reserve's Web site: http://federalreserve.gov/releases/h15/update/. Wall Street professionals can obtain swap rates via Bloomberg, Reuters, and other data providers.

The View from the Top Down: When debt obligors are concerned that the cost of their debt obligations might rise as a result of either a rise in interest rates or a rise in interest-rates spreads between corporate bonds and Treasuries, they will seek to minimize the impact by entering into a swap agreement whereby they swap out of their floating-rate obligations in exchange for fixed-rate obligations. When this happens on a large scale, swap rates rise because greater numbers of market participants are seeking fixed-rate obligations over floating-rate obligations, hence pushing up the swap rate, which reflects the fixed-rate portion of the swap. It is a sign for top-down investors to beware of the possibility of worsening conditions in the credit markets whereby credit spreads will begin to rise. This means, for example, that high-yield bonds will begin to underperform investment-grade bonds. In such an environment, the riskier the asset, the worse its performance is likely to be. Swap spreads will tend to widen when the Fed begins to raise interest rates, reflecting the desire to lock in rates and fears of future cash flows, which boost credit spreads and which also compel swap participants to lock in rates. Of course, tightening credit spreads reflect the opposite: expectations for lower rates, improved cash flows, and hence tighter credit spreads. In the months following the emergence of the 2007–2008 credit crisis, the Dow Jones Industrial Average gained over 1,000 points in the three times between August 2007 and May 2008 that swap rates fell from above average levels (in August and November 2007, and in March 2008). The interest-rate swaps market is such a gigantic worldwide market that its signals are very strong and reliable; it is an efficient market.

How to Nail It: For context, note that since 1991, the 10-year swap spread, which measures the number of basis points that the 10-year swap rate trades above the 10-year Treasury rate, on a weekly chart has averaged 55 basis points, trading at a low of 27 basis points in January 1994 and peaking at 135 basis points in April 2000 (Figure 14.2). In March 2008 the spread moved to as high as 91 basis points before falling sharply to about 60 basis points after the March 16 rescue of Bear Stearns. When swap rates climb, especially

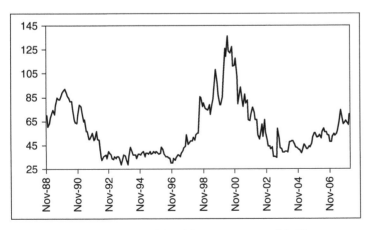

Figure 14.2 10-year swap spread (yield over comparable Treasury maturity in basis points).
Source: Bloomberg.

if by more than a few basis points in a single day, be leery of taking risks in corporate bonds, emerging markets bonds, and equities, as was the case in April 2000. Buy Treasuries in such a case unless the swap rate is rising because of Fed rate increases. Delay your Treasury purchases in this case. Buy equities and other risk assets when swap rates fall.

GOLDEN COMPASS 15: THE CORPORATE FINANCING GAP

Its Power: From this indicator you can make predictions about whether capital spending will have a tendency to be either strong or weak in the quarters ahead.

Where to Get It: Bear with me on this one. Go to the Web site of the Bureau of Economic Analysis (http://www.bea.gov/) and spot the link to "gross domestic product." Click on it and then click on the link "news release." From there, click on the link to "full release and tables," which is usually hidden on the right side of the Web browser. You are looking for two numbers: nonresidential fixed investment and corporate profits. For the former, look for the table called "Gross Domestic Product and Related Measures: Level and Change from Preceding Period." Under "gross private domestic investment" you will find the nonresidential number. You want the seasonally adjusted figure in current dollars (it was $1.53 trillion in the first quarter of 2008). For corporate profits, it is best to search for the word "corporate profits" within the PDF, where a number of pages after the nonresidential number you will find the figure for "Corporate profits with inventory valuation and capital consumption adjustments" (it was $1.57 trillion in the first quarter of 2008).

The View from the Top Down: The very reason that capital markets exist is that corporations do not generate enough internal funding to finance their expansions. Historically, there is typically a gap known as the *corporate financing gap*, amounting to about 2 percent of the nation's gross domestic product. In other words, capital spending, as measured by nonresidential fixed investment, typically runs higher than corporate profits by an amount equal to 2 percent of GDP. With companies spending more than they earn, they must raise capital, typically by selling stocks and bonds.

Fluctuations in the corporate financing gap can be used as a basis for constructing forecasts on capital spending. For example, when the financing gap grows larger than the norm of about 2 percent, this means that companies are spending far more money than they are earning, an unsustainable condition that portends weakness in capital spending in areas such as equipment and software. This is what happened in 2000 (see Figure 14.3). In recent times, a long stretch of strong corporate profits and attention to balance sheets eliminated the financing gap, a rare event. This should act as a significant buffer against lasting weakness in capital spending and portends a healthy trend in capital spending for many quarters to come (because companies have plenty of internally generated funds).

How to Nail It: As in 2000, when the corporate financing gap widens, unless there is a reason to believe that corporate profits will shrink the gap, expect weakness in capital spending. In such circumstances, underweight the technology sector as well as sectors tied to the production of capital equipment. Be leery of commercial real estate, where spending on structures could weaken; underweight the sector as commercial real estate investment trusts. Overweight Treasuries, and underweight corporate bonds.

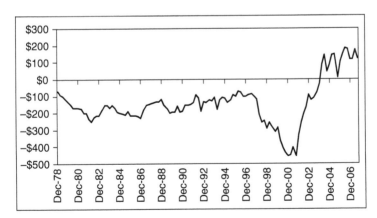

Figure 14.3 Corporate financing gap (in billions of dollars).

Note: The corporate financing gap is calculated by subtracting nonresidential fixed investment from corporate profits.

Source: Bureau of Economic Analysis.

GOLDEN COMPASS 16: COMMERCIAL AND INDUSTRIAL LOANS

Its Power: This indicator relies upon the principle that *money borrowed is money spent.* If lending activity picks up, you can bet that corporate spending will too. This indicator is therefore a good gauge of business confidence, which can be applied in many ways.

Where to Get It: On the Fed's Web site, www.federalreserve .gov, every Friday at 4:15 p.m. ET look on the home page for the link to "statistical releases," which is typically on the right side of the page. From there, under the category "bank assets and liabilities" click on the link to "assets and liabilities of commercial banks," the so-called H.8 release. Once there, click on the PDF for the most recent release, and on the first page, line six, you will find the figure, which stood at about $1.5 trillion in March 2008.

The View from the Top Down: Commercial and industrial (C&I) loans fluctuate with the business cycle, and historically these loans have been strongly linked to the inventory cycle, as many businesses utilize C&I loans to raise working capital for the production of goods. When the number of C&I loans increases at a healthy pace, it is rational to expect a healthy period of economic expansion. It is difficult to imagine, for example, how the economy could falter when corporate borrowing increases, not only because the borrowing means that companies are set to spend, but also because the borrowing signals that companies are confident and planning for economic expansion. As for what constitutes a healthy pace, note that in the heart of the past two economic expansions of the 1990s and early 2000s, C&I lending advanced at a pace that was in the high single digits. Notably, C&I lending fell during the past two recessions and was either flat or falling until job growth picked up again. It can therefore be said that there is link between C&I loan growth and the job market, which makes sense given the link between C&I loan growth and the inventory cycle, which has a substantial influence on the job market.

How to Nail It: Remember the linkage: C&I loans are tightly correlated to the inventory cycle, which means that C&I loans are tightly correlated to industrial output and to the job market. In turn, this means that you should expect the factory-laden economic calendar to be heavily affected and thus adjust your portfolio accordingly.

Invest defensively when C&I loan growth weakens; invest for economic expansion when C&I loan growth strengthens. Keep in mind, however, that although overlays on C&I loan growth and major equity indexes such as the Dow and S&P 500 show solid correlation directionally, equities sometimes inflect in a new direction before C&I loan growth does, so you must be on your toes. The easy trade here is to play equities in the direction that loan growth points to if equities seem to be trailing. Use this indicator also as a gauge of credit conditions.

GOLDEN COMPASS 17: COMMERCIAL PAPER ISSUANCE

Its Power: The commercial paper market was at the epicenter of the credit crisis when it began in the summer of 2007, underscoring its importance as a financial indicator. The commercial paper market is also an excellent gauge of the economy.

Where to Get It: The Federal Reserve releases data every Thursday at about 9:50 a.m. ET on its Web site at http://federalreserve.gov/releases/cp/. On that page, click on the link to "outstandings" to see the weekly figures.

The View from the Top Down: As with commercial and industrial (C&I) loans, the commercial paper market tends to fluctuate with the business cycle, and it is linked closely with the inventory cycle, which has a substantial influence on the job market. Commercial paper is short-term debt issued primarily by corporations and financial firms, with maturities of up to 270 days, although the average term is for 30 days. Companies will generally issue commercial paper to meet short-term needs. For example, a company might issue commercial paper to produce inventory for resale, using the proceeds to repay commercial paper investors. Toyota Motor Credit is an example. It borrows money to make cars, sells the cars, and repays investors. General Electric is the world's biggest issuer of commercial paper. When companies are confident that their sales will increase, they produce more, using commercial paper to finance the production. This is why the commercial paper market is strongly linked to the inventory cycle and why it is such an excellent gauge of both industrial output and business confidence. In recent times, the commercial paper market was watched closely for signs of strain in the credit markets. A plunge in commercial paper issuance signaled a major shift in risk attitudes, with the commercial paper market shaking out issuers whose paper was either backed by mortgage-related assets or contained assets deemed difficult to value. The commercial paper market is Darwinian, weeding out the weakest players, which is why the commercial paper market has seen only seven defaults since 1970.

How to Nail It: Always remember that the Securities and Exchange Commission (SEC) requires that all commercial paper issuance be for *transactions purposes only*. This highlights the fact that when a company borrows money in the commercial paper market, the money will result in economic activity—SEC rules dictate as much. This means that when commercial paper issuance is on the rise, you can probably bank on economic expansion. Also use these data to look for signs of strain in the money market, focusing also on commercial paper rates, which tend to trade close to the fed funds rate except when risk aversion increases.

GOLDEN COMPASS 18: FREE-TRADE AGREEMENTS

Its Power: When two countries sign a free-trade agreement, trade between the countries increases significantly, forging many opportunities for investors. As an illustration, see Figure 14.4.

Where to Get It: One source for past agreements and for agreements in progress is the Web site for the American State's Foreign Trade Information System: http://www.sice.oas.org/default_e.asp. There is a plethora of information there, including the details on the various trade agreements. There is also official information from the U.S. government available at www.tradeagreements.gov, which is "an interagency effort by the United States government to provide the public with the latest information on America's trade agreements." On that site pending agreements are also shown. There are also very useful data on the impact of free-trade agreements on specific sectors. You can also go here: http://www.ustr.gov/Trade_Agreements/Bilateral/Section_Index.html.

The View from the Top Down: In early 2008, the United States had signed 14 free-trade agreements (FTAs), up from 3 in

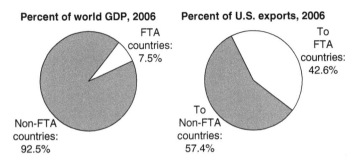

Figure 14.4 Most U.S. trade takes place with its free-trade partners.
Sources: U.S. Department of Commerce; International Trade Administration.

2000. Importantly, although comprising 7.5 percent of global GDP (not including the United States), the 14 FTA countries accounted for over 42 percent of U.S. exports in 2006. To enrich these data further, note that these FTA countries accounted for only 7.5 percent of the world economy. We note in Chapter 8 that according to the White House, recent research shows that after 5 years the average FTA increased trade between bilateral trading partners by 32 percent; after 10 years the increase bolted to 73 percent; after 15 years the increase surged to 114 percent. All these data clearly show that FTAs result in substantial increases in trade. Sometimes the agreements become hot political issues, as was the case with NAFTA in the 1990s and then again in the 2008 presidential campaign, but the fact is that since the signing of NAFTA trade between the U.S., Canada, and Mexico. trade has increased by 200 percent.

   How to Nail It: When two countries sign an FTA, find the industries and companies likely to benefit and weigh how important the new business might become to those industries and companies. Utilize the Web sites I cite above, which give detailed facts and statistics about which sectors will be affected by the FTAs. Another strategy is to buy an ETF for countries that stand to see a significant increase in economic activity as a result of the signing of FTAs. Finally, consider whether the signing of an FTA signals the type of shift to market capitalism that would make a country's foreign currency and its government bonds more attractive than they were before.

GOLDEN COMPASS 19: ENTRY INTO THE WORLD TRADE ORGANIZATION

Its Power: When a country enters the World Trade Organization, a powerful surge in economic activity for that country usually results. There are also benefits to countries already in the WTO when member countries agree to liberalize trade rules further.

Where to Get It: There is a wealth of information about the World Trade Organization on the WTO's Web site, www.wto.org. Very intriguing and useful to investors is the WTO's trade policy reviews, which discuss in simple language the economic situation of the country being reviewed, specifically with respect to trade. Additional details are available within the review, providing boatloads of information about the country's economy.

The View from the Top Down: The WTO is the successor to the General Agreement on Tariffs and Trade, which was signed in 1947. The WTO was officially established in 1995 as a result of the Uruguay round of negotiations on trade, which lasted from 1986 to 1994. The WTO's current round of negotiations, the Doha development agenda, was launched in 2001. As the WTO describes, its purpose is not solely to liberalize trade. At its heart are the WTO agreements, negotiated and signed by the bulk of the world's trading nations. These documents provide the legal ground rules for international commerce. They are essentially contracts, binding governments to keep their trade policies within agreed limits. These rules create confidence in dealing with countries in the WTO, primarily because the countries are bound by the agreements, which provide a legal basis for resolving disputes and ensuring fair trade. When combined with reductions in tariffs and other barriers to trade, countries that enter the WTO become fertile ground for businesses to establish ties with greater confidence than before. In addition, companies within the countries that enter the WTO are subjected to greater competitive pressures from outside their country, thus boosting efficiencies and spurring innovation within the WTO-entering country. Moreover, domestic interest groups become somewhat more neutralized by external pressures. All in all, the economies of countries that enter the WTO prosper. The latest example? China. It formally ascended into the WTO in December 2001 after about 15 years of trying.

How to Nail It: *Stay abreast of news on the World Trade Organization,* which will often wind up in the financial press, although it is probably best to go to the WTO Web site to monitor which countries are being considered for entry into the WTO. *Watch also for developments related to the Doha round,* which will have varied impact on WTO members. *Add exposure to countries that enter the WTO by buying ETFs and mutual funds meant to give exposure to the country chosen.* Assess whether to buy the country's sovereign debt and its foreign currency. Exporters should establish ties to the country.

GOLDEN COMPASS 20: INITIAL JOBLESS CLAIMS

Its Power: There is no timelier and more accurate gauge of the employment situation than the weekly release of initial jobless claims.

Where to Get It: Data on initial jobless claims are released every Thursday at 8:30 a.m. ET by the U.S. Department of Labor. You can find the statistics on the Department of Labor's Web site: http://www.dol.gov/opa/media/press/eta/ui/current.htm.

The View from the Top Down: So accurate are the jobless claims data that the Bureau of Labor Statistics reconciles its widely followed monthly employment statistics with them. The accuracy stems in part from the fact that each state collects its own data and because data on jobless claims are derived using very little estimation. By definition, jobless claims measure unemployment; only by inference do the claims data tell us anything about labor demand. This is important to remember because during turning points, say when the U.S. economy is shifting from expansion to contraction, the jobless claims figures won't necessarily capture it, since no layoffs will have occurred. Then again, the fact that hiring has stopped will keep more people on the unemployment line for longer, thus boosting claims. There is no denying, however, as was the case in late 2007 and in 2008, what an increase in jobless claims means: increased unemployment. There is no other reason why people file for jobless benefits. Keep in mind these few rules: (1) When claims move above 370,000, it tends to signal economic recession. (2) Only about 60 percent of the U.S. labor force is eligible for unemployment benefits. This means that if 100,000 additional people file for jobs during a given month, the actual change in trend for monthly payroll growth was probably about 160,000. (3) When looking at historical levels, remember that the U.S. labor force grows by about 1 percent per year, which means that jobless claims should rise by about 1 percent per year. Therefore a 300,000 reading from five years ago would be the same as a reading of about 315,000 today.

How to Nail It: Look closely at the weekly breakdown by states of the industries reporting increases and decreases in filings for initial jobless claims. This detail can be used as a basis for making decisions about which sectors to overweight and underweight. As it was important to do in the latter part of 2007, treat jobless claims as an important leading indicator of a change in the production cycle and hence the overall economy. Later, as the down part of the business cycle progresses, put jobless claims very low on your list of indicators, as employment conditions will lag improvements in the economy, with companies cautious about hiring even as their sales and output levels rise. This is why productivity tends to rise early in the cycle.

GOLDEN COMPASS 21: THE BALTIC DRY INDEX

Its Power: A gauge of global maritime shipping rates, the Baltic Dry index reliably depicts conditions in the global economy and trends in commodities prices.

Where to Get It: The Baltic Dry Index is available only to subscribers on the Baltic exchange's Web site, www. balticexchange .com, but it is widely reported in the financial news and can be obtained with a one-day lag from data providers such as Bloomberg, Reuters, and Dow Jones.

The View from the Top Down: The Baltic exchange dates back over 250 years and has been utilized since then as a place where merchants, sea captains, ship owners, and businesses could go to arrange for the oceanic transport of industrial bulk commodities from producer to end user. According to the Baltic exchange, the BDI provides "an assessment of the price of moving the major raw materials by seas. Taking in 26 key shipping routes measured on a time-charter and voyage basis, the index covers supramax, pana-max, and capsize dry bulk carriers," carrying a wide range of com-modities, fuels, foodstuffs and fertilizers, construction materials, and other raw goods. About half of sea cargoes are energy-related, but the value of container traffic, which accounts for a little over 10 percent of cargoes by weight, are much higher. The index therefore provides useful information on the pace of global economic growth. The index can be inflated by shipments of foodstuffs, but at the margin the bigger influence is the pace of global economic growth. It is important to note that because much of what is shipped repre-sents precursors to production—building materials, coal, and iron, for example—the BDI can lead changes in economic activity. Moreover, there is very little in the way of the speculative element in shipping rates because shippers do not book freighters unless they have cargo to ship.

The BDI tends to strongly correlate with industrial commodi-ties prices, at least in terms of direction of change, owing to its cor-relation with economic activity.

How to Nail It: When the BDI is trending upwards, overweight commodities and shares in basic materials companies as well as shippers and shipbuilding companies. Bet on strength in the global economy by adding exposures abroad, particularly in countries where exports make up a relatively large share of economic activity. Add exposure to the currencies and fixed-income securities for these countries, as their credit risks will decrease as a result of increases in their current account balances. Overweight TIPS relative to conven-tional Treasuries in anticipation of accelerating headline inflation.

GOLDEN COMPASS 22: INDUSTRIAL MATERIALS PRICE INDEXES (JOC AND CRB RAW INDUSTRIALS)

Its Power: Industrial materials prices are tightly correlated with global economic activity and can be revealing with respect to senti-ment regarding the U.S. dollar.

Where to Get It: For the Reuters/Jefferies CRB Raw Industrials index, go to the CRB's Web site, http://www.crbtrader.com/crbindex/default.asp, and click on "daily closing values." Also go to the JOC's Web site: http://www.joc.com/data/pricesindexes

.shtml. The JOC Industrial Price index is produced by the *Journal of Commerce* and the Economic Cycle Research Institute (ECRI).

The View from the Top Down: The correlation between factory activity and industrial materials prices is strong, which makes sense since it is the factory sector that is the largest consumer of industrial materials. Charts between industrial materials prices and major gauges of factory activity such as the Institute for Supply Management's monthly purchasing managers index illustrate the tight connection, although what is notable is the extent to which industrial materials prices have begun to diverge despite weakening of the U.S. economy. What this means is that now more than ever industrial materials prices are reflecting global conditions, not just conditions in the United States, making gauges such as the JOC and the CRB Raw Industrials excellent gauges of factory activity worldwide. Industrial materials prices also reflect investor sentiment in the foreign exchange market, with the declines in the value of the dollar used as a basis for bidding commodity prices higher.

Included in the JOC are cotton, burlap, steel, copper, aluminum, zinc, lead, tin, nickel, hides, rubber, tallow, plywood, red oak, benzene, crude oil, ethylene, and natural gas.

How to Nail It: Use trends in industrial materials prices as a means of assessing the strength of the global economy. When industrial materials prices are trending upward, overweight shares in basic materials companies and bet on strength in the global economy by adding exposures abroad, particularly in countries where exports make up a relatively large share of economic activity. Overweight TIPS relative to conventional Treasuries in anticipation of accelerating headline inflation. Short-term traders can make bets on the likely strength of purchasing managers indexes worldwide, as well as their price indexes, to which the JOC and the CRB correlate strongly. Treat extreme moves in industrial materials as a sign of extreme sentiment about the U.S. dollar, establishing a countertrend position in the dollar.

GOLDEN COMPASS 23: INTERNATIONAL RESERVES

Its Power: Buildups, draw downs, and shifts in international reserves can speak volumes about a country's economic situation, its economic outlook, and its ability to counter both economic weakness and unexpected shocks.

Where to Get It: Many of the world's central banks publish on their Web sites statistics on their international reserve assets, but there is a central location where statistics for most major nations can be obtained: the International Monetary Fund's Web site. The IMF keeps a page titled "Data Template on International Reserve and Foreign Currency Liquidity," which can be found at: http://imf .org/external/np/sta/ir/colist.htm. Notably, China's reserves, which are by far the biggest in the world, are not on the IMF's Web site. Instead, obtain the figures from China's National Bureau of Statistics, which although difficult to find, are available through a search on the Web. China's reserves totaled a whopping $1.68 trillion in March 2008.

The View from the Top Down: Simply put, international reserves are like money in the bank, and the more that one has the better. Countries obtain international reserves primarily from one of two sources: higher prices for the goods they sell (oil in particular) or by increasing their export volumes (China's route to riches). To illustrate the importance of international reserves, consider Russia. In the summer of 1998, Russia defaulted on its debt obligations. At that time, Russia held only $10 billion in reserves. Fast forward to today: Russia's reserves now total $500 billion. Which Russia would you rather invest in? Russia's economy is about $1.5 trillion in size, and the country is growing at a 7 percent pace, which means that if growth were to weaken sharply, say to 3 percent, the country could deploy $60 billion of its reserves to return growth to trend growth of 7 percent. The destination of such sovereign wealth is of importance to top-down investors. Countries on the receiving end of international reserves are likely to benefit, and investments in such countries could flag a liberalization of markets there. For the global economy, increases in international reserves act as a cushion against economic weakness. For context, note that world reserve assets grew from $2.3 trillion in 2003 to $6.8 trillion in June 2008.

How to Nail It: The vast amount of international reserves now in place will support the world's economy for many years to come. It is therefore rational to bet that any downturn in global economic activity will be short and shallow. Hence, be a buyer on weakness in risk assets worldwide if the weakness relates to worries about the resilience of the world's economy. Overweight sectors that stand likely to benefit from increased spending on infrastructures, which should be well supported by the abundance of reserves. Invest in countries on the receiving end of the world's excess supply of reserves. Eastern European countries have been recipients in recent years. Track these movements via data on cross-border deposits compiled by the Bank for International Settlements.

GOLDEN COMPASS 24: BANK CREDIT

Its Power: Data on bank credit can be used in a number of ways, including as a gauge of the amount of money flowing into the economy, the banking sector's willingness to lend, and, recently, as a gauge of the recapitalization of the banking sector following recent credit losses. Never forget that only banks can expand the money supply.

Where to Get It: Data on bank credit are released by the Federal Reserve every Friday at 4:15 p.m. ET in the Fed's so-called H.8 release. Go to page one of the following: http://federalreserve.gov/releases/h8/current/h8.pdf. For historical data start here: http://federalreserve.gov/releases/h8/.

The View from the Top Down: For many years, I have used the Federal Reserve's data on bank credit to gauge the health of the U.S. economy. The rationale is that when bank credit expands, whether it is in the form of securities purchases, loans, or leases, borrowers will inevitably put the money to work and spur economic activity. It is not difficult to imagine how an expansion of credit can signal economic growth, and that is exactly how it has paid to view it. For perspective, note that in the 15 years ended March 2008, bank credit expanded at an annual rate of about 8 percent. During the credit boom years of the early 2000s, bank credit expanded faster, at a 9.5 percent pace in the five years ended March 2008. Loans and leases account for the bulk of bank credit, at about 74 percent. About half of that tally is real estate loans, which makes it easy to see how increases or decreases in that category would be important. Another area of importance is the figure on commercial and industrial loans, which although just 15 percent of bank credit is one of the most important categories, as it speaks volumes about business confidence, inventory investment, capital spending, and hiring. A new way of looking at bank credit statistics emerged recently. Now, the data are an excellent gauge of credit conditions, specifically with respect to the recent credit crisis. In theory, if banks are choking off credit, bank credit will grow at a below-trend pace. In early 2008, this had not materialized, partly because banks were unexpectedly absorbing assets into their balance sheets, including structured investment vehicles and loans they were having difficulty unloading via securitization.

How to Nail It: When bank credit expands at a strong pace, bet on self-reinforcing economic expansion. Also, in general, growth in bank credit is good news for banks because when financial assets grow, bank profits tend to expand. Of course, recent times have been an exception, because the growth in financial assets has been forced. Nevertheless, Fed rate cuts should be expected to boost the money supply and spur growth in financial assets. Narrow in on the figures on commercial and industrial loans to gauge business spending.

GOLDEN COMPASS 25: THE YIELD SPREAD BETWEEN LIBOR AND THE FEDERAL FUNDS RATE

Its Power: The yield spread between the London Inter-Bank Offering Rate (LIBOR) and the federal funds rate is an important gauge of both risk attitudes and funding costs for vast amounts of debtors carrying debts tied to LIBOR.

Where to Get It: The federal funds rate is widely available on financial Web sites. Alternatively, go to the Fed's Web site and look for the Fed's most recent policy statement, which refers to the federal funds rate target: http://federalreserve.gov/monetarypolicy/fomc.htm. LIBOR rates are also widely available on financial Web sites and the Fed's Web site, although you can also go to the source: the British Bankers' Association's Web site, which sets LIBOR rates each day after 11 a.m. in London, and generally around 11:45 a.m. The most widely watched term is the three-month LIBOR.

The View from the Top Down: Vast amounts of debts are tied to LIBOR. To illustrate, consider the fact that one of the most actively traded futures contract in the world is one that is LIBOR-based—the Chicago Mercantile Exchange's Eurodollar contract, which is based on three-month LIBOR. The reason it is so actively traded is that most LIBOR-based debts are tied to three-month LIBOR. Debtors use the futures contract to hedge their risks, and others use it to speculate on where LIBOR might be headed. LIBOR tends to trade at a very tight spread compared to the federal funds rate, say about an eighth of a percentage point for three-month LIBOR. This obviously means that three-month LIBOR will move in ways that coincide with the Federal Reserve's interest-rate changes. This is your first reason to track LIBOR and in particular longer-term eurodollar contracts, which reflect bets on monetary policy. The 2007–2008 credit crisis illustrates the second way of using LIBOR, specifically by focusing on the yield spread between LIBOR and federal funds. During the crisis the yield spread between three-month LIBOR and federal funds widened dramatically to 86 basis points on December 2007 (see Figure 14.5). It did so because banks became unwilling to lend to each other and because many banks hoarded their cash. Obviously this means that the yield spread is an excellent gauge of risk attitudes. The spread is also an important

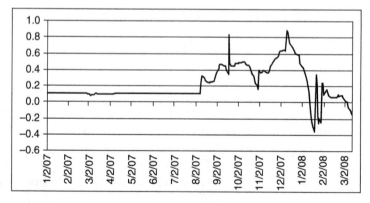

Figure 14.5 Three-month LIBOR minus the target fed-funds rate (in percentage points).

Note: The spread moved into negative territory in early 2008 in anticipation of interest-rate cuts from the Federal Reserve.

Sources: Federal Reserve, British Bankers Association.

gauge of funding costs because it reflects credit spreads and because it directly affects funding costs.

How to Nail It: Scan the monthly eurodollar contracts, particularly those that stretch out as far as about two years. Decide whether you agree with the market's bet on where the fed funds rate and credit spreads are headed, remembering to subtract an eighth of a percentage point from the implied yields from the contract to determine what the market expects of the Fed. Second, if the yield spread between LIBOR and the federal funds rate widens and you agree with the apparent premise, position your portfolio defensively, moving out of shares in cyclical companies and into defensive groups. In the fixed-income market, move up the credit-quality scale by buying higher-quality bonds.

GOLDEN COMPASS 26: THE INSTITUTE FOR SUPPLY MANAGEMENT'S MONTHLY PURCHASING MANAGERS INDEX

Its Power: Since the end of World War II, the Institute for Supply Management's monthly purchasing manager's index, which until January 2002 was known as the National Association of Purchasing Managers (NAPM) index, has accurately portrayed economic conditions in the United States and has served as a superior leading economic indicator.

Where to Get It: Go to the ISM's Web site, www.ism.ws, and do a mouse-over on the left navigation bar, highlighting the button "ISM Report on Business." Then click on "latest manufacturing ROB."

The View from the Top Down: There is perhaps no timelier and reliable economic indicator than the ISM index, which traces its roots back to the 1920s, when the local New York City purchasing managers association was polling its members about the availability of specific commodities. By the 1940s, the survey was molded into a format similar to today's ISM index. Figure 14.6 shows the tight correlation that has existed since the 1940s between the ISM's composite index, select components of the ISM index, and the U.S. gross domestic product. In a study, Harris, Owens, and Sarte conclude that the ISM provides "surprisingly accurate real-time information on the business cycle, essentially one quarter or more ahead of the release of the final GDP report."[1] Importantly, the researchers also found that the ISM's

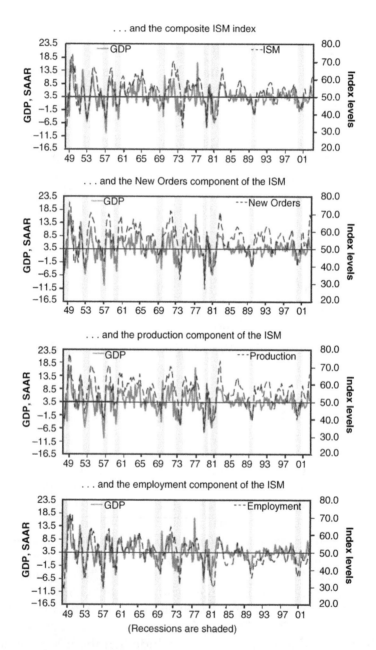

Figure 14.6 U.S. GDP growth.

Source: Harris, Matthew, Raymond Owens, and Pierre-Daniel Sarte,"Using Manufacturinig Surveys to Assess Economic Conditions," Federal Reserve Bank of Richmond, *Economic Quarterly*, Vol. 90', no. 4 Fall 2004.

production component, which accounts for 25 percent of the composite index (new orders rank highest at 30 percent), has shown the tightest correlation to GDP and personal income, which makes sense since it is production that affects GDP most, not orders, which predict future production. Few factors are more important to the economy and the financial markets than income growth, which is the fuel for sustained economic growth. In another interesting finding, Harris, Owens, and Sarte found that compared to other ISM components, the ISM's employment component had the weakest correlation to both GDP and personal income, underscoring the idea that employment is a lagging indicator.[2] Note that the ISM report contains an approximation for GDP derived from the historical correlation between that month's level for the ISM index and GDP growth.

How to Nail It: From this single indicator, an extraordinarily wide net can be cast for investment ideas. The strong historical correlation between the ISM index, GDP, and income growth makes this clear. The investment strategies that work best with the ISM index are plain vanilla. First, determine the economic growth rate implied by the ISM index. From there, position your portfolio accordingly, ever mindful of the predictive power of the ISM index and in particular its production component. This means that when the ISM index points to steady economic expansion, you should overweight procyclical industries, including companies in the following sectors: industrial, transportation, basic materials, consumer cyclicals, media, and travel and leisure. Utilize regional manufacturing surveys such as the New York Fed's Empire manufacturing survey, the Philadelphia Fed survey, and the Chicago purchasing managers index to project trends in the ISM index; the correlation is strong between these surveys and the ISM. Overweight commodities when the ISM index is running above its historical average, and underweight U.S. Treasuries in the fixed-income arena.

GOLDEN COMPASS 27: THE NATIONAL FEDERATION OF INDEPENDENT BUSINESSES' MONTHLY SMALL BUSINESS OPTIMISM INDEX

Its Power: The vast majority of net new jobs in the United States are created by small businesses, which are also big innovators—Microsoft and Apple are two goliaths that were essentially developed in garages. The NFIB survey captures sentiment and conditions in this critical sector extraordinarily well.

Where to Get It: NFIB's monthly survey is released on the second Tuesday of every month, and news of it will usually find its way into the financial press. Alternatively, go to the NFIB's Web site, www.nfib.com, and click on the "newsroom" button at the top of the page.

The View from the Top Down: Data from the U.S. Small Business Administration (SBA) indicate that 99.7 percent of all U.S. businesses are small businesses. Need I go on? In addition, data from the U.S. Census Bureau indicate that by a wide margin small businesses account for the bulk of U.S. job growth. In fact, Census Bureau data indicate that from 1990 to 2003, 79.5 percent of all net new jobs created (firm startups + expansions – jobs lost through firm closures and contractions) were created by businesses employing fewer than 20 workers (Figure 14.7).[3] In contrast, large firms (500-plus workers) accounted for only 7.3 percent of net new jobs created during the period. The small business sector is also a very innovative sector, as evidenced by SBA data indicating that small businesses apply for 13 to 14 times more patents per employee than do large firms. These data underscore just how important the small business sector is to the U.S. economy and why it is that investors should take seriously any

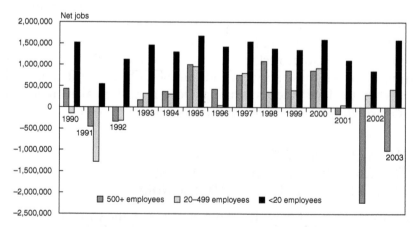

Figure 14.7 Net job creation by firm size, 1990–2003.

Sources: U.S. Census Bureau Statistics of U.S. Business.

developments in that sector. For example, in the early 2000s it was significant that Washington dealt significant tax cuts to the small business sector; it heralded a strong period for both the small business sector and for the U.S. economy. It also hinted at a more innovative period. Keep in mind that roughly 75 percent of establishments represent the self-employed. In addition, data from the Internal Revenue Service indicate that in 2004, 19.5 million individuals were self-employed, roughly 12 percent of the working population, a 26 percent increase from 1997. This underscores the importance of watching developments that could affect the self-employed.

How to Nail It: Be on the lookout for top-down developments, such as changes in tax laws, that could affect the small business sector and the self-employed; the impact on the economy and the markets can be substantial. There can also be impact on the tech sector, given the strong linkage between small businesses and innovation. Respect the NFIB survey as a reliable gauge of economic conditions; its correlation with government data is very strong, thanks to the work of the William Dunkelberg, the NFIB's Ph.D. chief economist, who has produced the data for years.

GOLDEN COMPASS 28: THE TRANSMISSION EFFECTS OF MONETARY POLICY

Its Power: When the Fed raises and lowers interest rates, the real action is what happens to financial conditions, which are affected through the transmission effects of monetary policy. Changes in aggregate financial conditions are far more relevant to the economic outlook than changes in the fed funds rate, the rate controlled by the Fed.

Where to Get It: There is no one gauge on this; it is a combination of gauges. Transmission effects are the means by which monetary policy is transmitted into the economy through the financial markets. The five ways in which the Fed's rate changes work their way into the economy are through stock prices, credit spreads, the value of the dollar, lending standards, and capital formation.

The View from the Top Down: The ability of the Federal Reserve to achieve a desired outcome from the rate changes it implements depends materially on the transmission effects of monetary policy. It is a mistake to consider the impact of interest-rate changes alone. Financial markets and the way that interest-rate changes affect the economy have become far too complex for such a narrow analysis as this, and it is awfully presumptuous to think that rate changes by themselves will achieve a desired outcome. This is why it is essential that investors track aggregate financial conditions by considering each of the transmission effects. When analyzing the impact from equities, the analysis is fairly simple. Basically, consider the wealth effects. For the U.S. dollar, keep this rule of thumb in mind: for every 5 percent change in the value of the dollar, see it as the equivalent of Fed rate cuts totaling 37.5 basis points, an amount enough to raise or lower industrial output by 0.4 percent over two years (output tends to increase by 1 percent per year in the United States). Moreover, a 5 percent change in the dollar's value will raise or lower manufacturers' profits by a similar amount. For credit spreads, consider that as much as $1 trillion of corporate debt could be sold over a given year and assess the dollar impact of any change in credit spreads. Also consider how credit spreads might be affecting bond issuance by tracking such, either via Bloomberg news or the quarterly report on the fixed-income markets prepared by the Securities Industry and Financial Markets Association (SIFMA), at www.sifma.org. To track lending standards, track bank credit and the Federal Reserve's quarterly survey of senior loan officers. These are a few of the quantitative things that you can do, but you also have to have a feel for whether it seems that the Fed's rate changes are working. For example, in 2007 and early 2008, there was no sense that the Fed's deep rate cuts were working, which meant that rate cuts would be deeper and that the Fed's objectives on reviving growth would take longer. This realization weakened the financial markets further.

How to Nail It: Be ever mindful to avoid the superficial analysis that far too many investors get lured into when they focus solely on the Fed's rate changes rather than on financial conditions on the whole. When the transmission effects of monetary policy are working well, expect the Fed to achieve its objectives on an accelerated timetable. For example, if the Fed begins a series of rate cuts and financial conditions loosen (stocks rise, the dollar weakens, credit spreads narrow), then bet on cyclical strength in the economy, shifting to an overweight on equities relative to bonds. If in the midst of the Fed cutting rates financial conditions tighten, the economy will be slow to strengthen and the Fed will likely need to cut rates more. In this case, overweight bonds relative to equities, investing in the short end of the yield curve.

GOLDEN COMPASS 29: DEMOGRAPHICS

Its Power: It is a fact of human and social life that people tend to engage in certain types of behavior at different points along the life cycle. If there are more babies in the world, companies will sell more diapers. If there are more senior citizens in the world, companies will sell more hearing aids, eyeglasses, and vacation homes. There is no escaping the power of demographics to predict consumption patterns across many industries.

Where to Get It: The U.S. Census Bureau is an importance source of demographic information. A variety of useful data can also be obtained from the U.S. Administration on Aging, particularly from the "newsroom" in the category "products and materials." Some of the publications are extensive. The Web sites for both agencies are a bit onerous to use, so you have to keep digging to find the specific information you want. Be patient.

One of the better resources is the Census Bureau's statistical abstract, which contains a very broad amount of information (over 1,300 pages!), including simple-to-find tables on birth statistics: http://www.census.gov/prod/www/statistical-abstract.html. Birth statistics can also be found at http://www.cdc.gov/nchs/births.htm. And here's a good page for trends in health and aging: http://www.cdc.gov/nchs/agingact.htm.

The View from the Top Down: In its most basic form, investing depends greatly upon predicting the actions of other people. When we invest, we must therefore ask many basic questions whose answers are often quite complex and very difficult to ascertain—this is what makes markets. The complexity of predicting the actions of people results from the fact that we are dealing with the human condition, which is quite complex, as we can see by the many different ways that people behave and the many different personalities and divergent cultures that exist throughout the world. Nevertheless, if we look at data that separate these complexities into groups containing similarities, it becomes easier for us to predict what people will do. Demographic information can empower us in this way, by giving us facts about very basic but critical attributes of the populace both here and abroad. The data also provide insight into herdlike trends whether in the form of consumption, investing, urban sprawling, or other forms of behavior that people latch onto for innumerable reasons.

Age demographics are one of the most useful kinds of data, as there is no denying that at certain ages people will do things that are fairly easy to foresee. For example, it is a fact that babies drink baby formula and wear diapers, that toddler girls play with dolls, that teenagers buy *Teen Beat* magazine and spend a lot of time on Myspace.com, that people tend to buy their first home between the ages of 25 and 29, that people aged 35 and over increasingly buy hair-coloring products, that people aged 55 and over tend to buy vacation homes more so than other age groups, that people 65 and over start spending their saving on such things as health-care needs, and so on. It is therefore critical to know the number of people entering the various age groups and to know as much as possible about what it is they consume. My favorite example applicable to the present is the fact that there will be good-sized increases amounting to close to 15 percent over the next 10 years in the number of people aged 25–29, the age group prone to buy new homes. (Less than 3 percent of new homes are bought by people aged 20–24, but about 25 percent of new homes are bought by people aged 25–34.) This means that the housing slump will be cushioned.

How to Nail It: Armed with demographic statistics, you can develop a very wide variety of investment ideas. Sometimes, these ideas might not fit with the mood in the markets, but therein you will find opportunities to beat the markets. For example, the pessimism surrounding housing will eventually have to give way to powerful demographic influences that will push demand for housing upward, a far different scenario from the early 1990s when demographic influences impeded the housing recovery from the bursting of the 1980s housing bubble. If you are investing from the bottom up and are therefore closely examining company balance sheets, use information that can be gleaned from demographics to project future sales trends. Seek out diversification benefits by choosing thematic investment strategies that depend heavily upon demographic trends. Utilize demographic trends abroad, but first delineate any differences between the ways people behave abroad compared to how they behave in the United States.

GOLDEN COMPASS 30: PERSONAL SPENDING ON SERVICES COUPLED WITH THE POINT SPREAD BETWEEN THE ISM'S NONMANUFACTURING AND MANUFACTURING INDEXES

Its Power: With scant figures available on the service side of the U.S. economy and scant attention paid to their importance, these two indicators pack a wallop, providing information about the service sector that can be used as a basis for assessing the U.S. job market.

Where to Get It: Data on personal spending on services are contained in the Bureau of Economic Analysis's monthly report on personal income and consumption, as well as the BEA's quarterly report on the nation's gross domestic product. Both reports can be found at this address: http://www.bea.gov/national/index .htm#gdp. Within the GDP report, look for the figure in Table 1 near the top of the page under the category "personal consumption expenditures." As for the ISM indexes, go to www.ism.ws and place your cursor over the button "ISM Report on Business," and click on both the "Latest Manufacturing ROB" and the "Latest Non-Manufacturing ROB," where you will find the main indexes for both near the top of the page.

The View from the Top Down: Very few investors pay heed to what is undoubtedly one of the most important factors influencing the labor market: the composition of GDP, particularly with respect to personal spending on services and how the nonmanufacturing sector is faring relative to the factory sector. Basically, the factory sector isn't hiring, so it's not the sector to watch. It is the service sector that creates the vast majority of jobs in the United States, accounting for 115.35 million, or 83.7 percent of the 137.75 million jobs in the country as of May 2008. To illustrate the importance of tracking the service sector, consider what happened at the end of the 2001 recession. In 2002 the U.S. economy began to recover from the recession, growing at an average pace of 1.9 percent during the year's four quarters. In 2003, growth sped up, moving along at a 3.7 percent pace. Despite the growth, the economic recovery was a jobless recovery, with the economy losing 45,000 jobs per month in 2002 and 9,000 jobs per month in 2003. Many were baffled by this, but the answers were staring them in the face. The problem was that although economic growth had picked up, it had done so in the wrong places, at least as far as job growth is concerned. In other words, the composition of the acceleration in GDP was skewed unfavorably away from the service sector, where most hiring occurs, toward other sectors such as the durable goods sector, which hasn't put up a help-wanted sign in 25 years. The growth divergence was stark. Personal spending on services advanced at a pace of just 2.1 percent in 2002 and 2003, which was well below the whopping 5 percent pace for spending on durable goods (in the second and third quarters of 2003, spending on durable goods advanced at a 16.8 and 16.7 percent pace, respectively). Only when personal spending on services jumped to a 3.4 percent pace in 2004 did job growth quicken.

Another way of tracking whether economic growth is skewing favorably in ways that will boost the job market is to compare the ISM's nonmanufacturing index to its manufacturing index. Typically, the nonmanufacturing business activity index runs at a spread of 5 points above the manufacturing index. This reflects the fact that the service sector tends to fare better than the factory sector, which has been in decline since the early 1980s. When the spread widens, job growth is likely to accelerate. When it narrows, job growth is likely to slow. Keep in mind that in February 2008, the ISM created a new index for the nonmanufacturing sector called the "composite index" (the business activity index is based on a stand-alone question; the composite consists of four subcomponents, including the business activity index). The ISM has built a data history for the new series, which appears to run at a three-point spread to the ISM manufacturing index.

How to Nail It: Diminish the importance of both the monthly data on personal spending and the quarterly GDP figures if the data on service spending conflict, recognizing that the figures on service spending are of utmost importance to the job situation. When service spending is strong relative to the rest of the economy, expect job growth to be faster than most anticipate. Conversely, when the composition of economic growth is skewed unfavorably toward spending on durable goods instead of services, expect the job market to be weaker than implied by the overall growth rate. When the ISM spread reinforces the conditions implied by the data on personal spending, position your portfolio more aggressively to fit with the conditions. Also, using this focus, either overweight or underweight the durable goods sector of the economy relative to other sectors, particularly the service sector.

GOLDEN COMPASS NO. 31: STEEL OUTPUT AND STEEL SCRAP PRICES

Its Power: The word "steel" has a connotation that few words can compare to. Steel has for ages been an enduring symbol of strength, and today it is playing an essential role in the surge in global economic activity. With steel at the heart of major projects throughout the world, the production of steel and steel scrap prices remain among the best indicators of economic activity available.

Where to Get It: Every Monday, the American Iron and Steel Institute releases on its Web site data on steel production through the prior Saturday. The data can be found at this address: http://www.steel.org/AM/Template.cfm?Section=Statistics. Steel scrap prices can be obtained from a number of Web sites, although most require a subscription: platts.com, chinascrapmetal.com, estainlesssteel.com, and metalbulletin.com are a few. *The Wall Street Journal* is one of the easier places to find the data, and they can also be found on the journal's Web site in its markets data center.

The View from the Top Down: During times of prosperity, steel demand soars as high as the buildings it supports. In weak economic times, projects stall, and steel rusts. Despite the slant toward a more service-oriented economy, steel production continues to correlate strongly with the overall economy. Today, as in decades past, steel is being utilized on a variety of fronts in the production of cars, cans, clothes hangers, appliances, heavy equipment, pipes, rail cars, train tracks, trucks, airplanes, bridges, ships, stadiums, skyscrapers, and much more. From this list it is easy to see why steel can be such a good economic indicator. For example, during times of economic prosperity, consumers tend to increase their purchases of durable goods, which of course affects steel demand and steel prices. Moreover, during prosperous times, tax revenues increase for state and local governments, which results in increased spending on infrastructure, boosting steel demand. Such is the case at the present time worldwide, with the domestic and external balances of vast numbers of countries on every continent in their best condition in decades, providing the impetus for a global surge in infrastructure spending that is still relatively young. Therefore, with this likely to continue for a while, the cyclical ups and downs of this secular uptrend will almost certainly be reflected in the production of steel and steel prices, making these indicators as valuable as ever.

There are many different types of steel, but the prices to watch are those for steel scrap. Steel scrap prices have long been a favorite of former Fed chairman Alan Greenspan, whose client list in the 1950s at his firm Townsend-Greenspan included more than 10 steel companies. In 1997 Greenspan told the American Iron and Steel Institute at its annual meeting, "Every day, I still look for the price of No. 1 heavy melt steel scrap," underscoring its importance. Steel scrap is in fact vital to the steel industry, as roughly 70 percent of all steel produced in the United States is recycled into steel scrap and because it is the steel industry's largest source of raw materials, according to the Steel Recycling Institute (recycle-steel.org). Another reason it is a good price gauge is that it is not yet traded on a commodity exchange, which means that its price is "pure," devoid of most of the speculative fervor that exists in commodities that trade on exchanges. This makes steel scrap an even better gauge of the economy than many of the more widely followed, exchange-traded commodities.

How to Nail It: As a gauge of the industrial sector, steel ranks extremely high. This is why trends in steel production and steel prices should be used as a basis for investing in the various industries that use steel, including those that are mentioned above. Be sure to take note of whether the driving forces behind steel demand reflect cyclical or secular trends, as steel plays an integral role in both. For example, the global infrastructure investment strategy is the result of a secular theme with immense staying power. This means that even if cyclical factors tell you to short names in industries such as those shown above, you should also be considering new long positions on any weakness in those names because, as a cyclical force moving against a secular trend, any dip is likely to be short-lived.

As a gauge of the economy, steel trends have been good pre-dictors for decades, which is why they should be used as a basis for positioning your portfolio for the ups and downs of the business cycle. This means that when the steel indicators point to cyclical strength, you should overweight cyclical industries and under-weight those considered more defensive. You should also under-weight Treasuries relative to other segments of the fixed-income market, betting on a flatter yield curve. As a high-frequency indica-tor, steel will keep you very much in tune with the latest develop-ments in the economy, but be ever-mindful of the secular trends likely to endure and affect the many steel-related sectors, especially in light of the global infrastructure play.

GOLDEN COMPASS 32: AUTOMOBILE PRODUCTION

Its Power: Swings in automobile production substantially influence the economy and the sense of the economy that investors glean from the monthly economic statistics because manufacturing-related sectors disproportionately affect the economic calendar.

Where to Get It: Ward's Automotive is a top source for data on automobile production. It can be found here: http://wardsauto .com/keydata/. Subscribers to the Ward's data can get more fre-quent (daily) and detailed data on both production and sales, including projections. Major economic services such as Stone & McCarthy Research provide additional insight into the impact of any changes in automobile production schedules.

Very important are data from automobile manufacturers, which each month include within their sales statistics information about production schedules. For example, General Motors reports on its sales and production data here: http://www.gm.com/ corporate/investor_information/sales_prod/. GM's production data are particularly good because they show the quarterly changes to production dating back several years and to the quarter ahead. Federal Reserve data on automobile production is contained in the Fed's report on industrial production: http://federalreserve.gov/ releases/ g17/Current/g17.pdf.

The View from the Top Down: The production of automobiles and parts accounts for about 5 percent of all industrial production, which is large enough to have a substantial impact on total output when the swings in automobile production are large. For example, at 5 percent of total output, a 10 percent change in automobile production over a given quarter affects total output by five-tenths of a percentage point, which is a large amount when you consider the fact that industrial production tends to increase by only about 0.2 percent per month on average. Importantly, when automobile production has such swings, the annualized impact is quite large, and this amplifies the market response to the impact. Swings in automobile production occur because production often gets out of sync with sales, which is why it is important to track the monthly sales figures. For perspective, keep in mind that sales of domestically produced vehicles ran at a pace of about 12.5 million per year over the two years ended March 2008, and overall sales ran at a pace of 16.6 million over the five years ended March 2008. Deviations from these levels, especially if they happen abruptly, are sure to affect production schedules and exert an important influence on the overall economy and the monthly economic statistics.

How to Nail It: When automobile production schedules are expected to exert a significant influence on the economy, expect market-moving data such as durable goods orders and the ISM manufacturing index to be affected, thus influencing the financial markets. Recognize that the extent to which markets are affected depends upon whether the impact on the economy is enough to be a game changer. In other words, if automobile production is expected to boost the economy by a percentage point during a particular quarter after having subtracted the same amount in a current or previous quarter, the two-percentage point swing might push GDP from running at a pace that is below the economy's 3 percent growth potential to a rate that is above it, boosting income growth in ways that fortifies an economic expansion and limits downside risks. This would be a strong basis for betting on an expansion of the economy by overweighting equities, corporate bonds, commodities, and the emerging markets. Treasuries would be underweighted and yields on short-dated maturities would be expected to rise faster than yields on longer maturities. Within the equity market, the automobile sector's influence on factory statistics will influence perceptions about a variety of sectors, including the durable goods, capital goods, and industrial sectors such as steel and heavy equipment. Also influenced is the commodities market, particularly for metals, platinum, and other industrials.

GOLDEN COMPASS 33: HOUSING—INVENTORIES OF UNSOLD HOMES

Its Power: At the heart of the recent housing crisis was a buildup of unsold homes. All that is needed to understand this powerful gauge is respect for the laws of supply and demand.

Where to Get It: To assess the inventory situation in housing, you need to look at both new and existing homes. For new homes, go to the Census Bureau's Web site, http://www.census.gov/cgi-bin/briefroom/BriefRm, and scroll down to find the link to the PDF for the data. Once there, look for the table titled, "New Houses Sold and for Sale by Stage of Construction and Median Number of Months on Sales Market." Look for the column showing the number of homes for sale. For existing homes, which account for the vast majority of unsold homes, go to the Web site for the National Association of Realtors and click on the link to the newsroom: http://www.realtor.org/press_room/index.html.

The View from the Top Down: When the housing market peaked in the summer of 2005, the most important metric from that point forward was the inventory of unsold homes. The related inventory-to-sales ratio had not moved much, mainly because home sales were still high at that point. This is why it is crucial when assessing housing to focus on the absolute number of homes for sale—the inventory-to-sales ratio is a lagging indicator. Sales trends can change, and when they do, the inventory-to-sales ratio will play catch-up with the trend in inventory levels.

When assessing inventory levels, for context keep in mind that in the 20 years ended January 2004, the maximum number of unsold new homes was 378,000 in May 1989. The average for the period was 325,000. In 2004, inventory levels began to climb, which was a red flag, beginning the year near the all-time high at 377,000 and ending the year at 431,000, a record high at the time. Inventories continued to climb in 2005 and 2006 until the peak of 570,000 in June 2006. To underscore the danger of focusing on the inventory-to-sales ratio alone, note that the inventory-to-sales ratio did not begin to climb until the end of 2005. Interestingly, it took almost two years to bring the number of unsold homes down at about 100,000 from the peak, which shows how lengthy the impact of the housing inventory cycle can be. In March 2008 inventories were still at about 160,000 above the long-term average, which meant that there was a ways to go still, although the progress made up until that point was promising. For existing homes, a normal reading for unsold homes is about 2.1 million or so. In 2005, the tally started to climb and eventually peaked at a whopping 4.56 million in July 2007 (Figure 14.8). One thing that is notable here is that both the climb and the peak lagged that of new homes, which makes sense since a home has got to be built first before it can be called an existing home. This obviously means you should watch the new home market more intensely, as it will turn before the existing home market.

To assess the amount of time that it might take to bring inventory levels down, always keep in mind the fact that, owing to population growth, household formation tends to run at a pace of about 1.2 million per year in the United States. Hence, if housing starts are running at a pace of 1.0 million, which equates to about 800,000 new dwellings (200,000 "starts" are teardowns and such), this would remove about 400,000 homes from the market per year, either through purchases or rentals.

How to Nail It: When inventory levels trend upward as they began to in 2004, take it seriously because it could take considerable time to get rid of the inventories, as recent times have shown. Focus during turning points on the number of unsold new homes, which tend to lead, as they did in 2004 and 2005. Be suspicious of inventory-to-sales ratios, which could hide both increases and decreases in inventories that could have major consequences for the next housing trend, as was the case in 2004 and 2005, and, possibly, early 2008, when absolute inventory levels were falling but inventory-to-sales ratios were still climbing. Obviously, when inventory levels climb, be leery of anything attached to housing, including sectors such as building materials, mortgage finance, home builders, furniture, and real estate investment trusts. In the current environment, when inventory levels show more meaningful signs of moving lower, overweight all of the sectors mentioned, and take your pick of the wide variety of securities affected by the recent housing crisis; there's plenty to buy amid the carnage.

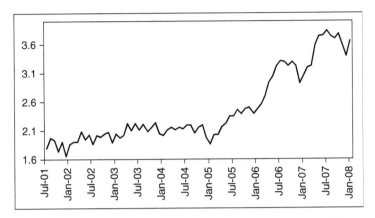

Figure 14.8 Supply of unsold existing one-family homes (in millions of units).

Source: National Association of Realtors.

GOLDEN COMPASS 34: PRODUCTIVITY CYCLES

Its Power: At the root of what boosts a nation's standard of living is productivity. History has shown that productivity trends are very long lasting—both up and down. The key is to figure out which way the trend is going and ride the wave.

Where to Get It: Data on productivity can be obtained from the U.S. Bureau of Labor Statistics, www.bls.gov. The link is readily visible on the home page.

The View from the Top Down: Productivity is at the heart of what makes a nation prosperous. For example, early humans who took hours to make a fire had time for little else. Today, we produce fire by turning a switch, and so we can put our time to many other things. Similarly, the amount of time that it takes to travel has been cut substantially compared to premodern times. The number of examples is endless, and it is easy to see how productivity improves the quality of our lives. For investors, there is a different tack. By reducing the amount of resources needed to produce goods and services, productivity results in increased profits. This is of course very good news for share prices. It is also good news for the bond market because low unit labor costs tend to result in low inflation. Productivity has advanced in the United States at an average rate of

2 percent over the past 40 years, which means that companies each year have the ability to produce 2 percent more in goods and services than they produced previous year without having to add to payrolls. This is why it is said about the U.S. economy that its growth potential is 3 percent per year: 2 percent productivity growth + 1 percent labor force growth. Growth that exceeds GDP potential results in decreases in the unemployment rate and increases in price pressures, while growth below GDP potential results in increases in the unemployment rate and decreases in price pressures. This is one of the reasons why higher levels of productivity are desirable to the markets—they boost GDP potential, helping to keep inflation low, which is good news for stocks and bonds.

Over the past 125 years, a pattern has emerged on productivity indicating that it tends to experience extended cycles. Former Federal Reserve governor Laurence Meyer highlighted this pattern in a speech I heard him give in New York in June 2001.[4] Meyer noted the fact that aside from a short cycle that occurred from 1914 to 1920, productivity cycles averaged 24 years in duration during the period 1889 to 2000. Figure 14.9 illustrates this pattern. At the root of what drives productivity above-trend is a more rapid pace of innovation. For example, in the 1910s, the automobile sector boosted productivity. In the 1920s, radio and electric utilities boosted productivity. Beginning in the mid-1990s, computers and the Internet began a technology shock that has been driving productivity sharply higher, with gains averaging about 2.5 percent since then. The key, then, is to decide whether the economy is in the midst of one of these cycles, primarily by focusing on whether the present era can be characterized as an innovative one.

How to Nail It: The only true way to play productivity cycles is by recognizing which type of cycle is in place and to position yourself aggressively in accordance with that cycle, adjusting positions during the cyclical ups and downs of the economy. For example, it is clear that since 1995 the U.S. economy has been in a productivity upswing, which could last until as late as 2020. This means that although there are almost certain to be weak periods of economic growth in the United States until 2020, these cycles are likely to be overwhelmed by the secular upswing in productivity. This is a reason to be very bullish on U.S. equities for years to come, and therefore a reason to buy equities and other risk assets on

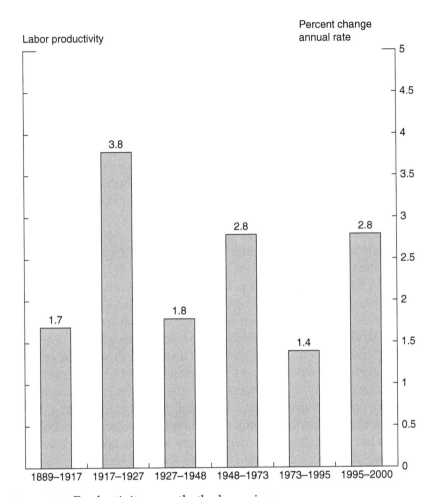

Figure 14.9 Productivity growth: the long view.

Source: Meyer, Laurence. "What Happened to the New Economy," speech before the National Association of Business Economists and the Downtown Economists, June 6, 2001.

weakness for years to come. As the super-cycle fades, expect yields on debt securities to rise because of the impact on inflation.

GOLDEN COMPASS 35: NONTRADABLE COMMODITIES

Its Power: Speculative fervor tends to reside most in assets that can be traded on exchanges. By gauging nontradable commodities, a clearer picture on underlying conditions can be obtained.

Where to Get It: In most cases you will be focusing on metals prices, which can be found on a number of Web sites, on Bloomberg, and in the *Wall Street Journal* (in the markets data center) and in Barron's. A few Web sites include platts.com, metalbulletin.com, and chinascrapmetal.com. There is also good reason, particularly in the current housing-obsessed environment, to focus on nonmetallic products such as stone, clay, glass, and concrete. An excellent source is the U.S. geological survey (USGS), which produces a monthly report that includes an index of leading indicators for the nonmetallic mineral products industry: http://minerals.usgs.gov/ minerals/pubs/imii/. You can also subscribe to obtain reports on more than 100 commodities, most of which are nontradable and are almost certain to give you an edge over other investors. This incredible resource can be found here: http://minerals.usgs.gov/minerals/ pubs/listservices.html.

The View from the Top Down: It is important from a top-down perspective to have a good handle on investor sentiment, which for centuries has been an excellent basis for countertrend trading and a valuable consideration for timing entry and exit points in the markets. To augment any analysis of market sentiment in the commodities markets, a focus on nontradable commodities is useful, particularly when prices are either soaring or plunging on exchange-traded commodities. The goal is to figure out the extent to which the price movements are related to excessive speculative fervor. This is not only an excellent way to trade commodities and other assets, such as corporate equities that are heavily influenced by commodities prices; but it is also an excellent way to gauge the underlying pace of the economy. One of these nontradable commodities is vanadium, a chemical element (atomic number 23), which is used mostly in the production of steel. Its price trends should mirror price trends for steel, since it is an important element in the production of steel. Steel and the elements that go into making steel are not readily traded, which makes them an excellent cross-check of price trends on exchange-traded commodities. At the same time, the price of vanadium and other nontradable commodities, such as *boron, cement, chromium, feldspar, manganese, nitrogen, potash, tungsten, and titanium,* all provide clues to the pace of economic activity.

How to Nail It: When the prices of nontradable commodities rise, take it as evidence that economic growth is increasing. Overweight the basic materials sector during such times, as well as the industrial sector, the automobile sector, housing-related sectors, commercial construction, export-related sectors, infrastructure, machinery, and heavy industry. When price trends in exchange-traded commodities outstrip those of nontradable commodities, bet against the sustainability of the divergence, trading commodities, related sectors, and all assets in commodity-based countries, including stocks, bonds, and the currencies of these countries.

GOLDEN COMPASS NO. 36: THE ART AND COLLECTIBLES MARKET

Its Power: Prosperity inevitably results in a spillover of capital into the art market, and art prices rise. In lean times, art prices fall, although they tend to provide good diversification benefits when equity prices fall. In recent times, the art and collectibles market has increasingly become a gauge of the global economic situation and of wealth creation abroad.

Where to Get It: One way to track art prices is to follow the major art auctions held by auction houses such as Sotheby's and Christie's. In addition to the Web sites for these companies, search financial Web sites for news on both, where recent auction information is bound to be given. Information can also be obtained from Artnet and Art Market Research, which has over 500 indexes on art and collectibles. You can view long-term indexes by following the Mei Moses art index. The *Financial Times* maintains a Web page devoted to the art market: http://www.ft.com/markets/wealth/art.

The View from the Top Down: Art is certainly more of a want than a need, which is why during the different points along the economic cycle art demand fluctuates, just like the demand for anything else that depends upon the allocation of discretionary income. By tracking art prices, a top-down investor can gain a better sense of the health of the economy in the United States, which has for many years dominated the art market. The art market has also become an increasingly good gauge of economies abroad, particularly with respect to gauging the amount of excess capital that exists there and any irrational exuberance that might be developing as a result of prosperity from the global economic boom, as the art market outside the United States has grown sharply in recent years. Art prices tend to rise at a similar pace to stock prices. Based on an index created by Mei and Moses covering a time as far back as 1875 (the work by Mei and Moses is the most extensive around), art prices are shown to have returned 8.2 percent in the 50 years ended 2000 compared to a return of 8.9 percent for the S&P 500.[5] Importantly, although art prices returned an amount similar to that of equities and tended to be more volatile during the period, the correlation between art prices and equities was small, less than 10 percent. For example, during many of the worst periods for the equity market over the past 50 years, art prices held up relatively better, including in 1987 and after the bursting of the financial bubble in 2000. This means that art is an asset class with significant diversification benefits, a substantial reason to track and invest in the art market.

How to Nail It: When art auctions are successful and there are other signs of rising art prices, it is a clear sign of economic prosperity and a reason to structure your portfolio for economic expansion. On the other hand, when auctions flop, position your portfolio defensively, especially if the flop is rooted in the global economic situation. Always consider art as a worthy asset class with significant diversification benefits.

GOLDEN COMPASS 37: PORT STATISTICS

Its Power: The United States is both the biggest exporter and the biggest importer of goods and services in the world. Moreover, as a percentage of the U.S. gross domestic product, U.S. exports are at a record high (see Figure 14.10). With substantial portions of these exports passing through just a few U.S. ports, investors focusing on data from these ports can gain an edge on this very important part of the U.S. and world economy.

Where to Get It: The two most important ports to obtain information from are the ports of Los Angeles and Long Beach, the two busiest ports in the United States. The Port Newark Marine Terminal is the third busiest port, but no data are available on the port's Web site. For the Port of Los Angeles, go to http://www

Figure 14.10 U.S. exports as a share of the U.S. gross domestic product.

Source: U.S. Department of Commerce, Bureau of Economic Analysis, from the economic report of the president to the Congress, February 2008.

.portoflosangeles.org/factsfigures_Monthly.htm. For the Port of Long Beach, go to: http://polb.com/economics/stats/default.asp. For additional transportation statistics and analyses, visit the Web site for the Bureau of Transportation Statistics, www.bts.gov.

The View from the Top Down: In the middle of 2008, U.S. exports were running at an annual pace of $1.9 trillion, and U.S. imports were running at an annual pace of $2.6 trillion, tops in the world for both categories. The export tally was $700 billion higher than it had been five years earlier. With figures like these, it is obvious that having a bead on the pulse of U.S. trade would be a good idea. Port statistics provide insight into U.S. trade in a timely manner, generally weeks in advance of the Census Bureau's monthly report on international trade. As an indicator, port statistics have grown in importance in recent years, as U.S. ports are now responsible for passing through about $800 billion, or 40 percent, of all U.S. trade on an annual basis.

Importantly, about 85 percent of U.S. container traffic is handled by just 10 U.S. ports, up from 78 percent in 1995, and the three busiest ports—Los Angeles, Long Beach, and Newark—handle 49 percent of U.S. container traffic (Figure 14.11).[6] This means that it

Thousands of 20-foot equivalent units

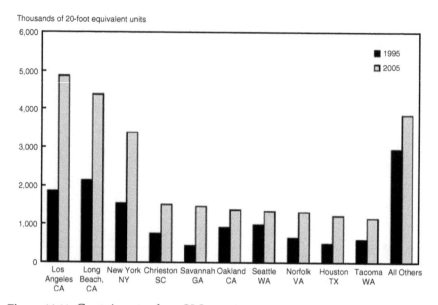

Figure 14.11 Container trade at U.S. marine ports.

Source: U.S. Department of Transportation, Bureau of Transportation Statistics, from the Economic
Report of the President to the Congress, February 2008.

does not take a lot of work to get a grip on the U.S. trade situation.
Of the three major ports, only Los Angeles and Long Beach provide
monthly statistics, but their proximity to Asia and massive container volumes make them extraordinarily representative of trends
in U.S. international trade, particularly with respect to exports to
India and China, which increased at rates of 27 and 25 percent
annually between 2003 and 2006. To further underscore this point,
consider the fact that the ports of Los Angeles and Long Beach
together handle about 10,000 truckloads per day in addition to
other forms of transportation. Aside from growth in world trade,
one of the reasons for the growth in trade through major U.S. ports
is the shift in the late 1980s to a new type of vessel known as "post-
Panamax" vessels, which are ships that are too large to pass
through the Panama Canal. These ships now account for 30 percent
of container-shipping capacity.

Tracking port statistics is pretty much plain vanilla. You
should track the figures on inbound and outbound containers as
well as the figures on "empties," which measure the amount of

containers sent back overseas to be refilled. In the first half of 2008, inbound and empties were down on a year-over-year basis, signaling continued weakness in U.S. demand for imports, a sign of weak U.S. consumer spending and impact from the weakening of the U.S. dollar, which makes imports more expensive to U.S. residents. Outbound containers continued to show strong year-over-year gains, underscoring both the vigor seen in recent years in U.S. exports, as well as the global economy.

How to Nail It: *Take a multipronged approach when absorbing port statistics.* First, use the data as a gauge of the strength of the U.S. economy, by focusing on inbound containers, which provide clues to the pace of consumer spending. Second, use the data on outbound containers to assess the pace of global economic activity. In both cases, drum up as many investment scenarios as you can squeeze out of the data. A third way to use the data is as a gauge of the maritime shipping industry and related industries such as cranes, warehouses, and ground transportation, which includes trucking and rail in particular.

GOLDEN COMPASS 38: THE JONESES

Its Power: The tendency is unmistakable. Consumer preferences toward fashion, automobiles, television programming, electronics, books, hairstyles, food, and many other goods and services are influenced significantly by the preferences of other consumers. Investors who understand the masses well improve their chances of choosing the best possible investments.

Where to Get It: This one is all around you. It starts with you and your own sense of people, what they like and don't like, and their changing moods. You also need a sense of the mood of the nation, which can be picked up in a wide variety of ways, whether from newspapers, magazines, comedians, YouTube.com, consumer sentiment indexes, political preferences, shopping tendencies, and much more. In the final analysis, you have to move out of the classroom and into the real world and align yourself with the masses.

The View from the Top Down: Duesenberry theorized that the inclination of people to spend is affected by the spending patterns of other consumers that they come into contact with.[7] This means that spending patterns are likely to be affected by trends that catch on. This is an important element of thematic investing, which we discuss in Chapter 4. There is plenty of evidence to support this idea; for example, when we refer to the decades of the 1940s, the 1950s, the 1980s, or the 1990s, we immediately recall the trends of those days, which are all very different from each other. What remains from those and other decades is embedded in the nation's culture, which can be used by today's investors to come up with investment ideas. For example, U.S. consumers have a tendency to spend rather than save, so the question should never be over *whether* consumers will spend earned income; it should be on *what* they will spend it. Some of what we learn by following the Joneses can be applied only for a short while, because many things that people buy reflect a passing fancy. In other cases, the Joneses make a fundamental shift in their preferences that have staying power. For example, peoples' fascination with Crocs shoes could either be a passing fancy or reflect a fundamental shift in the types of shoes people buy. The shift a few years ago toward Apple's iPods away from other types of MP3 players was obviously more than a passing fancy and certainly a game-changer for the music industry.

Keeping up with Joneses should be both easy and rewarding for most people. This must be true because by "most" I am referring to the masses. People know themselves, they know how others like them think, and they know their town, their city, their region of the country, and their country. Only those buried in textbooks or too draped in high society to know real people have the potential to misunderstand the Joneses. No amount of quantitative analyses or upper education can replace the power that ordinary people gain from their understanding of the masses—they are the masses. In John Lennon's song titled "Imagine," he declares that, "I am not the only one." This is something that I personally never forget, and so long as I am doing things that most everyone else likes to do, I am likely to always have an edge when trying to figure out what the Joneses will do next.

How to Nail It: As we discussed, it is crucial to decide whether consumer-driven trends are passing fancies or the start of something new that can shake up an industry. You can trade both of these scenarios, but those that have a faddish nature to them are likely to be duds after a while, so you have to be quick in and quick out and attach no diversification benefit to them. Invest with conviction on trends that look likely to last a while (buying Apple when iPods were first released obviously was a winner). Align yourself with the populace and feel what they are feeling. Doing so will help you to choose not only profitable companies, but it will also help you make a wide range of decisions about the pace of economic growth, inflation, investment trends, changes in the political landscape, and much more.

GOLDEN COMPASS 39: THE U.S. TREASURY'S INTERNATIONAL CAPITAL (TIC) SYSTEM

Its Power: Foreign investors do not determine the valuation of U.S. financial assets, but they have a substantial influence on valuations, both over the short and long term.

Where to Get It: The TIC data can be obtained from the Department of the Treasury's website at www.treas.gov/tic around the fifteenth of each month for the month that ended six weeks earlier. Look particularly at the statistics on "securities data," which is generally at the top of the page. Once there, look for the section for "transactions data" where you will find monthly flows into U.S. financial assets. Below the section on transactions is a section containing "holdings data," where you will find a table showing the major foreign holders of U.S. Treasuries.

The View from the Top Down: In the five years ended in 2007, data from the Bank for International Settlements show that cross-border deposits roughly doubled to about $30 trillion, highlighting the vast amounts of money flowing between nations. The United States is of course a major recipient of this money, which has helped it to finance its budget and trade deficits. These deficits in 2008 were expected to reach close to $1 trillion. In March 2008, foreign investors held $2.52 trillion of U.S. Treasuries, about half of the roughly $5.3 trillion outstanding at the time. These data underscore the massive influence that foreign investors have on the U.S. interest-rate environment, which is indelibly linked to the U.S. Treasury market. I have personally contended for a long time that while foreign investment is important, the biggest influence on interest rates both in the United States and abroad hinges on two factors above all others: the inflation rate and the benchmark rate set by the nation's central bank. Technical factors are not as powerful.

One example of the small influence that technical factors such as debts and deficits have on interest rates is illustrated by Japan's experience of the 1990s and early 2000s. Japan had massive budget deficits that brought its debt-to-GDP ratio to a massive 140 percent compared to the internationally accepted maximum of about 60 percent. This means that Japan needed money to finance its debt, which would lead one to think that Japan's interest rates would soar. That did not occur, of course, with Japan's interest rates then and now the lowest of the industrialized world. Why? Because the Bank of Japan has set interest rates close to zero, and Japan has experienced deflation. Hence, technical factors have played no role in determining Japan's interest-rate levels.

In the United States, the situation is a bit different because of the nation's current account deficit, but not materially different on the whole given that the U.S. budget situation is far better than Japan's. Moreover, far more foreign capital flows into the United States than flows into Japan. Nevertheless, we have witnessed in recent years the powerful influence that foreign capital flows can have on both the U.S. financial markets and its economy. The most glaring is what happened after Federal Reserve chairman Alan Greenspan began signaling in April 2004 the likelihood of a cycle of interest-rate hikes, which began two months later. One would think as Greenspan did that market interest rates would follow, but they didn't. Long-term interest rates actually fell after the Fed's hikes began. Greenspan called it a "conundrum" in a speech he gave before Congress in February 2005.[8] One major influence was foreign investment. In 2004, foreign investors bought $763 billion of long-term U.S. securities and about $100 billion in 2003. This included $352 billion of Treasury purchases, which were up $89 billion from 2003. Foreign purchases of U.S. securities increased another $76 billion in 2005. A consequence of the low interest-rate environment was that it kept mortgage rates low, which of course contributed to the housing and credit bubble, a powerful illustration of the influence of foreign investment on the U.S. economy and its financial markets.

How to Nail It: Utilizing the tables contained in the Treasury's TIC data, establish perspective on the inflows that have occurred historically into U.S. financial assets, in particular U.S. Treasuries, agencies, corporate bonds, and corporate equities. Weigh current and recent influences on U.S. markets and any factors that might cause the flows to change and upset the apple cart in terms of the economy and the markets. Get up to a six-week lead on the TIC data by looking each week at the Fed's data on foreign central bank holdings of Treasuries, which is released every Thursday at 4:30 p.m. ET in the H.4.1 release titled "Factors Affecting Reserve Balances," which can be found within the Fed's "statistical releases" on the Fed's home page. Within the release, look for the "memo" on off-balance-sheet items. The figure stood at $2.3 trillion in June 2008.

GOLDEN COMPASS 40: TRADE AND INDUSTRY GROUPS

Its Power: Few know the nation's industries better than those who work in them. From these industries, their trade groups, and the companies of these industries, investors can obtain vast insights and perspectives not easily obtained elsewhere.

Where to Get It: Everywhere on the Web! Where you go depends on what you want, but to guide you, let me give you a few suggestions. For starters, I would make it a point to at least once visit sites that represent major industry groups and sectors. In doing so, you can get a sense of what type of information is available to you, even if you are not interested in the information at the time. For example, you can learn more about copper and the copper market from the Copper Development Association, www.copper .org. Or you can learn more about the mortgage market from the Mortgage Bankers Association, www.mbaa.org. A couple of other examples include the National Federation of Independent Businesses (www.nfib.org), the International Council for Shopping Centers (www.icsc.org), the National Retail Federation (www .nrf.com), and the Fibre Box Association (www.fibrebox.org). On each of these sites and many others like them there is a plethora of information.

The View from the Top Down: When investing from the top down, it is important to have data in hand that will give you a perspective on things. Web sites such as those above give you that perspective. For example, years ago I learned from facts that I obtained on the Copper Development Association's Web site that the greatest source of demand for copper was residential demand, accounting for about 43 percent of all demand, and that about 400 pounds of copper are used in the construction of every new home. Armed with these figures, every wiggle in housing has led me to think about copper in one way or another and vice versa. So, what you should do on these sites is pile up a bunch of numbers and perspectives that will help you to draw a link between industries and the overall economy—something you could not do if you did not visit these sites. You should visit these sites also for information about conditions in the various industries, not only because you might invest in these industries, but also because each industry has a story to tell about the economy. Go to these sites and you will be amazed at all the information available, and much of what is there is in plain English, with plenty of tables, charts, and executive briefs to educate you in ways that are certain to make you an informed investor and give you an edge.

How to Nail It: If you are organized enough, keep a list or a folder in which you can keep a list of the favorites you keep on your Web browser of industry sites you feel are worth going to. Search these sites in-depth at least once to see what is available and revisit them whenever possible, particularly if the sites relate in any way to the industries you are invested in. Use information from the private sector as a cross-check against the government's regular releases of economic data. Amass a large number of facts and figures that will help you to more clearly see the interconnectivity that exists in the economy and to give you a better perspective on investing from the top down.

Notes

[1] Harris, Matthew, Raymond Owens, and Pierre-Daniel Sarte,"Using Manufacturinig Surveys to Assess Economic Conditions," Federal Reserve Bank of Richmond, *Economic Quarterly*, vol. 90, no. 4, Fall 2004.

[2] Ibid.

[3] Edmiston, Kelly, "The Role of Small and Large Businesses in Economic Development," Federal Reserve Bank of Kansas City, *Economic Review*, second quarter 2007.

[4] Meyer, Laurence. "What Happened to the New Economy?" Speech before the National Association of Business Economists and the Downtown Economists, June 6, 2001.

[5] Mei, J., and M. Moses, "Price Estimates and the Future Performance of Artworks," working paper, Stern School of Business, New York University, 2003.

[6] Economic report of the president to the Congress of the United States, 2008.

[7] Duesenberry, J. S., "Income—Consumption Relations and Their Implications," in Lloyd Metzler et al., *Income, Employment and Public Policy* (New York: W.W. Norton & Company, 1948).

[8] Greenspan, Alan, *The Age of Turbulence*. (New York: The Penguin Press, 2007), p. 377.

INDEX